A NEW WORLD ORDER?

A NEW WORLD ORDER?

Global Transformations in
the Late Twentieth Century

Edited by
David A. Smith and József Böröcz

PRAEGER

Westport, Connecticut
London

The Library of Congress has cataloged the hardcover edition as follows:

A new world order? : global transformations in the late twentieth
   century / edited by David A. Smith and József Böröcz.
         p.   cm.—(Contributions in economics and economic history,
   ISSN 0084–9235 ; no. 164) (Studies in the political economy of the
   world-system)
      "The chapters of this volume were selected from conference papers
   presented at the 1994 Political Economy of the World-System Annual
   Conference in April at Irvine, California"—Introd.
      Includes bibliographical references and index.
      ISBN 0–313–29573–5
      1. International economic relations—Congresses.   2. Economic
   history—20th century—Congresses.   I. Smith, David A. (David Alden).
   II. Böröcz, József.   III. Political Economy of the
   World-System Conference (1994 : Irvine, Calif.).   IV. Series.
   V. Series : Studies in the political economy of the world-system.
   HF1352.N47   1995
   337—dc20   94–47418

British Library Cataloguing in Publication Data is available.

A hardcover edition of *A New World Order?* is available from Greenwood Press,
an imprint of Greenwood Publishing Group, Inc. (Contributions in Economics and
Economic History, Number 164; ISBN 0–313–29573–5).

Library of Congress Catalog Card Number: 94–47418
ISBN: 0–275–95122–7 (pbk.)

First published in 1995

Praeger Publishers, 88 Post Road West, Westport, CT 06881
An imprint of Greenwood Publishing Group, Inc.

Printed in the United States of America

The paper used in this book complies with the
Permanent Paper Standard issued by the National
Information Standards Organization (Z39.48–1984).

10 9 8 7 6 5 4 3 2 1

for Bea

Contents

Illustrations

Acknowledgments

This volume is the final product of the eighteenth annual conference on the Political Economy of the World-System (PEWS), held each year by the American Sociological Association (ASA) section. The two-day meeting in April 1994 was hosted by the University of California at Irvine (UCI). Over fifty abstracts of papers were considered for inclusion, of which the coorganizers (and coeditors of this book) selected twenty for presentation at the conference; the volume's contents were further winnowed to twelve essays of the highest quality and fit. In addition to the authors included here, we wish to thank everyone who intellectually contributed, especially the other participants at the Irvine conference: their papers, questions, and comments made the conference lively and stimulating and, moreover, materially contributed to this book by sharpening the analyses offered here.

A conference and volume like these involve the hard work and support of a great number of people. One essential ingredient to make it all work is monetary resources. Despite relatively lean economic times, the meeting was entirely funded through organizations at the University of California, Irvine. The Department of Sociology, the Democratization Focused Research Project, the Program in Global Peace and Conflict Studies, the School of Social Sciences, and the Office for Research and Graduate Studies all contributed generously. The single biggest contributor, though, was the State Studies Focused Research Project. This group has provided a forum for discussion of political-economy research and theories by faculty and graduate students in a variety of social science and humanities disciplines over the last several years; we offer special thanks its cochairs, Dorothy Solinger and Steven Topik.

The project, from conference planning to the completion of the manuscript, was labor-intensive, too. A number of Social Relations doctorate students helped throughout, assisting us early on with our call for abstracts, ferrying participants back and forth to airports (sometimes at unreasonable hours of the day and night), and reading and critically evaluating the conference papers. Ku-Sup Chin and

Socorro Sarmiento-Torres deserve special thanks for helping during the conference itself. The formal graduate student "editorial advisory board" included Lionel Cantú, Angela Crowly, Dennis Downey, Jae Kwun, Yoonies Park, and Clare Weber. Their astute assessments of the papers were invaluable in selecting the chapters for the volume and offering the authors constructive criticism. Thanks, also, to several UCI faculty colleagues who generously donated their time and energy as speakers and presiders at the conference: Russell Dalton, Patrick Morgan, Nancy Naples, William Schonfeld, Dorothy Solinger, Judy Stepan-Norris, Steven Topik, Judy Treas, Alladi Venkatesh, and Doug White. All who were in attendance know that special accolades must also go to our distinguished guests, André Gunder Frank and Immanuel Wallerstein, who delivered an exceptionally fine opening plenary session under difficult circumstances. Finally, we must recognize the staff support that made the conference and this book possible. Linda Cleland, the Sociology Department administrative assistant, and Betty Simmes, our secretary, both worked tirelessly to make the project a success. Karen Sadler provided invaluable help setting up the hotel and conference logistics, Cheryl Larsson professionally designed and word-processed the conference program, converted and formatted the volume's entire text, and even created an attractive proto-type for the book's dust jacket. We especially appreciate the behind-the-scenes work of these UCI staff people.

Marcy Weiner at Greenwood Press deserves credit, too. She made sure that we had the information we needed when we needed it, and she helped us complete this book properly, efficiently, and on time.

Of course, no project like this can succeed without the support of friends and family, so we would like to thank Tonya Schuster and Judit Bodnár for their patience and understanding over the past year (and particularly in the last, frenetic months). Finally, we want to recognize the special contribution of Beatrice Davida Schuster Smith, who animated the social events at the Irvine conference and provided inspiration and encouragement in a way that is distinctive to a two-year-old! We dedicate this book to her, in the hope that there really will be a "new" and better world order in the twenty-first century.

A NEW WORLD ORDER?

1

Introduction: Late Twentieth-Century Challenges for World-System Analysis

József Böröcz and David A. Smith

The closing years of the twentieth century will be remembered as a time of tumultuous change. At the global level, the post–World War II "Pax Americana" and Cold War seem to be over. The unchallenged hegemony of the United States has given way to a multicentric world–economy in which both economic and geo-political leadership appear to be up for grabs. Meanwhile, a new international division of labor has emerged in the last two decades in which an increasing proportion of global manufacturing is now done in the semiperiphery and periphery. However, this "globalization" of industry has failed to either improve living standards for most of the world's population or lessen global inequality. Within the "advanced" capitalist core states, profound economic and political restructuring (and social polarization) are taking place, as economies shift from "Fordist" mass production/consumption to more flexible "post–Fordism." By the 1990s, the erstwhile East Bloc societies of "actually existing socialism" find themselves in the throes of convulsive change, as the communist parties of Central Europe and the Soviet Union have been routed and their putatively immutable totalitarian states dissolve, fragment, and undergo traumatic economic reforms or, alternatively, are subject to (or participate in) the horror of "ethnic cleansing." Further west, the European Community of long-established capitalist societies struggles with itself, its citizens, and its member states in arduous efforts to establish political and economic union. In the ever-volatile Middle East, on-again, off-again peace initiatives were interrupted by the Gulf War. Beyond the various regional impacts, the end of the Soviet-centered state socialist empire upset the bipolar equilibrium that had given structure to great power politics for over forty years, resulting in geo-political uncertainty, instability, and upheaval. Simultaneously, the growing economic power of Japan and the newly industrializing countries (NICs) of east Asia may be heralding the beginning of a true "Pacific Century" as the millennium approaches.

Ironically, in the midst of this multifaceted global crisis, shortly after the fall of the Berlin Wall and the East Bloc and during the international military buildup preceding the allied decimation of Iraq, U.S. president George Bush declared the beginning of "a new world order." This was consistent with the triumphialist assertions that the overthrow of European communism signaled an ultimate victory for the U.S., a sweeping vindication of global capitalism, and even "the end of history" (Fukuyama). Several years later, it is easy to forget that these views (and indeed, President Bush himself) were extremely popular with the general public, the mass media, and many members of the intellectual community. In retrospect, as the following chapters document, this vision of a new world order, with the U.S. the undisputed leader of a politically stable and economically prosperous world, was a chimerical one, and wrong on nearly every count.

The chapters in this volume debunk simplistic, conservative interpretations of the contemporary global situation. Given the ideological hegemony of "market-liberation theology" today, that is important in itself. However, it would not provide much of a theme for a scholarly collection. Rather, our goal is to promote theoretical discussion and debate, grounded in the context of the logic of the contemporary world-system and designed to clarify our understanding of the period of upheaval we are living through. Understanding the set of changes that make up the current world conjuncture and how they relate to one another is both a daunting and an urgent task for social scientists. It demands a well-informed, in-depth, empirically grounded analysis of various transformations and a sensitivity to how these are embedded in the wider logics of global system development. How is worldwide economic restructuring in the late twentieth century best understood? How is it related to simultaneous changes in states and geopolitics? Does the concatenation of ruptures, crises, and disjunctions mean that we are now in a "band of transition" in which the basic nature of the world-system is undergoing fundamental change, or is all the noise just another phase in the evolution of global capitalism? What types of differential impacts will these transformations have on regions, nations, cities, or world-system zones, and on relations of class, gender, and race within these various social formations? What are the prospects that popular social movements can successfully resist transnational capitalism, as epitomized in the ideologies of neoliberalism and privatization and embodied in such diverse forms as International Monetary Fund (IMF) "structural adjustment" programs, ecological pillage in the periphery, brutal "shock therapy" imposed on the former communist states, super-exploitative forms of "flexible accumulation" in the semiperipheral NICs, and the concomitant dismantling of the welfare state and rise of dualistic socioeconomically polarized cities in the core?

The chapters in this book divide into two main themes. One centers on the nature of structural transformations in the contemporary period (Part 1). How is the worldwide process of economic restructuring best conceptualized? Is the world-system undergoing a fundamental change, or is this just another phase of global capitalism? In this section of the book, some chapters will focus on the world-system as a whole (Ross, McMichael), while others examine the ramifications of global transformations in particular regions and countries. In particular, one examines the Persian Gulf War (Maki and Goldfrank), and a second, the internal "periphery" of the European Community (O'Hearn), while a set of chapters spotlights restructuring in East Asia and the Pacific Rim (Hill and Fujita, Bunker and Ciccantell, and Deyo).

The second theme will center on people's responses to global transformations, especially the way in which "anti-systemic" forces develop to counter restructuring (Part 2). One type of response involves labor and ethnic mobilization and resistance. Two essays on India explore these issues (Scrase, Ganguly-Scrase). An examination of the popular struggle against the capitalist restructuring of space in a "world city" like Zurich provides a glimpse of another form of resistance (Kipfer), as does a world-historical overview of ecological activism (Chew). This section of the volume will conclude with an essay that attempts to reconceptualize "the politics of resistance in the new world order" (Drainville).

MISSING ELEMENTS

The chapters of this volume were selected from conference papers presented at the April 1994 Political Economy of the World-System annual conference held at Irvine, California. We are confident that they address many of the most pressing issues raised by the global transformations of the late twentieth century, and that they do so in interesting, data-rich, and theoretically significant ways. At the end of this introductory chapter, we will return to a synoptical discussion of the volume's chapters and interwoven themes and provide our interpretation of their specific contributions.

However, we also think it is necessary to point to some crucial areas and issues that neither the conference nor this volume treat in much detail, but that world-system analysis ought to confront in the closing decade of this century. One major problem that we tried to address when we organized the conference and formulated the call for papers is what we see as the increasingly narrow specialization of scholarly writing and research. Immanuel Wallerstein's recent (1991) book provides a cogent critique of the pernicious effect of rigid disciplinary boundaries in the social sciences and argues that a world-system perspective must transcend the usual academic categories. We were pleased to see conference participants who identify themselves as sociologists, political scientists, anthropologists, historians, urban planners, and even business and management professors. This volume preserves at least some of that disciplinary diversity.

However, academic specialization today is much more narrow than one's discipline: it involves increasingly focused specialists in many subfields examining distinct aspects of social reality and different geographical regions of the world. Of course, expertise is always a valuable thing. However, it becomes counterproductive when scholars working in cognate areas or fields become so narrowly focused on their own literature that they are unaware (or decide to ignore) researchers in neighboring fields working on common empirical problems.

For instance, in studies of both Third World development and global economic restructuring, issues of race and gender are clearly of great importance. However, as Jeffery Paige's conference paper (which was not revised in time to be included in this book) makes clear, there is a great lack of dialogue between students of global political economy and those studying race, ethnicity, and gender. Indeed, "essentializers" in each of these areas argue that one or the other of those factors is the absolute starting point of any analysis. This kind of research makes it difficult, if not impossible, to speak through subdisciplinary boundaries—and it is an extremely self-limiting practice as it is difficult to see how the analysis of one sphere of human experience can be assumed to be fully determined by itself and itself only. We doubt that it is possible to explain race relations exclusively "from" race, gender only "from" gender, and so forth.

Another possible fallacy that occurs is in cases where analysis proceeds ruthlessly through boundaries of social experience, "finding" causation to point in one and only one direction. Ignorance and the assumption of one-directional overdetermination are quite akin. Staunch economic determinists—including some in the world-system tradition—argue that "culture" is epiphenomenal, while antistructuralist enforcers of the latest trend in identity politics are ready to jettison completely what they see as yesteryear's world-system considerations (having to do with flows of commodities, value, coercion, and physical violence) in favor of an exclusive focus on the globalization of culture and identity.

This could, incidentally, lead to a frustrating situation in which specialists in world-system analysis and research on women and development, for instance, work on common issues and may even arrive at mutually consistent conclusions, but are unable or unwilling to learn from one another. In a recent essay on this particular topic, Kathryn Ward diagnosed the problem well: "We may see the continuation of two parallel strands of theory: 1) international political economy where gender and race issues are ignored, and 2) women in development literature where international political economy is ignored" (1993: 60). However, that very essay also partly seems to perpetuate the problem by suggesting that current world-system analysis is fundamentally flawed and needs to be totally reconstituted, beginning with "race and gender at its center" (1993: 59–60). A more creative and constructive approach to this problem, from a global political economy perspective, would require redoubled efforts to incorporate race and gender issues into our research and theorizing in truly creative, mutually enriching ways. Only such endeavors could build bridges of dialogue among communities of scholars who already do work in the respective areas. While some of the essays in this volume attempt to "give voice" to Third World men and women (Scrase, Ganguly-Scrase), and while "ethnic division" was the central theme of a conference paper that does not appear here, one of the potential contributions of the conference and the volume was not realized in this area. Scholars working in world-system analysis ought to formulate more creative and intentionally inclusive intellectual strategies to incorporate culture and politics (including, but not restricted to, race and gender issues) into our understanding of the dynamics of global change without abandoning the already existing analytical power of the world-system paradigm.

Another area of fragmentation is the split between global political economy (and, indeed, other theory-driven perspectives) and area studies. For far too many U.S.-based social scientists, the term *area studies* has a pejorative connotation. It is seen as too idiographic in orientation and as unwilling or unable to contribute to theoretical generalization, and its practitioners are viewed with some suspicion. We could not disagree more. We do not see how meaningful generalization could be created without expert knowledge of ground-level reality. "Good" political intentions cannot substitute for thorough reality checks using empirical data, be they numerical, textual or otherwise. Almost every empirically oriented research chapter in this volume depends, to some degree, on the area or regional expertise of the authors.

However, we were a bit surprised after we issued the call for papers to find that there was very little interest in contemporary changes in the former Eastern Bloc societies: after all, it was the dramatic political and economic transformation of these societies that emboldened President Bush to declare a new world order in the first place. A political economy of the world-system approach should surely have much to say about this process of transition. We thus decided to include below a brief resume of the challenges that the historical developments due to the collapse of the state-socialist empire in central and eastern Europe present to world-system analysis.

THE CHALLENGE OF THE "TRANSITION" FROM STATE SOCIALISM

The collapse of state socialism was a world-systemic event, *par excellence.* Just as the creation and maintenance of the state socialist empire took place by military-geopolitical design and resulted in the rearrangement of the external linkages of the societies involved, the state socialist system's collapse was preceded by the reappearance of linkages of economic dependency on non–state-socialist actors, and the transition was managed on the highest levels of superpower cooperation. The structural conditions of the economic incorporation of the former Soviet bloc societies in the world-economy—spread out between the semiperiphery and the periphery and displaying disparities in per capita gross domestic product (GDP) figures on the magnitude of at least ten times—was thus hardly a surprise from a world-system perspective. It takes an overdose of either the free-market utopianism or mythical nationalism to expect that the societies of central and eastern Europe could rapidly assume core status. Indeed, a mixture of the two on the part of the (West) German political elite may well explain the inability of the planners of the unification to foresee the actual difficulties of the effort. The historical-comparative case material provided by the transition of central and eastern Europe provides a powerful challenge to most western social scientific theorizing, including the world-systems paradigm.

The first set of considerations pertain to variation in the changing mode of incorporation of the formerly state-socialist economies in the world-system. Until the collapse, the unique feature of the state socialist bloc was that the bulk of the formal external linkages of these societies to the capitalist world-economy were mediated through an institutional mechanism comprised by a complex interweaving of the Soviet imperial state and its subsidiaries, the local states (termed elsewhere the "comprador state"; see Böröcz 1992a, 1992b). The dissolution of that arrangement and the emergence of the new order are neither automatic, simple, nor obvious. The reintegration of the economics of the former Soviet Bloc into the new enlarged capitalist periphery (or semiperiphery) took extremely varied forms. These depended on a number of circumstances including, but not limited to, the economic-geographical location and the raw material and energy endowments of the given economy; its structures of specialization, inherited partly from the state socialist period and partly from before, the existence, timing, and characteristics of the economic, political, and social reforms during the socialist period; the size and degree of uneven internal development of the economy; the economic- and military-strategic importance of the location, and a host of other, noneconomic considerations. Contrary to widespread expectations and fears, direct foreign investment appears to be grossly lagging. Although indices of living standards, life expectancy, morbidity, and environmental conditions are declining all across the region, the deterioration is far from uniform: it is distributed quite unevenly and the resulting new inequalities cannot be simply explained away as determined by preexisting patterns of linkages to the core.

As anticipated easily by any simple application of the political economy of the world-system paradigm, the organization of regional economic integration, the Council for Mutual Economic Assistance (CMEA), was dismantled rapidly. However, that took place *not* via concerted action by core capitalist actors but via a joint motion by the central European states. As a result, the economies of those same states experienced the greatest losses of export and import markets, resulting in a harsher-than-necessary adjustment crisis, severe raw materials and energy supply problems, and, consequently, very high human costs for the transition. Were those states acting in a blatantly "irrational" fashion when they "shot themselves" in their own economic "foot," or, is there a set of important further considerations that such an analysis does not address? What can we learn from this case regarding the relationship among state action, regional integration, and structural adjustment?

The transformation produced a wide array of economic policies, ranging from the (in)famous Polish "shock therapy" through the Hungarian practice of small steps—some forward, some backward—to the apparently unstoppable Russian slide toward anarchy and primitive accumulation under mob control. Of particular theoretical importance to world-system analysis is the extreme variance in the modes and outcomes of the transformation of the property structure. Given the entire region's endemic capital shortage, the alternatives are (1) complete foreign sellout, (2) domestic privatization through extremely high subsidies, or (3) the preservation of the state's predominance as the biggest property owner in the economy. The task undertaken by the post-socialist states appears to be truly unique in that never before in human history has a set of states attempted to pass on, from public ownership to private hands, such a highly concentrated, relatively recent, usable, and hence, at least somewhat valuable, batch of assets.

The Czech and Slovak (and, in a somewhat less orderly fashion, also the Russian) coupon-privatization plans distribute formerly state socialist property initially to a very wide range of new capitalists, comprising, at least theoretically, the entire citizenry. The main theoretical question raised here is whether and how a reconcentration of productive resources will take place on such a basis. The other countries' privatization schemes include partial political *re*privatization (to previously disappropriated owners or victims of political terror), management and *nomenklatura* buyouts, the creation of complex organizational and management systems that leave ultimate state property largely intact while sharply detaching control from ownership, and/or buyouts through bankruptcy or domestic debt equity swaps. The role of foreign actors—states, manufacturing and finance capital, consultants and experts—is potentially an extremely important, and so far greatly unexplored, area of analysis.

The collapse of the imperial center and the transformation of the former comprador states has resulted in a rampant crisis of state formation in central and eastern Europe. This makes the post–state-socialist transition similar to the post–World War II collapse of the colonial empires: we are witnessing radical increases in the number of an increasingly unstable and frustrated set of state entities in the region. All the contemporary central and east European postcomprador states are asserting what appears as a caricatured, extravagant version of the Western formula of sovereignty and self-determination as the only acceptable form of statehood. Increases in the number of states due to multiplication by territorial division makes the arrangement of remaining borders appear arbitrary, questionable, conditional, and increasingly unjust. This mushrooming of states multipolarizes potential conflict. While the west European Union represents a move in the direction of the "spiritualization" of increasingly porous internal borders protected by an ever stronger wall around the union, the central and east European process points in the exact opposite direction: less and less permeable borders around ununified, increasingly small, and debt- and poverty-stricken states, which are extremely open to external economic and political penetration from the west. The reduction of the average size of states lends, finally, increasing strategic importance to those states that do not experience such splits, boosting the political attractiveness of territorial expansionism and further increasing the likelihood of military strife. A systematic account, let alone congenial understanding, of these processes in the world-system vein is overdue. The theoretical task is no smaller than that posed by the peace arrangements after World War II (resulting in such theoretical developments as the postwar resurgence of modernization theory, as well as the birth of dependency theory and world–system analysis itself).

Another feature of the crisis of state formation has to do with the peaceful or violent nature of the transition. Violent uprising and military coup in Romania, civil and interethnic war in the former Yugoslavia, and more armed ethnic conflict in the southern belt of the former Soviet Union contrast to the peacefulness of the collapse in the Baltic states, Poland, Germany, Czechoslovakia, Hungary, and Bulgaria. It would have been extremely difficult to produce a prediction expecting this particular combination of states as the location of an uneven distribution of violence. In retrospect, it is striking that the pattern of political violence follows very strictly the geographical position of the imperial army of the Soviet Union: generalized political violence has been only witnessed in those societies where the Soviet military was absent or conspicuously impassive. The world-system implications of this regularity are, again, far-reaching and beg for exploration.

In addition, a profound nation formation crisis is also haunting central and eastern Europe. The recent resurgence of the nation-as-community appears to be imagined (Anderson 1983) in a very specific fashion: its patterns follow the combination of definite historical configurations based, clearly, on foreign borrowing, creating an explosive mixture of two west European traditions. Contemporary post–state-socialist nationalisms combine a characteristically German preoccupation with the mythical notion of "blood" and purity with the French idea of tying nationhood to statehood through the symbolic assertion of a utopian concept, the ethnically pure nation-state. With the region's infinitely fragmented ethnogeographical patterns of settlement, central and east European nationalisms produce a barrage of mutually unsatisfiable, territorially fixed claims to statehood. Nineteenth-century French historian Pierre Miquel's depiction of the post–World War I destruction of the Hapsburg monarchy provides a very apt description of the ongoing "ethnic cleansing" on the Balkan peninsula: he remarked that "the injustice of the oppression of the peoples by the old empires was replaced by an arbitrary carving, inspired more by appetite than ethnic or linguistic realities" (see Fejtő 1988). In contrast to seventy five years ago, this time the no less arbitrary carving is done by the smaller states and not the Entente Cordiale of victorious Western great powers. The fact that the pattern-producing sources of Central and East European nationalisms are so eminently Western ironically mocks the typical West European "orientalist" reading (see Said 1978) of the ideological crisis in "their back yard." The eastern boundary of Europe is thereby mentally manipulated as a key element in the cultural construction of the new European (id)entity. The precise delineation of that entity will impact profoundly on the direction of the region's further economic, political, and cultural change.

Given the centuries-long discrimination against the Rom and the more recent traditions of anti-Semitism and other forms of xenophobia, all the so-far calm societies of the region appear to be ethnic powder kegs in search of a spark. If for no other reason than the approach's tacit tendency to endorse economic nationalism as an antidote to foreign exploitation, the dynamics of the crisis of nation formation constitute a formidable challenge to the world-system perspective. The analysis of "the nationality issues" promises to reveal enormous insight into a historical-comparative sociology of nationhood, ethnicity, and linguistic-cultural exclusion.

Exacerbating all those crises, central and eastern Europe's transition from state socialism reveals a profound crisis of class formation—which, needless to say, is a prime subject matter for world-system analysis proper. The transition to capitalism without a preceding private, primitive accumulation of capital poses the problem of the social sources of the new capital-owning class. Indeed, central and eastern Europe's states are faced, in a major way, with the problem described by Peter Evans as the Latin American states' dilemma of "reinventing the bourgeoisie" (Evans 1979). Various state-centered strategies of economic development are, of course, quite familiar to world-system scholars. However, the central and est European case involves not only the concentration of economic and other resources by strong states in favor of national growth. The task also involves the establishment of the very fundamental institutional structure of capitalist society, along with the creation of a capital-owning class (including the elites). This job is, of course, daunting, and the impoverished postcomprador states are in no position to hand out free goods as tools for class formation. The only available tools are their instruments for the monopolization of legitimate violence. However, the extremely strong anti*etatist* ideological climate of these post–state-socialist societies seems to constantly prevent the state from being able to use its oppressive resources for class and elite formation. The frustration of the formation of a propertied bourgeoisie appears to be a determining feature of the transformation.

Meanwhile, the sizable working classes of the region are in a state of near-complete disorganization. Due to the area's belated industrialization, working-class culture here has always been somewhat rudimentary. That weakness was further exacerbated by the rapid creation of the state socialist proletariat, which uprooted and forced to the cities enormous peasant masses; the disorienting system of multiple income earning strategies during the state socialist period; the complexity of the current transition, and the perceived moral and ideological corruptness of the trade union structures (largely inherited from the previous period). Putting together a comparative-historical interpretation of the crisis of class formation presents another intriguing puzzle for adventurous world-system analysts.

Finally, the post–state-socialist transformation is begging for an appraisal of its *global* impact. At least two substantive issues emerge. First, the conjuncture of the crisis of state formation, nation formation, and class formation is a historically novel, but theoretically fascinating, development. What are the implications of such a combination for global social change? Second, the systematic consideration of the (former) state socialist bloc in world-system terms is inescapable because of its sheer magnitude. After all, roughly one-third of the globe's population lived under this political system a decade ago, all of whom are now undergoing some degree of transformation. An extension of the questions about "transition" that we have raised in response to such Third World, (former) state socialist societies as China, North Korea, Angola, Ethiopia, Nicaragua, or Vietnam, when melded with issues raised more specifically from the experience of those societies, would, no doubt, enrich world-system analysis. On the other hand, a failure to seriously explore these issues would mean that the world-system perspective's comparative scope will fall short of the global promise of its analytical framework.

SYNOPTICAL OVERVIEW OF THE BOOK

Each of the following chapters challenges the world-system paradigm in its own distinctive way. A dominant theme of most world-system analyses is on the basic continuity of the capitalist world-economy over the past 500 years (Wallerstein 1974) or even longer (Frank 1992). However, the extent of global change and restructuring in the late twentieth century raises serious questions about what is, and what is not, new about the present world order. The volume's next two chapters both argue that things are quite different now.

Robert J. S. Ross's essay (Chapter 2) is a condensed and updated version of the theoretical view offered in *Global Capitalism: The New Leviathan*, the 1990 book he coauthored with Kent Trachte. Its basic argument is that in the last quarter of this century, a new, qualitatively different variant of capitalism has emerged. The distinguishing feature is the global mobility of capital, which changes the nature of capitalist competition and becomes "the major lever by which capital extracts surplus from labor and gains favorable policies from states" throughout the world. This formulation accurately captures the dilemma facing workers and governments subject to contemporary neoliberal economic restructuring. Whether the chapter sustains Ross's claim that his "theory of global capitalism" offers a better diagnosis of the contemporary global situation than theoretical alternatives, including the world-system approach, is less certain.

Like Ross, McMichael also claims that recent restructuring has led to a basic transformation of the global system. Chapter 3 is grounded in the logic of "regulationist theory," and documents the rise of "the new colonialism" under which various multilateral agencies, in the wake of the debt crises of the 1970s, have increasingly subsumed the powers of nation-states to police labor and enforce market discipline. The paradigmatic cases are the imposition of "structural adjustment" in Africa and Latin America, where agencies like the World Bank and the IMF dictated policy changes that seriously eroded the prerogatives of sovereign states. However, the chapter argues that this type of global regulation is much more pervasive, undermining the legitimacy of nation-states everywhere, including "the welfare/democratic state," and thus "shifting national policy discourse further away from constructive social policy."

While McMichael's chapter plumbs the intricacies of the recent history of international institutions, sometimes plunging into detailed discussions that may strike some as arcane, its conclusions resonate with Ross's much simpler argument. Both claim that in the new global situation, capital gains more leverage while workers and the state lose it. There is something to this statement, but claims about the fundamental newness of what they describe is more tenuous. We would simply point out that neither "global capital mobility" nor corporate "colonization" of states are entirely new, although the forms they take may be.

Moving from global to regional, Chapters 4 and 5 focus on two epochal, but sharply contrasting, geopolitical struggles popularly associated with the very emergence of a new world order. The 1991 Gulf War was a convulsive event, that occurred in a region that appears to perpetually teeter on the brink of violence and afforded both George Bush and the U.S. Cable News Network (CNN) an opportunity to demonstrate their global power. The peaceful constitutional (and, supposedly, orderly and predictable) consolidation of the European Union, on the other hand, was designated as heralding the beginning of renewed prosperity and enlarged community in an area that has been an industrial core region all along. Our authors demonstrate that in order to understand *both* these regional dynamics, we must see them in the context of global hegemonic cycles, competition, and decline.

The Maki and Goldfrank argument centers on the ambiguous, tenuous nature of both U.S. hegemonic decline and Iraqi semiperipheral mobility, as well the demise of the stabilizing Soviet counterbalance in the Middle East, as critical triggers to war. The oil-based "rentier state" in Iraq provided Saddam Hussein with the political maneuverability to attempt military conquest as a means of semiperipheral ascent (a historical route, followed, to varying degrees, by several current core powers)—but led to disastrous consequences. For the victors, the war led to uneasy core domination over the oil rich Gulf region via "the new U.S./UN mode of policing the world," which may become increasingly common as U.S. hegemony ebbs.

"Lean and mean" European firms, poised to lead the continent's hegemonic struggle with the U.S. and Japan, are the major forces determining the nature of economic integration and restructuring in the new Europe, according to O'Hearn. The liberalizing policies designed to foster economies of scale and scope in the "world's largest market" are designed to promote this hegemonic project. However, they are pushing the countries of "the European periphery" (defined as Spain, Portugal, Greece, and Ireland) toward continued economic marginality, poverty, and unemployment. European Union membership under these conditions provides no panacea for uneven development. Although the "other" European periphery, "east of the Elbe," receives only cursory attention in this chapter, O'Hearn's thesis offers cautionary lessons there, too.

Moving to the opposite side of the planet, one of the dramatic changes in the late twentieth century is the shift of the world-economy's center of gravity toward East Asia and the Pacific Rim. Three essays address this region's economic dynamism. Chapter 6 explicitly contrasts the overseas investment strategies of U.S. and Japanese firms, finding in the difference reasons for the continued economic success, not only of Japan, but of the entire East Asian region. Hill and Fujita claim that U.S. investors use "oligopolistic bargaining and location strategies," which lead to exploitation and underdevelopment in Third World manufacturing enclaves and deindustrialization at home. In contrast, Japanese companies, under the tutelage of state policies maximizing national comparative advantage, employ the "flying geese" logic of economic growth. In this framework, the technologically advanced nation of Japan leads the way with continuous industrial upgrading and new product development, while other East Asian countries follow along as recipients of industries that are no longer profitable in Japan itself. For the authors, one lesson is that the Japanese-style globalization of manufacturing has sustained, rather than weakened, Japan's home industries. The other is that Japanese foreign investment "complement[s] and strengthen[s] the comparative advantage in investing and receiving countries alike." This benign view of Japanese investment is likely to be controversial among those familiar with the rest of East Asia, where memories linger of the last Japanese attempt to establish an "East Asian Co-Prosperity Sphere."

Bunker and Ciccantell are also interested in explaining Japan's successful bid for competitive advantage, but they focus on a completely different (and often overlooked) aspect of economic development: secure access to relatively cheap raw materials. Indeed, Chapter 7 argues that this is a crucial element in struggles for global economic hegemony, which world-system analysts often ignore. The key (especially for resource-poor Japan) was the development of a transportation infrastructure. The bulk of the chapter describes the recent geometric expansion of the volume of world raw materials trade, explains Japanese government policies promoting the development of giant ports, and documents how the promotion of a world-class shipbuilding industry was an essential component of Japan's development strategy. While the main theme highlights raw materials and transportation as key factors in economic growth, this chapter, once again, emphasizes the crucial role of the Japanese state.

The final chapter on East Asia shifts attention geographically to Thailand and analytically from national economic policies to the behavior of firms and the way in which they structure labor relations on the shop floor. Deyo reports on efforts by Thailand-based automobile manufacturers to meet the pressures of global competition by resorting to techniques of "flexible production." While the firms use some elements that foster worker participation and cooperation among skilled workers and engineers, cost-cutting measures such as "labor casualization," the use of temporary workers, and subcontracting remain prevalent. The political weakness of workers and the failure of the Thai state to enforce even minimal labor standards results in a very limited "top-down model of flexibility," which inhibits industrial upgrading. While a low-wage regime of "market despotism" may result in high short-term profits and growth, Deyo is skeptical about its long-term prospects for sustaining Thai global competitiveness.

The remaining essays in the volume address how people respond to or resist global restructuring. Chapters 9 and 10 both examine India's experience with globalization. Scrase (Chapter 9) takes a subcontinental view of a variety of national struggles for labor, ethnic, and environmental justice. He maintains that approaches to globalization that privilege "culture" encourage the commodification of the causes of indigenous people and the environment (via the selling of "native" or "green" products) and obfuscate the political-economic underpinnings of "new social movements." In the Indian case he shows that insurgent groups that seem to be based on religious fervor or ethnic chauvinism are responding to material deprivation and inequities generated by capitalist restructuring. We are left with an image of politically mobilized Indian masses resisting the pernicious effects of globalization.

The companion chapter on India (Chapter 10) is an ethnographically focused examination of the impact of neoliberal policies on a particular urban community of leather workers. Ganguly-Scrase portrays the Rabi Das people as profoundly and negatively affected by the opening of the Indian economy, and particularly the transnationalization of the footwear industry, which destroyed their livelihoods as traditional artisans. Structural adjustment policies leading to the devaluation of the rupee exacerbated the problem of household survival. This grim economic situation, in concert with fundamentalist ideologies, reinforced gender hierarchies: Rabi Das women find themselves in a particularly difficult situation. Nevertheless, Ganguly-Scrase, in interesting contrast to the previous chapter, argues that the particular history of the Rabi Das (and especially the inculcation of middle class values by Gandhian social reformers after Indian Independence) led them to respond to their plight with despair and accommodation rather than resistance. The lesson of this chapter is that, just as we should avoid arguments about the structural necessity of underdevelopment that ignore the *possibility* of resistance, we also need to guard against the "valorization of resistance" by assuming that people will *inevitably* mobilize against capitalist exploitation. Methodologically, it is essential to study the interplay between global and local political-economy and ideology.

Chapter 11 also focuses on a community and stresses the need to understand the global-local dialectics (termed "glocalization" here). Kipfer's empirical case is Zurich, Switzerland, which he conceptualizes as a "global city." However, he wants to avoid structural determinist interpretations of global city formation and instead emphasizes "the relevance of local politics in the process of transnationalization" of urban space. The chapter sketches the dynamics of Zurich political life since the 1960s in terms of struggles between a corporate "growth coalition," pushing development and internationalization of the central business district, and popular forces intent on preserving the neighborhoods and urban ecology of the "city of living." Actors resisting globalization included the "institutional left" and reformist political parties as well as new social movements of squatters, radical students, anarchists, and other "countercultural" elements. While the chapter tells an interesting story and convinces the reader that the internationalization of Zurich was a contested process, it may be telling that, in the end, the oppositional forces won few real victories and were in disarray by the 1990s. Despite an energetic, valiant effort to resist, the juggernaut hegemonic project of international finance reshaped Zurich according to its needs.

The global ecological movement is another potentially potent anti-systemic force that world-system analysis has yet to fully explore. Chapter 12 provides a sweeping (but preliminary) attempt to redress that lacuna. Chew begins with a brief history of 5,000 years of exploitation of nature, the ecological crises that resulted, and the periodic "environmentalist" social movements that arose in response; ecological degradation and deforestation frequently led to the collapse of empires and civilizations. Accumulation that exploited nature played a critical role in the rapid economic growth of certain nations in this century (descriptions of Japanese strategies for securing access to lumber dovetail with the themes of Bunker and Ciccantell's earlier chapter). Significantly, however, environmental degradation consistently engenders social movements that resist the destruction of nature. Chew catalogues the range of contemporary ecological movements, from "deep ecologists" and "direct action" groups in North America to indigenous people in the Brazilian and Malaysian rain forests, and indicates, albeit in a preliminary way, how international linkages are being cultivated between activists. He suggests that "ecological movements have the potential to be transnational . . . and transformative."

The final chapter returns the discourse to a high level of abstraction and the substantive focus to the entire globe. Drainville attempts nothing less than a reconceptualization of "the politics of resistance in the New World Order." His chapter provides a stylized sketch of the world economic crisis attendant on the decline of U.S. hegemony and the rise of a neoliberal global regulation. The chapter turns to a synoptical discussion of the history of "left internationalist" thought from the "socialists, Marxists, anarchists, collectivists and mutualists in the nineteenth century" up to various "international solidarity" movements of the present. These contemporary "new social movements" are based on a variety of issues that connect concerns about global capitalism with struggles for labor rights, gender equality, environmental protection, racial/ethnic equality, and so forth. Drainville sees in this new left internationalism a movement of resistance by marginalized or threatened people against global restructuring. He sees little prospect for these varied movements to coalesce into any grand anti-systemic movement to dislodge global capitalism. Instead, "the 'new' internationalism has radical implications because it reveals how fragile are the social foundations of the New World Order." The power of global capital, in other words, is forced to rely increasingly on raw coercion rather than cultural legitimacy to maintain authority. This opens up new possibilities for oppositional political organization and action.

The chapter (and the volume) end on the hopeful note: the current global conjuncture may be more brittle than it seems, offering spaces for "the construction of a socialist framework for local, national, and regional attempts to build counter-hegemonies." For now, that is about as far as world-systems theorizing goes via of verifiable predictions.

REFERENCES

Anderson, Benedict. 1983. *Imagined Communities: Reflections on the Origin and Spread of Nationalism*. London: Verso.

Böröcz, József. 1992a. "Dual Dependency and Property Vacuum: Social Change on the State Socialist Semiperiphery." *Theory and Society* 21:77–104.

———. 1992b. "Dual Dependency and the Informalization of External Linkages: The Case of Hungary." *Research in Social Movements, Conflicts and Change* 14:189–209.

Evans, Peter. 1979. *Dependent Development*. Princeton, NJ: Princeton University Press.

Fejtő, Ferenc. 1988. *Réquiem pour en empire défunt: histoire de la destruction de l'Autriche-Hongrie*. Paris: Lieu Commun.

Frank, A. G. 1992. "World System Cycles, Crises, and Hegemonal Shifts." *Review* (Fernand Braudel Center) 15, no. 4:179–191.

Fukuyama, Francis. 1992. *The End of History and the Last Man*. New York: Free Press.

Paige, Jeffery. 1994. "Intimacy, Identity and Dignity: Human Needs and the Primacy of Production in Marxist Social Thought." Paper presented at PEWS XVIII Conference, Irvine, CA.

Said, Edward. 1978. *Orientalism*. New York: Vintage Books.

Wallerstein, Immanuel. 1974. *The Modern World-System, I*. New York: Academic Press.

———. 1991. *Unthinking Social Science: The Limits of Nineteenth Century Paradigms*. Cambridge: Polity Press.

Ward, Kathryn. 1993. "Reconceptualizing World System Theory to Include Women." In Paula England, ed., *Theory on Gender/Feminism on Theory*. New York: Aldine de Gruyter, 43–68.

Part I

STRUCTURAL TRANSFORMATIONS OF THE LATE TWENTIETH CENTURY

2

The Theory of Global Capitalism: State Theory and Variants of Capitalism on a World Scale

Robert J. S. Ross

THE SETTING

The twenty-first century began in 1989, with the end of the Cold War and, for the time being, the collapse of socialism as a competing mode of production on a world scale. A period of aggregate stagnation and recession in the older industrial regions of Western Europe and North America joined the longer-term stall and decline in working-class wages and incomes. Together with growing inequality dating from the mid-1970s (Harrison and Bluestone 1988), this is an era of changing economic structure and political situation at the "core"—the older industrial regions.

Growing inequality also characterizes the broader interstate system, as does structural change. In particular, industrial growth in the semiperiphery, the NICs, has propelled these countries into new roles in world trade in manufactures.(Dicken 1992). This chapter uses and revises the theory of global capitalism (Ross and Trachte 1990) to erect a framework within which the global social order of the new century may be analyzed.

THE THEORY OF GLOBAL CAPITALISM AS A FRAMEWORK

The theory of global capitalism contends that the mobility of capital, on a global geographic scale, has grown in scope, speed, and volume. The result is everywhere an increment in the social, economic, and political power of capital in relation to labor and to states. The increase in relative strength of capital in the era of global capitalism is particularly notable in relation to well-organized national fractions of the working class in the nations of the core. The global scope of capital mobility and the shifting nature of commodity chains (Hopkins and Wallerstein 1986; Gereffi and Korzeniewicz 1994) have changed the nature of capitalist competition. While, as an abstract proposition, the use of *space* as a resource for power in the struggle between capital and labor is not new, the new conjuncture gives the use of space new—or, at the least, renewed—strategic primacy in the ability of firms to realize profits.

Published in monograph form in 1990, the theory of global capitalism had been expressed in a number of early formulations before then (e.g., Ross, Shakow, and Susman 1980; Trachte and Ross 1985; O'Keefe 1984). The widely adopted phrase, "global capitalism," and Ross and Trachte's particular theoretical formulation for it, were part of a general current of ideas, grappling with the empirical phenomena associated with the globalization of production and the rise of the Multinational Corporation (MNC).

Since then, new empirical practices such as the study of commodity chains (Gereffi and Korzeniewicz 1994) have been applied to this problem and new applications of the approach used by Ross and Trachte have been published (Noponen, Graham, and Markusen 1993).[1] Together with reviews of the original monograph, the new empirical work and the new political economic setting of the post–Cold War world now prompt a broad-scale review of the contemporary nature of capitalism and, in particular, the relation of state institutions to global and national class structures. This volume, which is based on the world-system approach to global analysis, is a highly appropriate occasion for this assessment, as the original formulations of the theory of global capitalism depicted it as a competing perspective. While significant differences do remain, these shrink in the relative perspective of contemporary social studies, where the very endeavor to analyze *structures*, analyze them on a *global* scale, or even conceive of a *science* of social or class relations is to declare a certain skepticism in relation to (or against) the fashion of "postmodern" approaches to the human sciences.

VARIANTS OF CAPITALISM: GLOBAL CAPITALISM

Some aspects of capitalism are historically specific products of evolutionary change, as distinct from those that are constitutive. The theory of global capitalism accepts a concept of capitalism that defines it as commodity production for exchange, where labor is a commodity and where a capitalist class owns and controls the means of production, extracting value from a working class by purchasing its means of survival—labor power—through the payment of wages. This is among the areas of difference with world-system analysis, which does not use a concept of hierarchical articulation of modes of production. In contrast to world-system theory, then, the theory of global capitalism did not depict the world-system as a single mode of production, but rather a hierarchy of pre- and (prematurely) postcapitalist modes of production.[2]

The invariant social relationships of capitalism are relatively abstract. Through the history of capitalism, however, particular forms, or variants, of capitalism have emerged during great moments of restructuring, responding to barriers to accumulation that might have otherwise threatened the mode of production itself.

At an intermediate level of abstraction, the concept of variants or submodes of capitalism thus generalizes from national circumstance. It clarifies the successive responses to developmental crises of the mode of production, responses that "restructure" capitalism but do not end it. This, then, is the basis for conceiving of historical stages of capitalism. Without some concept like a variant or submode, practically all discussion of twentieth-century capitalism (in relation to the century that preceded it) would be unintelligible.

The theory of monopoly capitalism articulated by Baran and Sweezy (1966) focused on the ways in which twentieth-century capitalist competition differed from that of the previous century. Although Baran and Sweezy were criticized for their specification of the dynamic problems of monopoly capitalism, broad agreement has emerged on two points. First, many analysts concur that the history of capitalism can be fruitfully analyzed by distinguishing stages of capitalist development. Second, political economists have accepted the notion that a new structural form—monopoly capitalism—became dominant *within* the capitalist mode of production during the course of the early twentieth century.

"Monopoly capitalism," as used by Baran and Sweezy, designated that moment of capitalist development in which key markets were dominated by a handful of firms. The variant of capitalism called "monopoly capitalism" focused on oligopolistic competition as its defining characteristic.[3] Maturing as capital came to be invested in the "assembly line" method of organizing work for the mass production of standard consumption goods, recent usage has termed this moment of capitalist development "Fordism." In other influential contexts (e.g., Aglietta 1979), this usage implies Henry Ford's additional *social* innovation—wages that allowed his employees to buy the cars they made. This relation between wages and prices for large segments of the rich countries' working class made possible Keynesian regulation (i.e., the attempted stabilization of the business cycle and the social system). In other contexts (Dicken 1992), the *Fordism* refers more simply to the mass production of standardized goods and the long production runs and rigid division of labor inherent in its cost control strategies. The theory of global capitalism targets the *social* dimension of the Fordist, or monopoly capitalist, regime for special attention; the collapse of Keynesian, social democratic solutions to "underconsumptionist" tendencies of capitalism is a structural, rather than merely a political, phenomenon in the theory of global capitalism.

Post-Fordism, in recent contexts, refers to production techniques and organization in which specialized, "batch" or job lot production, rather then standardized production, is the key to industrial dominance within the contemporary variant of capitalism. "Flexible accumulation," the companion concept, implies rapid innovation and market sensitivity—said to be lacking in the Fordist organization of production, which is posited on an assumption of mammoth production runs and economies of very large scale.

The theory of global capitalism begins its own, somewhat different, approach to modern capitalism, as do the Baran and Sweezy and "regulationist" (Aglietta 1979) views, by distinguishing a competitive from a monopoly variant. In the framework of the theory of global capitalism, the distinguishing characteristics of competitive capitalism are the *bundle*: small firms, regional trade, price competition, and an undifferentiated labor force disciplined by the existence of a large labor reserve.[4] The state in competitive capitalism was, to be sure, a vigorous ally of capital, but its social and economic bulk were smaller than they would become under monopoly capitalism. Government's regulatory functions, in the era of competitive capitalism, were fewer and less intensive, its fiscal and monetary policies were less central, and it was everywhere less accessible to the working class than it was to become later, under monopoly capitalism.[5]

By contrast, from the end of the nineteenth century through the first two-thirds of the twentieth, the dominant mode of capitalist organization was national in scope and multilocational, and the oligopolistic nature of major commodity markets gave rise to administered prices. Labor forces were elaborately segmented, with some workers (those in the primary sector of large firms and strong unions) able to "ride" the price-making powers of their employers to middle income by mid-century (O'Connor 1973; Gordon, Edwards, and Reich 1982). The enlarged state, especially after World War II, allowed organized workers points of access to press their interests. Social safety nets of various extent were the product of the resultant social democratic politics.

Two very important qualifications to these characterizations must be made in order to proceed. When a new variant of capitalism rises to dominance, the older one does not simply disappear. Sectors of late capitalist economies still exhibit features of the competitive mode of capitalism, which is only gradually giving way to the change in scale and scope of the monopoly mode. Competitive relations lasted, for example, in the apparel and food retailing sectors long after other key commodity markets in consumer durables and producer goods had become oligopolistic.

Furthermore, specific industries, like the garment industry, may "skip" stages and, for example, become globalized *before* they become concentrated or monopolistic.[6] The claim that the competitive mode of capitalism gave way to the monopoly mode merely notes that the dominant firms and mode of accumulation were monopolistic and, in principle, the flow of value was *to* the monopoly form of organization *from* the competitive (small) firms and sectors (Ross and Trachte 1990; pace Agnew 1991). Thus, contrary to some arguments (Agnew 1991), the global capitalism perspective does not assume that all, or even most, firms are global or large.

Crisis as Restructuring

The monopoly variant of capitalism was dominant through the 1960s, and it was pervasive throughout the advanced capitalist countries. In world-system terms, the period of monopoly capitalism encompasses the apogee of Western imperialism and conquest in the late nineteenth century, its political retreat, and then the neocolonial or economic domination of the core over the periphery which characterized this century through the late 1960s. Throughout this period the characteristic form of core dominance was the unequal exchange of primary commodities for manufactured goods, which certainly worked to the advantage of the investor class in the core. Others have argued that it buffered the standard of living of core workers as well (Emmanuel 1972; Chase-Dunn 1989; cf., Szymanski 1981). Two kinds of forces disrupted the stability of this moment.

Inherent contradictions of capitalist accumulation appeared in new forms, and new entrants to world capitalism's competitive system forced change in the market and the political behavior of the older oligopolists. The crises of the 1970s and 1980s have not been of the "breakdown" nature such as Marxist theory had anticipated. Rather, similar to the structural crises of the late nineteenth century, the recent period has been one of "restructuring" (Frank 1987). Just as the turmoil of the earlier period witnessed the emergence of monopoly capitalism out of the shell of competitive capitalism, so this era is one in which global capitalism is succeeding monopoly capitalism.

The Transition from Monopoly to Global Capitalism

The assertion that we now live in an era of transition to a new variant of capitalism is supported by the following propositions:

1. American, and European economic *hegemony is in relative retreat*, challenged by Japanese and East Asian economies in world export markets;
2. *Price competition* appears on a global scale, including a vital component in which differential labor costs in different geopolitical regions is central to world market competition;
3. Working-class *levels of living* in the formerly rich countries are stagnating or *declining*;
4. Rather than a segmented labor force and monopolistic pricing as the chief lever of surplus extraction, the threat and reality of *capital mobility* on a global scale is the major lever by which capital *extracts surplus from labor and gains favorable policies* from states, both in the older industrial regions and in the periphery and semiperiphery.

None of these observations or propositions is consistent with a model derived from the theory of monopoly capitalism. However, the relation of these developments to world-system theories is more complex. From a world-system perspective, while contested hegemony is expected, the working class of the core is almost always depicted as relatively privileged. Competition is common, but the world-system perspective also notes that core nations and firms normally strive for monopolistic pricing powers (Chase-Dunn 1989). The contemporary courtship of capital by peripheral states reverses the observation in the original world-system views of imperialism which, along with other critical theories, saw the capitalist powers as coercive penetrants of "external" formations.

The bargaining power that the threat—and promise—of capital mobility gives to firms is the force, our theory contends, that causes the stagnation of working-class economic and political advance in the old core. While world-system theory notes that capital might migrate outward from the core, this movement is cyclical, taking place during long wave downturns and, paradoxically, if not in contradiction, it helps to restore working-class purchasing power in the core.[7]

The mixed and ambiguous response of world-system analysis to these pressing developments is the warrant for pressing the claim that the perspective of global capitalist theory more clearly and directly addresses the big changes in global political economy than do either of the older approaches. In addition to world-system analysis, however, another complex of ideas attempts to capture recent changes in world production and trade. "Post-Fordism" and the attendant idea of flexible specialization or accumulation refers to a complex of labor and technology utilization, accompanied by market segmentation. Flexible production eschews the long production runs of standardized products and fixed division of (routinized, semiskilled) labor that characterized of the dominant sectors and firms of the monopoly or Fordist era.

In the paradigmatic case, flexible specialization or production uses teams of workers who have been prepared by their training and organizational culture to constantly engage in new and varied tasks for a changing product line. Firms respond quickly to changing market demand and are able to recoup investments with relatively short production runs (Dicken 1992; Piore and Sabel 1984).

Also associated with the analysis of post-Fordist industrial change and global commodity chains is the practice of international subcontracting as an alternative to foreign direct investment and, thus, an alternative to fixed capital in a technique or product line. To the theory of global capitalism, subcontracting (as an alternative to direct investment) poses difficulties for accountants of capital mobility, but not to its sociological identification. To the extent that an investor is able to move the burden of capital investment and direct supervision of labor onto another capitalist's account book, and thus to avoid hiring workers on his own account at the metropolitan core is, for the theory of global capitalism, a register of 1) the power of the investor in relation to the contractor and 2) the lower cost of the direct laborer, as distinct from those in the investor's home country (or the location of final sale). Both these elements are fully consistent with the global theory vision of capital mobility, though the phenomenon presents obvious difficulties to empirical study.

As for flexible specialization, three comments are relevant. First, many products that fit this description are the result of combining diverse, but routinely produced, parts. Second, others may be made, albeit responding rapidly to market changes, with older techniques (e.g., fashion garments) by poorly paid workers (e.g., electronics components). Third, while these techniques may be used in very high value-added products in the older industrial regions, as with German machine tools (Piore and Sabel 1984), major industrial complexes, such as those in the Korean automobile industry, have been constructed along older lines (Kim and Lee 1994). In short, the facts of flexible specialization do not constitute a theory of the new world's system.

From the perspective of the global firm, the regions of the world form a mosaic of differentiated sites of potential investment. Wage rates and labor militancy are two important dimensions of that mosaic, and the policy output of national states or subnational bodies of government are another. The political or policy environment of a given locality becomes an important variable in a firm's location decisions.

Part of this political environment is state policy in regard to industrial relations, policies, and laws that mediate the capital-to-labor relation. No longer held hostage to unique local agglomerations of infrastructure and labor, global capital can now threaten to withdraw investment from localities or nation-states whose governments adopt policies that are relatively favorable to labor. Global capital and its local allies are in a strategic position that allows them to demand the repeal or rollback of programs adopted during the monopoly era, but that global capital no longer regards as necessary.

This view of contemporary capitalism results in a thesis distinguished from the extensions of structuralism, and from the "orthodox" criticism of that work (Block 1977, 1981; Poulantzas 1973, 1975; Berberoglu 1981). In particular, the theory of global capitalism rejects the proposition that the relative autonomy of the state declined under monopoly capitalism. In contrast to the structuralism of the 1970s, this perspective asserts that state autonomy *does* decline under global capitalism.

The era of monopoly capitalism was once characterized in both European and North American political economic theory as one in which the state was thoroughly and instrumentally dominated by "big" capital, to the exclusion of the "broad masses."[8] However, in retrospect, it becomes clear that the transition to monopoly capitalism entailed, in the long run, an *increase* in the political influence of organized labor in the advanced industrial nations. In all of them, the monopoly era witnessed the limited ability of unions, usually in consort with a mass political party, to influence labor legislation, trade policy, and other policies surrounding the social wage.

The result included expansion of the social expenditures of the state, driven in part by the uneasy political accord between monopoly capital and monopoly labor (O'Connor 1973; Bluestone and Harrison 1982). This accord entailed a relative increment in the capacity of organized monopoly-sector labor to influence state policy, both for itself and for the broad penumbra of its allies.

Competitive sector capital, and especially small firms, did not participate fully in this accord. In a price-competitive environment, without the ability of larger firms to pass on the costs of labor legislation, taxation, or regulatory burdens, competitive industries and small firms opposed the social policies and regulatory environment of monopoly capitalism. However, the secular trend was toward the concentration of capital and the apparent marginalization of the national political influence of such forces.

Accommodation with labor was a *political* requisite to governing in North America and Western Europe in general. Examples include the ferocious struggles in the United States over social insurance and medical benefits, health and safety regulation, and labor law. In Europe, nationalization and income policies saw uneasy, and often temporary, compromises between capital and labor. Thus, under monopoly capitalism, the state was relatively autonomous from the momentary interests and direct political intervention of particular fractions of capital.

However, autonomy from the more "conservative" preferences of competitive capital was a function, in large part, of the relative dominance of monopoly capital within the capitalist class and the relative ability, in turn, of monopoly capital to make concessions to labor. Labor's enfranchisement was both the predicate and the motivation for these concessions. It should be recalled that the original concept of "the relative autonomy of the state" under monopoly capitalism denoted relative autonomy of state behavior from:

1. the transient will of fractions of the capitalist class and
2. the direct intervention or influence of incumbency by capitalist class personnel.[9]

As Ralph Miliband (1977, 74) put the first proposition: "While the state does act . . . *on behalf* of the 'ruling class,' it does not for the most part act *at its behest*."

In this context, autonomy implied discretion for decision makers. The derivation of state discretion rests on the heterogeneity of the capitalist class and the necessity to compose differences among its contending fractions in a manner that preserved the social order. The zone of discretion produced state policy that, under the conditions of monopoly capitalism appeared to be imposed on various fractions of capital. Thus occurred those instances in which "enlightened" capitalist class leadership implemented or tolerated policies rejected by that class's numerical majority: for example, many Progressive Era and New Deal reforms in America and a variety of social and industrial policies in Western Europe.

The relative autonomy of the specifically capitalist character of the state was tested by the second assertion: the independence of state policy from the biographies of official incumbents. This was borne out by the continuity of state policies when governments have been formed by social democratic and labor parties while cabinets have been recruited from outside the ranks of corporate leadership.

In addition to the two widely accepted aspects of relative autonomy just noted, this analysis includes a third, concluding observation:

3. Relative autonomy also entailed discretionary power of state managers to accommodate some of the needs and demands of labor in the political system.

The older excoriation of monopoly "domination of the state" may have been true—but it was less so than of the era before and after it. The owl of Minerva takes flight at dusk: as the moment of labor's apogee passes, and as the advanced capitalist countries reverse the moderate post-war trends toward equality, only now does analysis become cognizant of the relative uniqueness of that moment.

Implications for State Institutions

With the transition from monopoly capitalism, the emergence of global capitalism shifts the balance of class forces toward capital and the result is decline in the relative autonomy of the state from transient capitalist class will and ideology. The concept of relative autonomy implies that if autonomy is not absolute but, rather, relative, then it may vary. The possibility of variation implies a historic, developmental dimension. The question of autonomy thus has a historical specificity shared by the general question of change in the state and by class and social relations therein.

The logical implication is that important changes in the state will occur when the underlying relations between, and among, classes are transformed. The obvious qualifiers are two: first, while such underlying changes are *sufficient*, they may not be necessary—(i.e., there are other sources of state change), and second, changes in the form, process, and policy outputs of states clearly *lag* behind changes in underlying class relations. States will change after the underlying balance of power between different classes or class fractions has been restructured. Within capitalism, such changes eventually result from obstacles to accumulation. Though "crisis" theory has gone in and out of respectability in both Marxist and non-Marxist theory, it has focused on a "breakdown" problematic, namely, the analysis of those dynamics within capitalism that will, or might, produce its historical termination as a mode of production.

However, capitalism has survived its crises through structural changes that preserve its general characteristics. Restructuring crises are the midwives of transition to new variants of capitalism. State policy and political processes become responsive to newly dominant class fractions—or new bases of unity among them. Under global capitalism political change is influenced by a new strategic aspect of political within the capitalist class. This political unity consists of common concern with price competition based in part on a global search for appropriate, but often lower-waged, labor or a less burdensome regulatory environment (i.e., price competition with a geographic expression). This unites the political agendas of otherwise competing (both large and small, whether diversified or specialized) firms who share the same labor market and political jurisdictions.

The global scale of this competition grants new strategic resources and compels this new unity in capital's demands on state policy. The threat and practice of *global mobility of capital* disciplines both labor and state decision makers, who lose discretionary power over some major matters—such as taxation, social policy, and entitlements—lest investment decline within their areas of jurisdiction. The implicit, and explicit, threat of capital flight gives capital leverage to prevail more frequently than before over labor and other "cost" factors (e.g., consumer or political interests).

The political regime of monopoly capitalism was characterized by activity that, throughout the core, ameliorated the condition of the poor—surplus laborers concentrated in the secondary labor market and the competitive sector. The expenses of these activities both facilitated accumulation (by supporting aggregate demand) and legitimated the system by promoting social peace through welfarist policy and ideology (O'Connor 1973, 1–12). The programs that ameliorated the condition of the poor, it should be noted, bolstered the bargaining power and potential militancy of workers in general, for the consequences of striking or changing one's employment were thus buffered by the variety of income mainte-nance and social transfer programs (Piven and Cloward 1982).

As monopoly capitalism gives way to global capitalism, all sectors of labor decline in bargaining power, social potency, and political influence. Social expenditures give way to market coercion as the mode of enforcing discipline, and the threat of penury rather than the promise of social justice maintains order. Workers (and others) support market-oriented regimes through a blend of motives. Without relinquishing their preferences for welfarist policies, they nevertheless are persuaded in some degree, and in previously unheard of numbers, that conservative regimes can best attract the golden goose of investment, which lays the egg of jobs.

The articulation of capitalist class interests with the state also changes in the transition from one submode to another. At the turn of the century, finance and monopoly capital began the construction of an institutional relation to state power which supplanted the personalistic advantages enjoyed by the entrepreneurial founders of family fortunes (Useem 1984). The institutional order that prevailed by mid-century throughout the capitalist West afforded special access and favorable policy for the monopoly sector.

Now, spurred by competition, which includes the search for low-wage labor, and constrained by access to finance, large-scale capital becomes global—the multinational conglomerate replaces the monopolistic firm as the dominant form of enterprise. Politically, however, the project of producing abroad has a domestic face of coalition with competitive sector conservatives in an assault on the social wage, and on the discretionary expenditures of the state. Capitalist class unity in the core is reforged around resistance to the organizational and policy demands of labor.

Combined, these changes can be grossly summarized as:

1. a relative increase in the power of investors and employers in relation to labor; and
2. the increasingly transparent shift from legitimation activities to those state activities that attempt to facilitate capital accumulation (cf. O'Connor 1973).

The regime of monopoly capitalism entailed some degree of political influence going to the organized working class. The influence of the political parties and civic associations of the working class required state managers to engage in social expenditures that legitimated the state and the broader social system (O'Connor 1973). However, the heightened strategic clout of investors and employers provides the capitalist class with alternatives to social expenditures to obtain social peace. Now, instead of state activity that demonstrates compassion, democracy, and equity, the threat of job loss and economic stagnation serves to obtain compliance and political acquiescence. The vision of equity is replaced by the threat of homelessness as the means of enforcing social order.

With labor in decline and capital struggling to cope with changes in its competitive environment, state managers have less leeway to take actions that meet either the long-term needs of the social formation or the demands of labor. The autonomy of the state declines in relation to the period in which national oligopolies were the dominant form of enterprise.

GLOBAL CAPITALISM AND THE STATE IN EAST ASIA

The model of global capitalism just put forth has its origin in reflection about the industrial West—the erstwhile core. Agnew (1991) and Jennings (1991) appropriately observed that the weak state–weak labor movement of the Anglo-American (Margaret Thatcher and Ronald Reagan) era is not the whole world's way. In particular, the nationalist, state-interventionist development policies of Taiwan, Korea, and Singapore are put forward as the actions of strong, autonomous states whose behavior is counter to the general outline proposed here (cf. Amsden 1989).

The degree of state intervention taken to contrast with current state practices in the core varies. Singapore, which engages in welfarist state provisions (e.g., housing) is highly authoritarian and free trade–oriented; South Korea is nationalist in industrial and trade policy, and labor, while repressed until recently, became active in the last decade. Taiwan has benefited from egalitarian land distribution.

From the perspective of the theory global capitalism, the relevant distinction is certainly *not* "liberalization" versus statism. Rather, the distinction between core and East Asian capitalism in the era of global capitalism appears, in light of this theory, to consist of the direct versus indirect nature of state intervention on behalf of the capitalist class in the two areas. The *direct* nature of state intervention on behalf of the capitalist class, in East Asia, is part of a historical package which, under current conditions in the global system, includes *low* political efficacy of the working class. Eckert (1993) and Koo (1993b) see South Korea as having an authoritarian state, a contentious (but politically excluded) working class, and a capitalist class that was politically dependent early in the post–World War II era but is now increasingly interventionist and growing in potency in relation to the state. What characterizes all the examples of East Asian capitalism in the expansionist period of 1970–1990 is the close dedication of state policy to local capitalist class interests interpreted as national capitalist expansion (Koo 1993a).

The era of global capitalism was characterized in *Global Capitalism: The New Leviathan* (Ross and Trachte 1990) as one in which, in the older industrial regions of the core, the state *reduced* its overhead of social expenditures. The import of this trend was that the state became subject to a new constellation of pressures and workers' potency was reduced. Criticisms of the thesis noting that states in the semiperiphery are the more activist are literally irrelevant to the extent that these states are staunch defenders of local (or other) capitalist classes.

In many of the expanding, formerly agrarian or colonial economies, the state is less influenced by empowered national fractions of the working class and its local vigor is more nearly devoted to local capitalist class interest (compared to those social formations whose working classes have, over four generations, wrested some political influence from their rulers). This difference in local history and developmental stages accounts for the different ways in which the same (global) era in world capitalist history effects state behavior in different areas.

In the older industrial areas, where the various national working classes have a history of self-organization and enfranchisement, the current moment witnesses the reduction of the attack on their political and economic power and influence and the detachment of state policy from their interests. The phenomenal appearance of this change is the "retreat" of the state and the increased of the importance of market forces. The language used by Ross and Trachte's 1990 formulations may not have clearly enough marked the differences in class relations to the state in the different regions of the global system. In particular, among the East Asian newly industrialized countries (NICs), the state is available to the capitalist class without the same level of political competition for it as in the West. The capitalist class has more uninhibited access to state power.

Thus, the development of a global capitalist successor to the monopolistic stage of capitalist development leaves all previous forms of capitalist enterprise present—including competitive firms and sectors and national oligopolies; however, it changes the nature of the dominant forms of organization—the global conglomer-ate—and the nature of competition. Price competition returns, labor loses bargaining power, and state autonomy and state social interventions decline in the older regions and may rise in the NICs, but everywhere capital's interest has new prevalence over labor. This summary is broadly suggestive of an approach to the issues involved in the incorporation of the formerly "socialist" countries into the global order.

It is a matter of some irony that conventional, anti-Communist Sovietology and East European political economic studies, as of the early 1990s, proceeded quite apart from what sociologists, political scientists, and others called development studies (no less, world-system or other analytical systems). The conventional *political* view, as enshrined in the mass media, conflated democratization and market liberalization. The privatization of industry and the creation of Western-style markets and financial instruments were widely depicted as sure and certain paths to prosperity. Individuals with such views might have profitably attended to the great variety of studies of penetration by transnational corporations (TNCs) and investment dependence (e.g., Bornschier, Chase-Dunn, and Rubinson 1978; London and Smith 1988; London and Robinson 1989; London and Williams 1988) which suggest the hazards which loomed before middle Europe.

How will nations such as Poland, the Czech Republic, or Hungary be incorporated into the global capitalist order? While the new capitalist countries of Central Europe may hope for a role analogous to that of Portugal, Spain, or Greece (Böröcz 1992, 206), they may be in danger of the dependence, volatility, inequality, and large-scale poverty of Mexico. While this matter cannot be taken up here, the critical point is that there is now only one global alternative, global capitalism, and those who direct its investment flows are the key to each regions' fate and fortune. In the past, their logic has not been a portent of good fortune for each of the world's regions, and it is not apt to bear magical healing for Middle Europe.

CONCLUSION: INTEGRATION VERSUS CHAOS

The tumult of this era includes the collapse of the Communist parties and the states they led. As this book comes to press, ethnic war is afire in Europe, Africa, and Asia. In the older industrial regions, economic stagnation presages political change, and the end of rapid growth in the periphery has brought about yet another round of political instability.

Rather than systemic breakdown, however, these events mask the reintegration of capitalism into a new, global, variant. Based on the ability to evade labor and politically efficacious workers, this historical moment of capitalist development will itself eventually pass. Potential political hegemons will contest one another, no doubt in epochal struggles, and they too will change.

Someday, if not soon, the world's laborers will find the elements of unity that will permit them to address in common their employers and governors. Whether this will then herald the end of global capitalism as capitalism's last variant in human history cannot now be known, but it is a result for which many will hope.

NOTES

1.   This approach uses a region-by-industry approach to the analysis of social change. It sees the local-global change relation as best expressed in the analysis of local industry in a global context.

2.   While capitalism may be articulated with subsystems based on coerced labor, it has historically always come to dominate them. The straightforward empirical test of "domination" is the flow of value: value (surplus labor) flows *from* subordinate modes of production (or subordinate variants of a given mode) *to* dominant ones. Of course, empirically, this is not so easy to establish. A different

view, the orthodox world-system starting point (which defines capitalism as commodity production using any means of appropriating the product of labor) may be found in Chase-Dunn (1989), who defended, articulately, world-system theorists' preference for defining capitalism as "commodity production for exchange," in which coerced labor may be part of the capitalist mode of production.

3.   Baran and Sweezy's other technical innovation was top claim that a "rising rate of surplus" had supplanted a "declining rate of profit" as a key, problematic process for capital accumulation.

4.   The labor *shortages* that accounted for the comparatively better conditions of American as compared to European, workers, motivated industry's support for immigration and the strategy of ethnic division, which was extremely useful to employers in mass production industries during labor conflicts starting in the last decades of the nineteenth century (see, e.g., Kornblum 1974). That the immigration of former peasants could be such a corrective is accounted for by the relatively undifferentiated nature of labor demand.

5.   Among the current core nations, the arguable exception is Japan, where state institutions exerted more intensive and extensive influence during the period referred to as the Meiji restoration (which corresponds to parts of the competitive era in the West) but did so, of course, in very different structural settings. The Japanese working class, however, was, similar to those in the West, excluded from political or social influence.

6.   Though Waldinger (1986) found evidence of increasing concentration in the garment industry, Taplin (1994), citing Office of Technology Assessment (OTA) (1987), showed the opposite; in any case it is still a small firm, fiercely price competitive industry.   However, Taplin (1994) and Appelbaum, Smith, and Christenson (1994) showed that apparel production is thoroughly internationalized.

7.   See Ross and Trachte (1990, ch. 4, 5) for a discussion of the contrast between global capitalism and world-system theory on this matter.

8.   Although they are by no means distinct in this approach, see, for example, Baran and Sweezy (1966) and O'Connor (1973).

9.   See the Poulantzas-Miliband debate; in part, Miliband (1973), on Poulantzas (1973); Miliband (1969); and Poulantzas (1975).   Also see Kasinitz (1983).

REFERENCES

Aglietta, Michel. 1979. *A Theory of Capitalist Regulation: The U.S. Experience.*
        London: New Left Books.
Agnew, John A. 1991. Review of Ross and Trachte (1990). *Economic Geography*
        67, no. 3:262–63.
Amsden, Alice. 1989. *Asia's Next Giant.* New York: Oxford University Press.
Appelbaum, Richard P., David A. Smith, and Brad Christenson. 1994. "Commod-
        ity Chains and Industrial Restructuring in the Pacific Rim: Garment Trade and

Manufacturing." In Gary Gereffi and Miguel Korzeniewicz, eds., *Commodity Chains and Global Capitalism*. Westport, CT: Praeger, 187–204.

Baran, Paul, and Paul Sweezy. 1966. *Monopoly Capital*. New York: Monthly Review.

Berberoglu, Berch. 1981. "The Capitalist State: Its 'Relative Autonomy' Reexamined." *New Political Science* 2:135–40.

Block, Fred. 1977. "The Ruling Class Does Not Rule: Notes on The Marxist Theory of the State." *Socialist Review* 33 (May-June): 6–28.

———. 1981. "Beyond Relative Autonomy: State Managers as Historical Subjects." *New Political Science* 2:33–49.

Bluestone, Barry, and Bennett Harrison. 1982. *The Deindustrialization of America: Plant Closings, Community Abandonment, and the Dismantling of Basic Industry*. New York: Basic Books.

Bornschier, Volker, and Christopher Chase-Dunn. 1985. *Transnational Corporations and Underdevelopment*. New York: Praeger.

Bornschier, Volker, Christopher Chase-Dunn, and Richard Rubinson. 1978. "Cross-National Evidence of the Effects of Foreign Investment and Aid on Economic Growth and Inequality: A Survey of Findings and a Reanalysis." *American Journal of Sociology* 84:651–83.

Böröcz, József. 1992. "Dual Dependency and the Informalization of External Linkages: The Hungarian Case." *Research in Social Movements, Conflicts and Change* 14:189–209.

Chase-Dunn, Christopher. 1989. *Global Formation: Structures of the World-Economy*. New York: Basil Blackwell.

Dicken, Peter. 1992. *Global Shift: The Internationalization of Economic Activity*. 2d ed. New York: Guilford.

Eckert, Carter J. 1993. "The South Korean Bourgeoisie: A Class in Search of Hegemony." In Hagen Koo, ed., *State and Society in Contemporary Korea*. Ithaca, NY: Cornell University Press, 95–130.

Emmanuel, Arghiri. 1972. *Unequal Exchange: A Study of the Imperialism of Trade*. New York: Monthly Review.

Frank, André Gunder. 1987. "Global Crisis and Transformation." In Richard Peet, ed., *International Capitalism and Industrial Restructuring*. Boston: Allen and Unwin, 393–412.

Gereffi, Gary, and Miguel Korzeniewicz, eds.. 1994. *Commodity Chains and Global Capitalism*. Westport, CT: Praeger.

Gordon, David, Richard Edwards, and Michael Reich. 1982. *Segmented Work, Divided Workers: The Historical Transformation of Labour in the U.S.*. Cambridge: Cambridge University Press.

Harrison, Benjamin, and Barry Bluestone. 1988. *The Great U-Turn*. New York: Basic Books.

Hopkins, Terence K., and Immanuel Wallerstein. 1986. "Commodity Chains in the World Economy Prior to 1800." *Review* (Fernand Braudel Center) 10, no. 1:157–70.

Jennings, P. Devereaux. 1991. [Review of Ross and Trachte (1990)] *Contemporary Sociology* 20, no. 5:710–11.

Kasinitz, Phillip. 1983. "Neo-Marxist Views of the State." *Dissent* 30:337–46.

Kim, Hyung Kook, and Su-Hoon Lee. 1994. "Commodity Chains and the Korean Automobile Industry." In Gary Gereffi and Miguel Korzeniewicz, eds., *Commodity Chains and Global Capitalism*. Westport, CT: Praeger, 281–96.

Koo, Hagen. 1993a. "Introduction: Beyond State-Market Relations." In Hagen Koo, ed., *State and Society in Contemporary Korea*. Ithaca, NY: Cornell University Press, 1–12.

———. 1993b. "The State, *Minjung*, and the Working Class in South Korea." In Hagen Koo, ed., *State and Society in Contemporary Korea*. Ithaca, NY: Cornell University Press, 131–62.

Kornblum, William. 1974. *Blue Collar Community*. Chicago: University of Chicago Press.

London, Bruce, and Thomas D. Robinson. 1989. "The Effect of International Dependence on Income Inequality and Political Violence." *American Sociological Review* 54:305–8.

London, Bruce, and David A. Smith. 1988. "Urban Bias, Dependence, and Economic Stagnation." *American Sociological Review* 53:454–63.

London, Bruce, and Bruce A. Williams. 1988. "Multinational Corporate Penetration, Protest, and Basic Needs Provision in Non-Core Nations: A Cross-National Analysis." *Social Forces* 66, no. 3:747–73.

Miliband, Ralph. 1969. *The State in Capitalist Society*. New York: Basic Books.

———. 1973. "Poulantzas and the Capitalist State." *New Left Review* 82:83–92.

———. 1977. *Marxism and Politics*. Oxford, UK: Oxford University Press.

Noponen, Helzi, Julie Graham, and Ann R. Markusen. 1993. *Trading Industries, Trading Regions*. New York: Guilford.

O'Connor, James. 1973. *The Fiscal Crisis of the State*. New York: St. Martin's Press.

O'Keefe, Phil, ed. 1984. *Regional Restructuring under Advanced Capitalism*. London: Croom Helm.

OTA. 1987. *The U.S. Texztile and Apparel Industry: A Revolution in Progress*. Washington, D.C.: Office of Technology Assessment.

Piore, Michael, and Charles Sabel. 1984. *The Second Industrial Divide*. New York: Basic Books.

Piven, Frances Fox, and Richard Cloward. 1982. *The New Class War*. New York: Pantheon.

Poulantzas, Nicos. 1973. *Political Power and Social Classes*. London: New Left Books.

———. 1976. "The Capitalist State: A Reply to Miliband and Laclau." *New Left Review,* 95:63–83.

Ross, Robert, Don Shakow, and Paul Susman. 1980. "Local Planners—Global Constraints" *Policy Sciences* 13:1–25.

Ross, Robert J. S. and Kent C. Trachte. 1990. *Global Capitalism: The New Leviathan.* Albany: State University of New York Press.

Szymanski, Albert. 1981. *The Logic of Imperialism.* New York: Praeger.

Taplin, Ian M. 1994. "Strategic Orientations of U.S. Apparel Firms." In Gary Gereffi and Miguel Korzeniewicz, eds., *Commodity Chains and Global Capitalism.* Westport, CT: Praeger, 205–22.

Trachte, Kent, and Robert J. S. Ross. 1985. "The Crisis of Detroit and the Emergence of Global Capitalism." *International Journal of Urban and Regional Research* 9, no. 2:186–217.

Useem, Michael. 1984. *The Inner Circle: Large Corporations and the Rise of Business Political Activity in the U.S. and U.K.* Oxford, UK: Oxford University Press.

Waldinger, Roger. 1986. *Through the Eye of the Needle.* New York: New York University Press.

3

The New Colonialism: Global Regulation and the Restructuring of the Interstate System

Philip McMichael

This chapter argues that the world is on the threshold of a major transition in the political regulation of economic activity: from a primarily national to a primarily global form of regulation. Recent episodes of restructuring undermine *national* forms of political-economic organization. Under the pressure of multilateral agencies, global firms, and global and regional free trade agreements (FTAs), nation-states increasingly surrender the organizational and ideological initiative to transnational forces. In short, nation-states face a form of colonization, distinct from previous forms.

Colonialism historically involved episodes or combinations of expansion of nations (settler colonialism) and expansion of states, as in late nineteenth-century imperialism (Arrighi 1978, 36–37). The objects of colonization were territories and peoples. However, in the late twentieth century *nation*-states, the regulators of territories and peoples, are being colonized. The colonization now is essentially by capital, under the banner of liberalization.[1] While it is a universal process, it has taken its most virulent forms in the financial conditions imposed on southern states during the 1980s. An equally far-reaching, and arguably intentional, consequence of the debt regime (notably, global labor-cost reduction) is the challenge to the managed economies and social and political democracies of the metropolitan states. As global circuits of capital destabilize nation-states by restructuring production, markets and class relations, new ideologies of nativism, ethnocentrism, and racism have emerged, as communities and labor forces compete for economic survival. Such ideologies substitute separatist politics for the inclusive politics of social democracy.

These trends unravel a century-long process of construction of citizenship and its social and political entitlements in the formation of *nation*-states. The current restructuring of states proceeds via limitation of democratic politics, declining economic sovereignty, and the enlistment of state administrations in the service of global circuits. In this sense, states increasingly assume, albeit unevenly or incompletely, the colonial posture: administering the colonizer's needs by organizing the exploitation of labor and natural resources for global banks and corporations. This includes proclaiming an ideology of service to these projects, namely, the ideology of global (price) efficiency, as the national goal is redefined as viability in a global economy. It is analogous to the historic subordination of indigenous cultures to the civilizing mission of Western rationalism. The rationalism of contemporary neoliberal ideology, with its price fetishism, is nonterritorial. That is, the "new colonialism" represents a distinctly postnational phase of world-capitalist history.

WORLD HISTORICAL CONTEXT

The history of the capitalist world-economy constitutes a succession of political forms of capitalism, including dominant and opposing models. Recent episodes of hegemony reveal these contradictory dynamics especially well. For British hegemony, which was an attempt to impose a colonial system writ large via the role of "workshop of the world," the countermovement was the rise of the nation-state (McMichael 1985). For U.S. hegemony, which stabilized a system of *nation*-states via the Bretton Woods institutional complex, the countermovement was transnational integration (Friedmann and McMichael 1989). The dominant principle—which was freedom of trade under the British and freedom of enterprise under the United States—generated countermovements that simultaneously eroded hegemony and shaped the post-hegemonic period (Polanyi 1957, Arrighi 1982). For example, British-sponsored free trade generated a protective movement of national economic management on the part of Britain's rivals, while U.S.-sponsored free enterprise encouraged the transnational integration of productive circuits. The latter, in generating offshore capital markets, has spawned a direct challenge to national economic management. The last two decades have seen a dramatic reorganization of capitalism and state forms, with a mutual conditioning of global markets and the political deregulation of national economies.

Arrighi argued that transnational enterprise "marks the end of the process of supersession of the Westphalia System and the beginning of the withering away of the interstate system as primary locus of world power" (1990b, 403). Certainly, the Westphalian concept of a system of sovereign states is increasingly outmoded. However, the interstate system, such as it is becoming, continues to be a significant locus of world power. The issue here is the difference between states and *nation*-states. My argument is that while the nation-state itself is losing salience, the state itself is by no means in decline.[2] It is, rather, being transformed. Not only is governance itself redistributed among agencies operating above and below the nation, but the policy agenda is also undergoing a fundamental redefinition. The result is less and less a nationally organized state, and more and more a transnationally organized one. To explain this shift, I will summarize the history of the *nation*-state.

The *national* form of the state is a mere *moment* in the history of the world capitalist economy. It reached its greatest coherence in the metropolitan world and has, more or less, been compromised in the former colonial regions (Migdal 1986, Hobsbawm 1991). It stemmed from the process of development, organization, and regulation of wage labor in the nineteenth century. Earlier, the colonial system was the principal mechanism generating surpluses for the metropolitan economy and markets for metropolitan manufacturing. This global process anticipated, and then coexisted with, wage labor, as the foundation of industrial capitalism (and British hegemony). Here capital now controlled, rather than mediated, production, and the enhanced scale and productivity of wage labor generated new (extracolonial) markets and a mode of self-expansion leading to the relaxation of mercantilist regulations (Marx [1867] 1965). The resulting free trade regime precipitated the national movement, emerging within the dynamic of British hegemony. The British attempt to establish a self-regulating (world) market via the gold standard, as anchored by the pound sterling, institutionalized national banking and political constitutionalism (see Polanyi 1957). Britain's global engineering to become "workshop of the world" provoked rival national capitalisms, which were anchored in the new, central banking. This produced a specific coupling of capital with the state, which regulated it nationally (McMichael 1987).

The national movement reached its apogee in the post–World War II global order under U.S. hegemony. The principles of liberal democracy and national economic management defined the North Atlantic bloc of the Cold War. The opposing bloc, that of Warsaw Pact socialism, similarly practiced national economic organization (Friedmann 1994). The countermovement *within* the U.S. hegemonic bloc (as part of its political-economic cohesion) was the transnational integration of capital, which has since undermined capital's national form (Arrighi 1982, Friedmann and McMichael 1989).

We are presently witnessing a rearguard move by the United States to consolidate a postnational order, with states submitting to the rules and culture of the market on a world scale. If such an economic liberal order were instituted, it would constitute an Anglo-American global regulatory system. To accomplish this requires the complicity of states, with international rules displacing national regulation. The vehicle of such complicity is multifaceted: from the debt regime through new global and regional economic arrangements, such as the General Agreement on Tariffs and Trade (GATT) and the North American Free Trade Agreement (NAFTA) and to America's recent sabre-rattling by threatening rival trading states with retaliation through the Super 301 Law. Because all of these measures would, and already do, subordinate all states to market rules (corporate power), I refer to them as the new colonialism.

POSTNATIONAL CAPITALISM

The American hegemonic project involved the reconstruction of the international economy under the principles of "embedded liberalism," where "multi-lateralism would be predicated upon domestic interventionism" (Ruggie 1982, 393). Bretton Woods Agreement, which was institutionalized in stable currency exchanges supported by the IMF and the World Bank and underwritten by U.S. deficits, framed the consolidation of national (largely metropolitan) capitalisms anchored in Keynesian policy. The principle was to secure macroeconomic policy instruments by controlling domestic rates of interest, "without interference from the ebb and flow of international capital movements or flights of hot money," as Keynes himself put it (quoted in Crook 1992, 10). This international/national institutional complex anchored a nation-centered social contract between capital and labor, stimulating the consumption of mass-produced commodities via policies promoting high wages, full employment, and farm subsidies. The national model of economic growth, epitomized by the United States and institutionalized in Bretton Woods, was projected into the expanding state system via decolonization and a discourse of "development." Strategies of import substitution in both industry and agriculture (the "green revolution") were adopted in the name of national development (Senghaas 1988, 46–47; Friedmann and McMichael 1989).

Within this "development regime," in which nation-building was a key geopolitical project within the Cold War context (Block 1977; Kaldor 1990), the countermovement of the internationalization of economic relations gathered weight. Transnational economic integration, linking subsectors with consumers and producers across national boundaries, occurred under the combined activities of multinational corporations and aid programs. The replication of this model of economic integration, in both industry and agriculture, underlay the intensified trade and investment patterns among metropolitan states in the postwar era. This mosaic of exchanges underwrote a period of prosperity for national capitalisms. It also underwrote a growing offshore dollar market, the so-called Euromarket. The Euromarket was a direct financial outgrowth of the global operations of transnational corporations (TNCs), and it also became the repository of American imperial spending abroad.

The burgeoning Euromarket symbolized the destabilizing of the Bretton Woods system, as American deficits ballooned in the late 1960s (Kolko 1988). As a facility for the redistribution of world liquidity, it substantially transformed the global order during the 1970s. Pressure on the dollar, excabated by a growing competition among rival TNCs investing in the periphery (Arrighi 1982), forced the U.S. government to declare the dollar nonconvertible in 1971. This released global economic forces. The offshore capital market, fueled by petro-dollars, grew from $315 billion in 1973 to $2,055 billion in 1982, and the seven largest U.S. banks saw their overseas profits climb from 22 percent to 60 percent of total profits between 1970 and 1982 (Debt Crisis Network 1986, 25).

The collapse of the Bretton Woods monetary regime ushered in a profound crisis of national regulation. Not only have nation-states been set adrift to negotiate their own competitive position within the world economy, but in doing so they have capitulated to the rule of the market. As the *Economist* stated, in its own inimitable way: "Exposed to offshore finance, controls fail; without controls, the boundaries between market segments cannot be defended; and without segmented markets, relationship-finance gives way to price-based finance. In short, market forces break in and run riot" (Crook 1992, September 19, 12). Alternatively, social priorities yield to private initiatives, which are increasingly concentrated and centralized under the new market order. As social priorities have evaporated, so have the illusions about development (as a publicly managed process of rising material living standards). These illusions nourished the period of national capitalism during the heyday of American hegemony. Moreover, when monetarism (e.g., credit restraint to curb inflation) pulled the rug from the debt financing enjoined by global enterprises, metropolitan farms and newly industrializing countries (NICs), it precipitated a debilitating debt crisis. This crisis, and the management of debt repayment with draconian conditions, revealed the limits and illusions of the development regime (cf. Arrighi 1990a).

This shift, from the development regime of the postwar era (1950–1970) to the debt regime (1980s), is at the heart of the reorganization of the interstate system. The fundamental shift was from state to capital as the organizing principle of international political economy. That is, the goal (and initiative) of economic management passes from national coherence to enterprise competitiveness in a global market. Finance capital has orchestrated this passage. Banks and financial institutions have emerged as the leading fraction of capital, with a global reach allowing them to uncouple from national regulation as well as productive capital. As Keynesianism disappeared and metropolitan economies slowed, declining consumption produced excess liquidity, elevating the power of the financiers already emboldened by the Euromarket (Arrighi 1978, 132). In turn, as unregulated global banking proliferated, the multilateral financial institutions (the World Bank and the IMF) have assumed a central banking role for the world. From being the handmaidens of national development under Bretton Woods, they have become the henchmen of transnational investors.

The growing power of financial capital in the 1970s and its newfound global mobility fundamentally altered the interstate system in both form and content. In *form*, finance capital restructured the interstate system in sponsoring the rise of the NICs. Such sharp differentiation among peripheral states undercut the political solidarity of the Third World in its mid-1970s bid to install a "new international economic order" (NIEO). During the 1970s, global financiers bankrolled industrial and agroindustrial developments in "middle-income" states, where 60 percent of foreign direct investment in the periphery was concentrated in just six countries: Hong Kong, Singapore, Malaysia, Argentina, Mexico, and Brazil (Daly and Logan 1989, 64). The rise of the newly industrializing (and agricultural and oil-producing) countries served to divide the south and legitimize a new export-oriented development strategy (Hoogvelt 1987). In consequence, a relatively tidy division of the world between northern and southern states is rendered more problematic. This has significant political effects—an obvious one being that such political fragmentation is fertile territory for imposing a new GATT, as well as new regional rules on the southern states.

In terms of the changed *content* of the interstate system, the greater power and mobility of finance capital has been deployed against the institutional complex of social democracy in metropolitan states. Offshore export platforms, bankrolled via international capital markets and organized by TNCs, routinely undermine the viability of metropolitan firms and industries and/or the power of organized labor. The social contract underlying national economic management has been steadily dismantled as industrial jobs have moved offshore or been deskilled. The universal spread of low-wage production and structural unemployment, which presently dominates state policy concerns of the Organization for Economic Cooperation and Development (OECD), results from the collapse of postwar systems of nationally regulated capitalism. Under the conditions of global finance, mass production for the regulated high-wage economy is no longer an adequate model. New forms of global accumulation uproot production systems from their linkages within mature home markets, reattaching them to more competitive and unstable global circuits of consumption and production. Sassen observed, "By the late 1970s, the wage-setting power of leading industries and their shadow effect had eroded significantly in both the United Kingdom and the United States, and by the mid-1980s it was becoming evident in Japan" (1991, 219). The resulting erosion of metropolitan social-democratic constituencies has had a profoundly conservative political fallout, as ethnic tensions surrounding immigrant labor, for example, have increased.

Finance capital has not simply restructured states from within, it has also appropriated power from states themselves (see Bienefeld 1989, 1992), most notably in the debt crises of the early 1980s, when some Eastern European and Third World countries failed to meet their debt obligations (Cox 1987, 301–2). At this juncture, as banks lacked the capacity to discipline their debtors, the IMF assumed the role of debt manager, affirming the state/international finance nexus (Wood 1986, 286; Cox 1987, 302). In centralizing the enforcement of debt repayment, the IMF also obtained the financial resources to play a central banking role for the world (Wood 1986, 301). The power of the IMF to compel state subordination to finance capital thus institutionalizes the trend toward postnational capitalism (McMichael 1992).

THE DEBT REGIME

Collectively, the debtor countries entered the 1990s "fully 61 per cent more in debt than they were in 1982" (George 1992, xvi). The (net) extraction of financial resources from the south during the 1980s exceeded $400 billion. Meanwhile the banks, protected from debt loss by northern governments, earned vast profits on the order of 40 percent per annum on southern investments alone (George 1992, 97). Not only did northern governments accept the status as lenders of last resort, Third World debt rescheduling embodies a clear policy choice in favor of finance capital. The premium on debt repayment, on a case-by-case basis (which individualizes the problem), amounts to a decision to restrict markets for northern exports. The debt crisis has been "policed mainly as a banking crisis, and secondarily, as an export crisis for some U.S. companies" (Corbridge 1993, 129). The imposition of deflationary conditions on southern states slowed economic growth rates and middle-income consumption, thereby reducing imports. Overall, the rate of growth of world exports to the south fell from 7.9 percent to minus 0.2 percent between the periods of 1969–1981 and 1981–1988 (George 1992, 103).

The impact on northern economies was significant, especially in further dismantling the economic sectors associated with the nationally organized capitalism of the postwar period. Estimates indicate that up to 3 million person-years of employment were lost in North America in the 1980s as a result of declining exports, and Great Britain lost exports equivalent to 49 percent in real terms between 1980 and 1983 (Corbridge 1993, 131–32). One calculation is that between 1980 and 1984, while manufacturing profits were negative, U.S. banks' direct investment in the Third World grew by 26 percent (Overseas Development Council 1986, cited in George 1992, 97).

Metropolitan denationalization mirrors a more extensive process in the south, where the privatization of public assets in most states (sometimes via debt-equity swaps) replaced the prior trend of nationalization under the aegis of the develop-mental state. In the 1980s, nationalizations disappeared as the average number of privatizations expanded on the order of about 700 percent across the decade (calculated from Crook 1993, 16): thus, "the only thing that was socialized rather than privatized was debt itself" (George 1992, 106) This swelled the power and scope of finance capital: the stock of international bank lending rose from 4 percent to 44 percent of the OECD's GDP between 1980 and 1992 (Crook 1992, 9). Whereas global foreign direct investment (FDI) declined from a peak of $234 billion to $150 billion between 1989 and 1992, during the same period FDI in the south (especially Mexico, China, Malaysia, Argentina, and Thailand) increased from $29 billion to $40 billion (Crook 1993, 16). The inescapable conclusion is that the debt regime is making the south safe for capital, footloose as it may be.

What is commonly referred to as a "lost decade" for the Third World needs to be understood more as a decade of financial terrorism. The imposition of global austerity at the same time restructured power relations across the interstate system. For the south, debt rescheduling and economic liberalization (e.g., competitive devaluation) consolidated the disunity stemming from the defeat of the NIEO initiative and the atomizing consequences (and intent) of monetarism.[3] The debt crisis (as an individualized crisis) enabled debt managers to end the illusion of national development and to institute the export-led growth model in the service of repayment. This, in turn, ensured the reorganization of political and economic power within individual states.

State restructuring required a reversal of the Bretton Woods legacies. Two related shifts in the early 1980s monetarist counterrevolution expressed an Anglo-American for power.

First, the rejection of *multilateral* management of the world economy was orchestrated by the United States through a devaluation of the (overvalued) dollar at the close of the 1970s, which precipitated a global recession (Wood 1986, 262). A new politics of austerity, based on tight credit policies, undermined the global debt structure. A significant redistribution of power followed as U.S.-dominated multilateral institutions such as the World Bank and the IMF assumed new powers. This involved the replacement of individualized short- and long-term loans by standardized packages dictating financial orthodoxy as the mechanism of debt repayment.[4] So-called "structural adjustment" loans replaced traditional IMF liquidity lending and World Bank project lending. Universal financial rationalization, managed by the multilateral agencies on behalf of the banks and their Group of 7 (G-7) governments (the U.S., Canada, Japan, France, Italy, Germany and the United Kingdom), replaced national development projects.

Second, the suspension of *development planning* in the debtor countries was accomplished partly by defining debt as a liquidity problem rather than a structural one (Economic Commission 1989, 123), locating the blame in debtor country policy rather than in the system at large. The financial agencies applied an increasingly restricted theory of sovereign immunity, whereby "sovereign borrowers could be requested to waive their immunity in loan contracts and thereby open up their foreign property used for commercial activity in the United States and United Kingdom to attachment, and execution" (Economic Commission 1989, 108). Such waivers were given in exchange for higher volumes of credit in the 1970s. When the crunch came, however, this practice rebounded. Responsibility for the repayment of debt devolved upon individual countries, via the balance-of-payments policy, with some emergency assistance from the OECD states.

THE NEW COLONIALISM

The debt regime has been the pretext for dismantling the development regime. As I have argued, this has involved a rollback of public policies geared to national economic management, under the banner of liberalization. I consider this a form of colonialism for the following reasons. States have surrendered powers of economic sovereignty, most notably in the management of national currencies, production priorities, and natural resources. State managers have collaborated in this project of privatization (dismantling public assets and facilities). Social-democratic constituencies have been undermined as a result, thereby exposing the political process to transnational forces that tend to reorient national economies to global markets. This fragmentation of national political and economic complexes releases subnational forces such as ethnonational separatism and microregional economic niches, thus privileging supranational forces (whether TNCs or multilateral managers of disintegrating states). To the extent that national organization subsides, the centralization of global economic management by the G-7 powers proceeds, largely in the service of powerful financial interests. In this section, I illustrate this process as it unfolds at the national and the global levels.

At the *national level*, structural adjustment policies pursued by the multilateral agencies in Africa reveal a telling redefinition of the problem of the state.[5] Initially, under the 1981 Berg Report from the World Bank on development prospects in sub-Saharan Africa, the goal of 'shrinking' the state was justified on grounds of efficiency and reducing urban bias (Bernstein 1990, 19). Structural adjustment programs (SAPs) directly challenged the class (e.g., wage earners) and political coalitions and discourses, thus sustaining the developmental state and its national projects. At the same time, SAPs strengthened finance ministries in the policy-making process (Gibbon 1992, 137). Overall, the Berg Report expressed a shift in the World Bank's lending practice from project aid toward tying aid to "comprehensive policy reform" (Bernstein 1990, 17).

The World Bank's premise was that the states experiencing postcolonial development were insufficiently indigenous in structure and policy. They were, therefore, overbureaucratic and inefficient, on the one hand, and unresponsive to civil society, on the other. In the World Bank's major report of 1989 on Sub-Saharan Africa, "shrinking" the state was reinterpreted politically, as a device to release populist initiatives. According to Beckman, the bank's democratic posturing is a form of "managerial populism" in which the World Bank attempts to undercut the opponents of structural adjustment programs by promoting community-level entrepreneurship. In effect, this interpretation considers the World Bank's recent position as a deeper challenge to the African nation-state by legitimizing a postnationalist (globalist) mentality: "Donors and bankers feel free to justify intervention with reference to their own notions of desirable development, rather than the development objectives of national governments" (Beckman 1992, 92, 99).

During the 1980s, World Bank Structural Adjustment Loans (SALs) (usually complemented by IMF conditionality with respect to financial stabilization) were used to extract and underwrite policy changes such as market liberalization, sectoral restructuring, privatization, and the promotion of exports to service debt. The story, for example, of how the World Bank negotiated with the Mexican government to restructure its agricultural policy in the 1980s is well known: the outcome was the reversal of an initiative to stabilize small-holding and medium-size capitalist family farming, along with the promotion of large-scale, foreign financed agroexport production. In these kinds of adjustments, domestic food security is redefined such that agroexports finance imports of cheap grains from the North American "breadbasket" (see McMichael and Myhre 1991; Myhre 1994). In the process of sectoral restructuring, SALs also enable a redistribution of power within the state from program-oriented ministries (e.g., social services, agriculture, and education) to the central bank and to trade and finance ministries (Canak 1989).

In its 1989 report entitled, significantly enough, *Sub-Saharan Africa from Crisis to Sustainable Growth: A Long-Term Perspective Study*, the bank advanced the notion of "political conditionality," whereby it proposed "policy dialogue" with recipient states, which would lead to "consensus forming." In effect, this involves a more sophisticated agenda of constructing cadres within the recipient state who embrace economic reforms proposed by the multilateral agencies (Gibbon 1992, 141). Stephany Griffith-Jones observed, "It has become an explicit target of the institutions, and the World Bank in particular, to shift the balance of power within governments towards those who expect to gain from the policy reforms encouraged by the institutions and/or those who are in any case more sympathetic towards such changes" (Rodriguez and Griffith-Jones 1992, quoted in Crook 1991, 19).

Deploying financial leverage to advance liberalization not only subordinates national sovereignty, such as it is, to institutionalized conditions favoring globalization. It also remakes the state. The internalization of global financial dictates is reflected in policy, as well as in the structure and allegiances, of the "reform" administrations. The structure may well be partly the creation of the bank itself, through its "institution-building" operations. In an account of the conditions imposed on an unnamed debtor country, which was derived from confidential bank documents, Jonathan Cahn detailed how the bank funded (to the tune of U.S. $9 million) an interministerial commission to manage the structural adjustment process, with a "technical committee" established to perform the commission's work (1993, 179). In the bank's words, this new administrative unit was "designed to assist . . . the Government in implementing its structural adjustment program successfully" (World Bank 1989, quoted in Cahn 1993, 180). Bruce Rich documented such Trojan horse activity as a routine operation by the bank in shaping conditions for lending capital to states (1994).

On the *global level*, this kind of new trusteeship role assumed by the multilateral agencies complements the imposition of global market rule. It is part of the emergence of global regulatory mechanisms that replace national forms of capitalist regulation and have increasingly begun to override national sovereignty (see McMichael and Myhre 1991). The World Bank, which is now the principal multilateral agency involved in global development financing, plays a definite governing role.[6] Not only does it "dictate legal and institutional change through its lending process" (Cahn 1993, 161), but also, since its 1989 report, it now asserts that evaluating governance in debtor countries is within its jurisdiction (Cahn 1993, 163; Rich 1994).[7]

However, despite the new emphasis on human rights and democratization as conditions for reform and financial assistance, the World Bank remains "structurally and operationally unaccountable to the citizenry in developing countries" (Cahn 1993, 165). Moreover, when the IMF and the bank, through convening a meeting of the Paris Club, stabilize and lend long-term to a debtor, they assume "a governance role that may best be likened to that of a trustee in bankruptcy"—except that trustees are accountable to the bankruptcy court, while the IMF and the World Bank (WB) remain unaccountable, other than to their powerful underwriters (Cahn

1993, 172).[8] On the other hand, on approval of a loan, U.S. corporations and citizens are given access to economic (and political) intelligence reports prepared by the bank. The political asymmetry is obvious enough, and it lends support to Stephen Gill's (1992) notion of the "new constitutionalism," in which parallel to economic globalization trends there is an internationalization of (public and private) political authority.

The attempt to establish world market rule, as Polanyi (1957) reminded us, requires an institutional framework, which in turn must be anchored in a powerful state. Having lost the unqualified commercial and financial supremacy of a hegemonic state, the United States has sought other enforcement mechanisms to assert its power in the world. In particular, in the 1980s it led the struggle to instrumentalize GATT as the third leg of a powerful "new institutional trinity" (as the recent chair of the G77 (the Third World Political Caucus established at the UN in 1963), Luis Fernando Jaramillo, called the WB, IMF, and GATT) dedicated to establishing a neoliberal discipline in the interstate system (McMichael 1993). In the 1990s, as undisputed military super-power in the post–Cold War era, the United States set up a tributary system, led by Japan, to offset its recently acquired financial deficit, while other states must submit to the discipline of finance capital (Cox 1992, 37). The structure of global power, at this level, is quite unstable, for while the G-7 acts as a collective world-economic management team, asserting market rules, the United States, as a recalcitrant super-power, flouts them.

Recent neomercantilist threats by the United States to deploy Super-301 against Japan, hard on the heels of the provisional completion of the Uruguay Round of GATT, illustrate this dual power. Another episode, this time directed against a German pretender, involved the struggle over the recolonization of Eastern Europe. The Deutsche Bank, seeking to integrate Central European as an independent German base in the world market, was outflanked by the Anglo-Saxon capitalist elite (originating in the 1920s) in the successful incorporation of Eastern Europe into the IMF/GATT-based economic sphere (Van der Pijl 1993, 20–21). As Jeffrey Sachs reminded us, this was possible because the multilaterals "could make loans that did not require Congressional and parliamentary authorization" (1994, 17).[9] Van der Pijl's conclusion that this dramatically illustrated planning by the U.S. security state to integrate German and Japan into a U.S.-led system of collective security was confirmed on August 3, 1993 by the *New York Times*, quoting a Pentagon document titled, "Defense Planning Guidance," which proposed:

> The U.S. must show the leadership necessary to establish and protect a new order that holds the promise of convincing potential competitors that they need not aspire to a greater role or pursue a more aggressive posture to protect their legitimate interests. Second, in the non-defense area, we must account sufficiently for the interests of the advanced industrial nations to discourage them from challenging our leadership or seeking to overturn the established political and economic order (quoted in Van der Pijl 1993, 30).

CONCLUSION

The current political and economic order, such as it is, and as secured by a GATT regime, would institutionalize the rules of a neoliberal world order matching the market integration already underway and privileging metropolitan states and their core classes.[10] The internationalization of productive and financial capital is expressed in TNC strategies to remove national regulations limiting trade and investment and to codify a new protectionism to secure intellectual property rights. Arthur Dunkel's "final act" (in the Uruguay Round) created a new global trade agency with unprecedented powers to enforce GATT provisions. The new super-agency, the World Trade Organization (WTO), is to have independent jurisdiction, like the United Nations, and to oversee trade in manufactures, agriculture, services, investments, and intellectual property protection. Its considerable power resides in an integrated dispute settlement mechanism, which allows a cross-conditionality process whereby a state's perceived violation of obligations in one area can be disciplined by the application of sanctions against another area of economic activity.

Through the WTO, state and local powers to regulate environmental, product, and food safety can be overruled by unelected trade bureaucrats with the power to require nations to "take all necessary steps, where changes to domestic laws will be required to implement the provisions [GATT] . . . to insure conformity of their laws with these [GATT] Agreements" (Burrows 1993). The GATT regime would complement and intensify the power of the multilateral agencies to discipline states, and withdraw Third World special treatment (e.g., agricultural protection and technology transfer). Like national regulation, global regulation involves formal rules and a set of substantive relations. That is, while members formally codify multilateral rules under "the new constitutionalism," the rules themselves would institutionalize a specific social structure of global accumulation in the interstate system (McMichael 1993).

Arguably, this structure will remain increasingly unequal and nonuniform. That is, while the metropolitan trend may be from welfare- to competition-state (Cerny 1991), a more profound disintegration of peripheral states is likely. This is already evident in the NAFTA configuration, whereby Mexico is dismantling its national institutional complex (notably the *ejido* system of peasant landholding collectives) and selling off its public assets to prepare the ground for the expansion of U.S. state power and capital via a regional trade and investment agreement. A similar pattern is evident in the European Community–Eastern Europe regional reconfiguration, which has been intensified by the proliferation of republics and territories competing for supplies of international capital (Gill 1992, 185). Even though there are different political and social effects across the metropolitan-peripheral divide of state restructuring, in each case a process of denationalization is evident. Expanding resource-exports (agricultural, labor, and mineral) from the south and the downward revision of minimum wage levels in EC states, are two substantial cases in point (Gill 1992, 172).

Denationalization is by no means a uniform, or inevitable, process. In the north, the recomposition of oppositional classes and of civil society is politically indeterminate (see Arrighi, Hopkins, and Wallerstein 1989), especially with new macro-regional trends. Meanwhile, the south confronts the incompleteness, and possible inappropriateness, of the nation-state in postcolonial regions (see, e.g., Davidson 1992; Leys 1994). The completion of the state system via decolonization was largely a formal process by which new states, incorporated into the United Nation's family of nations, engaged in what Vieille termed development "mimetism": "While affirming their nationhood, States could see no other way of developing as nations except imitating States which had been successful, i.e., Western countries; popular culture was seen as unfitted for development, as primitive and irrational . . .. The rejection of popular culture by the nation State was accepted for some time by the peoples concerned because it was underpinned and counterbalanced by the promise of development" (1988, 237–38). With the crisis of the developmental state, this mimetic moment unravels, generating new expressions of cultural identity and political withdrawal from the state (e.g., Cheru 1989). Withdrawal is symptomatic of the legitimacy crisis of southern states, and has undoubtedly been exacerbated by their participation in the restructuring project.

The dismantling of the southern developmental state in the debt regime has had a reflexive effect on northern nation-states, largely via the growing world labor surplus. Moreover, with rising right-wing movements, the state policing of labor surpluses empties national political discourse of constructive social policy. It is ironic that the nation-state that arose via the creation of the wage relation now must submit to a maturing *global* wage relation. The global wage relation unifies diverse labor forces into a competitive global labor market—organized by states to facilitate increasingly unregulated global capital accumulation. This, and the accompanying politics of intolerance, constitute the new colonialism, which is itself a new moment in the history of capitalism.

NOTES

The author acknowledges the helpful suggestions made by David A. Smith, József Böröcz, and the University of California at Irvine collective for revising an earlier draft of this chapter.

1. The argument of this essay turns on the historical specificity of the "nation-state." I do not accept the rather more abstract concept of a world-system governed by an elemental antinomy between "states" and a world division of labor. I seek to specify political organization at the national and the global levels. States became nations first in the nineteenth century, with the formation of national industrial classes, constitutional rule, and the establishment of national currency regulation via financial institutions such as central banks (Polanyi 1957; Hobsbawm 1991; McMichael 1987). These political-institutional developments conditioned the rise of the social-democratic movement. This movement, which was never

completed in the Third World (see, e.g., Migdal 1986), was generalized in the twentieth century with the maturation of industrial capitalism and the institutional facility of the Bretton Woods system of national currency stabilization. It preserved a national space for economic policy within a global capitalist system (Block 1977; Ruggie 1982). I argue that this movement, anchored by powerful working class political coalitions, 'socialized' capital by regulating it at the national level. I also argue that capital is reversing this movement now, largely because it has escaped the bounds of national currency and capital controls with the collapse of the Bretton Woods *system* in the 1970s. That is, capital is "resocializing" nation-states (as historic political formations) by dismantling the power of organized labor, and the institutions of social welfare and by attempting to incorporate states into world market relations (McMichael and Myhre 1991). This process is, of course, uneven and hotly contested.

2. The statement that the nation-state itself is losing salience raises problems of interpretation—not only because the usual reflex is an assertion that nation-states still rule, but also because such rulership is both uneven across the interstate system and changing in function. David Marquand captured this problematic when he argued that the European Community has, while appropriating sovereign powers to supranational institutions, in fact strengthened the core European nation-states—Germany and France, in particular. "They remain sovereign: indeed, they cling to their sovereignty . . . .. Yet the very processes through which they have regained the legitimacy and efficacy which they lost during the Second World War have made it increasingly difficult for them to act in the ways in which the social-democratic state of the postwar period used to act" (1994, 24). That is, Marquand was arguing that the stabilization of the European states required a certain supranational regulation, cradling economic integration and, hence, the process by which markets have undermined welfare democracy as the project of the nation-state.

3. Van der Pijl argued that the global banks, projecting a *rentier* perspective separate from the long-term interests of productive capitalists, "were in fact instrumentalized by the newly industrializing capitalist periphery in their struggle against the multinationals, and unwittingly financed the NIEO system" (1988, 350), thereby exacerbating the conflict between the industrializing south and the stagnating north. I would add that the NICs, in borrowing from the global banks, were also seeking autonomy from the bilateral and multilateral money managers in their bid to industrialize. The monetarist counterrevolution in 1980 not only politicized finance capital's power, leading the IMF to assume the role of securing debt repayment, but in doing so restored metropolitan power to manage the world economy along nonmultilateral lines.

4. For a detailed review and critique of the standardizing thrust of World Bank policies of economic reform with respect to African agricultural modernization, see Bernstein (1990).

5. African debt is predominantly public debt owed to multilateral agencies such as the World Bank and the IMF, unlike Latin American debt, much of which is owed to private financial institutions (even though the ability to repay necessitated official loans to Latin American states).

6. Under the Bank's Articles of Agreement, the five principal shareholders (currently the United States, Japan, Germany, France, and the United Kingdom, with a combined share of total capital stock of 43.28 percent) appoint the first five executive directors and, with support from several other developing countries, this five can assemble a working majority, thereby controlling the Bank (Cahn 1993, 162n).

7. This overt political role was elaborated in the Baker plan (originating at the 1985 joint meeting of IMF and the World Bank), where U.S. Treasury Secretary James Baker endorsed the suggestion that multiyear rescheduling arrangements be offered "as rewards for countries that had made strong progress on policies to deal with their balance of payments problems" (Corbridge 1993, 127).

8. The Paris Club is convened by the multilateral financial community to reschedule official debts of countries in imminent default and willing to submit to reform conditions, including the requirement that the debtor country commit a greater proportion of national income to debt repayment (Cahn 1993, 171–2). Participating governments include the United States, Germany, Japan, Britain, France, Italy, Canada, Austria, Belgium, the Netherlands, Norway, Spain, Sweden and Switzerland.

9. Note that Sachs, who was frustrated with the irresolution of the IMF in bankrolling its economic shock therapy in Russia, declared:

> Why was the I.M.F. so inept? For 50 years, it has been nearly as secretive and monopolistic as the Central Committee of the Communist Party . . .. The I.M.F. is cut off from independent professional scrutiny and from competition. It alone determines whether Western aid will flow. Like any longstanding monopoly, it has grown arrogant, self-protective and sloppy (1994, 17).

10. In his outgoing speech of January 1994, Luis Fernando Jaramillo, chair of the G77, claimed: "According to some estimates, the industrialized countries, which make up only 20 percent of the GATT membership, will appopriate 70 percent of the additional income that will be generated by the implementation of the Uruguay Round" (quoted by Ritchie 1994).

REFERENCES

Arrighi, Giovanni. 1978. *The Geometry of Imperialism*. London: Verso.
———. 1982. "A Crisis of Hegemony." In Samir Amin, Giovanni Arrighi, André Gunder Frank and Immanuel Wallerstein, EDS., *Dynamics of Global Crisis*. New York: Monthly Review, 55–109.

————. 1990a. "The Developmentalist Illusion: A Reconceptualization of the Semiperiphery." In William G. Martin, ed., *Semiperipheral States in the World Economy.* Westport, CT: Greenwood Press, 18–25.

————. 1990b. "The Three Hegemonies of Historical Capitalism" *Review* (Fernand Brandel Center) 13, no. 3:365–408.

Arrighi, Giovanni, Terence K. Hopkins, and Immanuel Wallerstein. 1989. *Anti-Systemic Movements.* London: Verso.

Bangura, Yusuf, and Peter Gibbon. 1992. "Adjustment, Authoritarianism and Democracy in Sub-Sharan Africa: An Introduction to Some Conceptual and Empirical Issues." In *Authoritarianism, Democracy and Adjustment: The Politics of Economic Reform in Africa.* Uppsala, Sweden: Nordiska Afrika-institutet, 7–38.

Beckman, Bjorn. 1992. "Empowerment or Repression? The World Bank and the Politics of African Adjustment." In Peter Gibbon, Yusaf Bangura, and Arne Ofstad (eds.), *Authoritarianism, Democracy and Adjustment: The Politics of Economic Reform in Africa.* Uppsala, Sweden: Nordiska Afrikainstitutet, 83–105.

Bernstein, Henry. 1990. "Agricultural 'Modernisation' and the Era of Structural Adjustment: Observations on Sub-Saharan Africa" *Journal of Peasant Studies* 18, no. 1:3–35.

Bienefeld, Manfred. 1989. "The Lessons of History" *Monthly Review* 41, no. 3:9–41.

————. 1992. *Rescuing the Dream of Development in the Nineties* Institute of Development Studies, paper no. 10. University of Sussex.

Block, Fred. 1977. *The Roots of International Economic Disorder.* Berkeley: University of California Press.

Bovard, James. 1991. *The Farm Fiasco.* San Francisco: Institute for Contemporary Studies.

Burrows, Beth. 1993. "Op-ed on GATT." Trade Strategy Electronic Network, 8 Dec.

Cahn, Jonathan. 1993. "Challenging the New Imperial Authority: The World Bank and the Democratization of Development" *Harvard Human Rights Journal* 6:159–94.

Canak, William L. 1989. "Debt, Austerity and Latin America in the New International Division of Labor." In W. Canak, ed., *Lost Promises: Debt, Austerity and Development in Latin America.* Boulder, CO: Westview Press, 9–27.

Cerny, Philip. 1991. "The Limits of Deregulation: Transnational Interpenetration and Policy Change" *European Journal of Political Research* 19:173–96.

Cheru, Fantu. 1989. *The Silent Revolution in Africa: Debt, Development and Democracy.* Chicago: Zed Press.

Corbridge, Stuart. 1993. "Ethics in Development Studies: The Example of Debt." In Frans J. Schuurman, ed., *Beyond the Impasse: New Directions in Development Theory.* London: Zed Books, 123–39.

Cox, Robert. 1987. *Production, Power and World Order.* New York: Columbia University Press.

————. 1992. "Global Perestroika." In Ralph Miliband and Leo Panitch, eds., *Socialist Register 1992.* London: Merlin Press, 26–43.

Crook, Clive. 1991. "Sisters in the Wood. A Survey of the IMF and the World Bank" *Economist*, 12 Oct., 1–48.

————. 1992. "Fear of Finance: A Survey of the World Economy" *Economist*, 19 Sept., 1–48.

————. 1993. "New Ways to Grow: A Survey of Third World Finance" *Economist* (supp.), 25 Sept., 1–44.

Daly, Maurice, and Malcolm Logan. 1989. *The Brittle Rim: Finance, Business and the Pacific Region.* Harmondsworth, UK: Penguin.

Davidson, Basil. 1992. *The Black Man's Burden: Africa and the Curse of the Nation-State.* Harmondsworth, UK: Penguin.

Debt Crisis Network. 1986. *From Debt to Development: Alternatives to the International Debt Crisis.* Washington, DC: Institute for Policy Studies.

Economic Commission for Latin America and the Caribbean (ECLAC). *Transnational Bank Behaviour and the International Debt Crisis.* Santiago, Chile: ECLAC/UN Center on Transnational Corporations.

Friedmann, Harriet. 1982. "The Political Economy of Food: The Rise and Fall of the Postwar International Food Order" *American Journal of Sociology* 88 (supp.):248–86.

————. 1994. "Warsaw Pact Socialism: Détente and Disintegration of the Soviet Bloc." In *Rethinking the Cold War: Essays on Its Dynamic, Meaning, and Morality.* Philadelphia: Temple University Press.

Friedmann, Harriet, and Philip McMichael. 1989. "Agriculture and the State System: The Rise and Decline of National Agricultures" *Sociologia Ruralis* 29, no. 2:93–117.

Friedman, Thomas. 1994. "Africa's Economies: Reforms Pay Off" *New York Times*, 13 Mar., A2.

George, Susan. 1992. *The Debt Boomerang.* Boulder, CO: Westview Press.

Gibbon, Peter. 1992. "Structural Adjustment and Pressures toward Multipartyism in Sub-Saharan Africa." In Peter Gibbon, Yusaf Bangura, and Arne Ofstad, eds., *Authoritarianism, Democracy and Adjustment: The Politics of Economic Reform in Africa.* Uppsala, Sweden: Nordiska Afrikainstitutet, 127–66.

Gill, Stephen. 1992. "Economic Globalization and the Internationalization of Authority: Limits and Contradictions," *Geoforum* 23, no. 3:269–83.

Harvey, David. 1989. *The Condition of Postmodernity.* Oxford, UK: Basil Blackwell.

Hobsbawm, Eric. 1991. "The Perils of the New Nationalism" *Nation* 253, no. 15:537, 555–56.

Hoogvelt, Ankie. 1987. *The Third World in Global Development.* London: Macmillan.

Kaldor, Mary. 1990. *The Imaginary War: Understanding the East-West Conflict.* Oxford, UK: Basil Blackwell.

Kolko, Joyce. 1988. *Restructuring the World Economy.* New York: Pantheon.

Leys, Colin. 1994. "Confronting the African Tragedy," *New Left Review* 204:33–47.

McMichael, Philip. 1985. "Britain's Hegemony in the Nineteenth-Century World Economy." In Peter Evans, Dietrich Rueschemeyer, and Evelyne Huber Stephens, eds., *States versus Markets in the World-System.* Beverly Hills, CA: Sage, 117–50.

———. 1987. "State Formation and the Construction of the World Market." In Maurice Zeitlin, ed., *Political Power and Social Theory.* Greenwich, CT: JAI Press, 187–237.

———. 1992. "Tensions between National and International Control of the World Food Order: Contours of a Third Food Regime" *Sociological Perspectives* 35, no. 2:243–65.

———. 1993. "World Food System Restructuring under a GATT Regime" *Political Geography* 12, no. 3:198–214.

McMichael, Philip, and David Myhre. 1991. "Global Regulation vs. the Nation-State: Agro-Food Systems and the New Politics of Capital" *Capital and Class* 43:83–106.

Marquand, David. 1994. "Reinventing Federalism: Europe and the Left" *New Left Review* 203:17–26.

Marx, Karl. [1867] 1965. *Capital.* Vol. 1. Moscow: Progress Publishers.

Migdal, Joel. 1986. *Strong Societies and Weak States.* Princeton, NJ: Princeton University Press.

Myhre, David. 1994. "The Politics of Globalization in Rural Mexico: Campesino Initiatives to Restructure the Agricultural Credit System." In Philip McMichael, ed., *The Global Restructuring of Agro-Food Systems.* Ithaca, NY: Cornell University Press, 145–69.

Overseas Development Council (ODC). 1986. "Working Paper, Number 10." Washington, DC: OCD.

Polanyi, Karl. 1957. *The Great Transformation.* Boston: Beacon.

Rich, Bruce. 1994. *Mortgaging the Earth: The World Bank, Environmental Impoverishment, and the Crisis of Development.* Boston, MA: Beacon.

Rodriguez, Ernio, and Stephany Griffith-Jones (eds.). 1992. *Cross-Conditionality, Gank Regulation, and Third World Debt.* Hampshire, UK: Macmillan Press.

Ruggie, John G. 1982. "International Regimes, Transactions and Change: Embedded Liberalism in the Postwar Economic Order" *International Organization* 36:397–415.

Sachs, Jeffrey. 1994. "The Reformers' Tragedy" *New York Times*, 23 Jan., A17.

Sassen, Saskia. 1991. *The Global City.* Princeton, NJ: Princeton University Press.

Senghaas, Dieter. 1988. "European Development and the Third World: An Assessment," *Review* (Fernand Brandel Center), 11:1.

Van der Pijl, Kees. 1988. "The Era of Transition from Capitalism to Social-ism—Myth or Reality? Notes on the Struggle over World Order in the Current Period." In Lelio Basso International Foundation for the Rights and Liberation of Peoples, eds., *Theory and Practice of Liberation at the End of the XXth Century.* Bruxelles, Belgium: Bruylant, 329–58.

———. 1993. "Capitalist Rivalry in the New World Order: Transnational Forces and the Reconquest of Eastern Europe." Paper presented to the International Symposium on Global Political Economy and a New Multilateralism, Oslo, Norway, 15-17 Aug.

Vieille, Paul. 1988. "The World's Chaos and the New Paradigms of the Social Movement." In Lelio Basso International Foundation for the Rights and Liberation of People, ed., *Theory and Practice of Liberation at the End of the XXth Century.* Bruxelles, Belgium: Bruylant, 219–56.

Wood, Robert E. 1986. *From Marshall Plan to Debt Crisis: Foreign Aid and Development Choices in the World Economy.* Berkeley: University of California Press.

World Bank. 1989. "Memorandum and Recommendation of the President of the International Bank for Reconstruction and Development to the Executive Directors on a Proposed Loan in an Amount Equivalent to U.S. $9.0 million for an Economic Management Project." June 29.

4

Lessons from the Gulf Wars: Hegemonic Decline, Semiperipheral Turbulence, and the Role of the Rentier State

Cynthia Siemsen Maki and
Walter L. Goldfrank

In 1992, Wallerstein published a provocative essay asserting that the collapse of communism marked the end of an old era, a liberal era that began in 1789. Almost simultaneously, the Persian Gulf crisis marked the beginning of a new, postliberal era in which the modernizing program of the French revolution for national progress had been decisively left behind, whether in its social-democratic, communist, or national-development guise. Not only is liberal ideology finished; the capitalist world-economy is disintegrating. The war for Kuwait was pure realpolitik, he wrote, Saddam Hussein having understood that only by military might could change occur in the world hierarchy of power. Wallerstein asserted that the Iraqi ruler did not miscalculate, since he had an even chance of winning in the short run if the United States did not respond quickly. And, "the U.S. had a 100% chance of losing in the middle run" (105), because with relatively declining global economic weight, it would be saddled with increased regional responsibilities. Note that he did not claim that the winner would be Saddam Hussein, Iraq, or the unified Arab nation dreamt of by its would-be Bismarck/Nebuchadnezzar (or, needless to say, the peoples of the entire global south). Wallerstein went on to find in this military challenge one of three postsocialist, post-antiimperialist forms of struggle from an increasingly marginalized south.

This symptomatic reading of events against a background of epochal transformations may or may not prove cogent in the long run, but we do not believe that it accurately captures the causes and consequences of the second Gulf War. It turns a grandiose fantasist and desperate opportunist into a clever strategist. It implies a more solid Iraq than has yet existed. It neglects the dependence of the U.S. on quite willing core country partners concerned both with the rules of the game of sovereign states and with assuring that oil supplies and prices remain amenable to core power influence. It also ignores the dimension of intrasemiperipheral competition and the ability of the U.S. to organize astonishing regional cooperation, involving not only Israel and Turkey, but also such disparate

Arab states as Saudi Arabia, the United Arab Republic (UAE), Syria, and Egypt. Wallerstein's interpretation, then, leaves ample room for analysis based on more conventional Wallersteinian concepts, some of which were implicit in the original essay.

To put it another way, the epochal interpretation invokes trends and, especially, discontinuous changes in the overall historical trajectory of world-system development, whereas our own analysis deals rather more cautiously with cyclical processes and familiar world-system patterns. These two modes of world-system analysis, the historical and the systemic, can in principle be reconciled, but we do not attempt to do that here.

Rather, in this chapter we deploy the concepts of hegemonic cycles and semiperipheral mobility to explore some of the causes and consequences of the Iraqi wars with Iran (1980–1988) and with Kuwait and the U.S.-led/UN-sanctioned coalition (1990–1991). We focus first on global changes related to the decline in U.S. hegemony, including the end of the Cold War. We highlight the ambivalence of the U.S. turn to multilateral financing and multinational forces, ambivalence that was recently displayed in the acrimonious debate over intervention in Somalia and Bosnia, and that we hold to be characteristic of a declining hegemon. We then trace Iraq's semiperipheral ascent, as its attempt to consolidate semiperipheral mobility was first encouraged, and then thwarted, by shifting combinations of core powers and semiperipheral competitors. We argue that the postwar continuation of Saddam Hussein's regime owes itself to such a combination. Meanwhile, for Iran and Turkey, the dissolution of the Union of Soviet Socialist Republics (USSR) (and, in the former case, a wish for rapprochement with the West) has induced a redirection of their primary energies toward competition for influence in Central Asia. We imply that one way to understand Middle Eastern regional instability is in terms of the multiplicity of competing semiperipheral countries. Throughout we reflect about the limited utility of the rentier state as an analytic tool.[1]

HEGEMONY AND GULF WARS

Many analysts have written that the war for Kuwait represented a reassertion of U.S. hegemony in a postcommunist, unipolar world. Some give this reassertion a global cast, seeing messages to Europe and Japan (as well as to any lesser country) contemplating a military adventure destabilizing the world order. Others give this reassertion a regional cast, focusing on the completion of a transition from British to U.S. domination of the Persian Gulf. This approach would seem to contrast sharply with our own, which sees a decline in U.S. hegemony. However, the apparent contrast is primarily due to our use of a different conception of hegemony, one in which the current politicomilitary superiority of the U.S. is readily acknowledged, and even expected.

As we understand it, the world-system perspective sees recurrent hegemonic cycles in modern history, which are distinct from the better known long waves of rapid and stagnating capital accumulation. In each hegemonic cycle, a technologically advanced country first pushes its economy to world dominance, which is defined as the ability to undersell competitors in their home markets. With a time lag, it then gains politicomilitary dominance during a period of major war (the Thirty Years War, the Napoleonic Wars, and World Wars I and II). Finally, its culture and ideology assert themselves across most of the world. The fully hegemonic moment occurs when all three aspects coincide—when cultural hegemony has been established but economic hegemony has not yet been lost. By the same token, hegemonic decline follows the same pattern, with economic competition from other core states, then politicomilitary rivalry and eventual parity, and finally a fading of cultural prominence. The declining hegemon becomes just another core country.

For the twentieth century, the moment of full-blown U.S. hegemony was 1950 through 1970. Over the next twenty years, relative economic decline has been unmistakable and widely remarked. Recently compiled data for this period show the U.S. losing ground to its competitors in productivity considerably faster than Britain did a century ago (Peterson 1994). Meanwhile, to recoup lost hegemony, U.S. president Jimmy Carter emphasized the ideology of human rights and President Ronald Reagan emphasized military strength. This odd couple found its sublime union in President George Bush's war against Saddam Hussein, who conveniently embodied both the antithesis of human rights and the capacity for military mischief. Despite relative economic decline, U.S. politicomilitary leadership continues, perhaps artificially extended by the peculiar post–World War II burdens borne by Japan and Germany. Evidently, U.S. culture continues to attract much of the world as well. Moreover, in an era when both armaments and culture are big business, there is an economic dimension to these aspects of US hegemony, even in a period of overall decline: U.S. corporations control large shares of the world market in both areas, thus contributing to the motivated capacity for rebelliousness that leads, in turn, to U.S. military interventions. At some point in the not-too-distant future, military might and culture-as-industry may become mere sectoral specializations of the U.S. economy, but we do not think that this point has been reached: they are still aspects of a waning hegemony.

In a similar way, our view of the Cold War and the demise of the USSR differs from the conventional perspective. The usual view is that the US and USSR were, for forty years, superpower rivals in a bipolar world. Each nation was capable of destroying the other and the rest of the world along with it, while competing for hearts and minds—and clients. This is, after all, what the superpowers said they were doing, and it is not entirely fanciful. When the USSR collapsed back into Russia and sought U.S. help to manage the transition to a market economy, the Cold War was over; the U.S. had won. However, as the Chinese leadership perhaps saw first, there had been much collusion as well. The Cold War was, in fact, part of the structure of U.S. hegemony, in which the Soviet role was threefold: to police vast territories and numerous peoples not then necessary as workers and customers, and to provide both a threat around which the U.S. could discipline its allies and a socialist alternative that increasingly seemed unattractive. Starting from a vastly inferior position, the USSR declined further and faster than the U.S. during the world-economic downturn of the 1970s and 1980s, making the advantages of Cold War arrangements less apparent to the Kremlin. No wonder President Mikhail Gorbachev opted out: even the Soviet military agonized over the poor quality of the human and material resources it received from the economy and the educational system. The demise of the USSR brought joy to some and sadness to others, but it meant difficult reorientations for all who had been connected, in one way or another, to the USSR—as dependencies, clients, or allies.

What lessons about the Gulf wars can we draw from the causal relevance of hegemonic decline and the end of the Cold War? We start with the heyday of hegemony, and move quickly through the rise of the Organization of Petroleum Exporting Countries (OPEC), the buildup of the shah of Iran as a regional policeman, the threat posed by the Iranian revolution, the sponsorship of Iraq as a counterpoise during the first Gulf War, and its punishment for insubordination during the second one.

In the decades of hegemonic apogee, the Middle East supplied the core countries with vast quantities of oil at low prices, while slowly, more advantageous rents and, eventually, nationalization enabled the producing states to increase the standard of living for many of their subjects. Politically, the U.S. and the USSR cooperated in settling the Suez Crisis. The U.S. intervened successfully in Lebanon and in overthrowing the nationalist-populist Mossadegh government of Iran. Junior partner Great Britain's armed mobilization dissuaded Iraq from attempting to annex Kuwait. Radical Arab nationalism was the principal ideological threat to the status quo, which included U.S. sponsorship of an aggressively defensive Israel, a modernizing Iran, and the conservative monarchies and emirates of the Gulf. The Soviets had their clients but were not about to encourage destabilizing adventures.

The rise of OPEC in the early 1970s profoundly altered the picture, both globally and regionally. Oil price rises redistributed income to the producing states, at the expense of almost everyone else. For the U.S., it was a question of coping with a balance of power that was shifting against it. Since the U.S. domestically produces a higher proportion of its petroleum than most other core states, it stood to gain, relatively, by the price increases. Europe and Japan pushed energy conservation and new sources of supply to counteract the ill effects. Nonproducers in the south were hit particularly hard. Meanwhile, the two principal U.S. clients in the Gulf, Saudi Arabia and Iran, would also gain and, not incidentally, spent many of their new petrodollars on U.S. armaments. In the Iranian case, oil-fed inflation, urbanization, and university expansion had hugely destabilizing effects. In Saudi Arabia, Kuwait, and the emirates, the vast increases in wealth led to massive labor migration from Egypt, Jordan, Palestine, and Yemen (and parts of South and Southeast Asia as well), making those countries heavily dependent on wage remittances and, despite Saudi largesse to governments and movements, fanning the flames of popular resentment. Although little remarked at the time, the oil price rise also facilitated the semiperipheral advance of Iraq, thereby adding a new ingredient to the regional stew.

OPEC's price increases were instrumental in the U.S. strategy of sponsoring Iran as a regional policeman. However, that gambit of hegemony through proxy collapsed when the Iranian revolution overthrew the shah, held U.S. hostages, and resulted in the installation of an anti-Western (and anti-Soviet) Shiite theocracy. This was at once a blow to U.S. domination and an indication that the Cold War was an increasingly irrelevant framework for containing the threat of anti-systemic insurgency. In its way, the universalizing thrust of the Iranian revolution challenged all the regional props of core domination. The Soviets, who soon invaded Afghanistan to defend a client regime, feared the effects of radical Islam there and in the Central Asian republics. The Saudis faced threats to their guardianship of the holy places as well as a new surge of antimonarchic populism. Fresh from the Camp David Peace Accords, the Israelis faced new levels of attack from militant groups, while the Egyptians were isolated from other Arab states and threatened by home-grown Islamic radicals. The U.S. itself foundered badly in a new attempt to intervene militarily in Lebanon—a telling contrast to the situation in the late 1950s.

Enter Iraq. The decision to invade its revolutionary neighbor and historic rival had tangled roots. The immediate spurs included geoeconomic and intra-Arab ambitions, political and ideological defensiveness, and the aim of ousting the Ayatollah Khomeini from power (Hiro 1991). What was planned as a quick and decisive seizure of land, oil, and ports turned into a stalemated, eight-year, million-casualty war that severely weakened both countries economically while enriching the arms industries of many core powers and some semiperipheral ones as well (Timmerman 1991). Politically repressive regimes entrenched themselves in both combatant states. Iraq ended up heavily indebted to the West, the USSR, and its temporary allies in the Gulf. So long as neither side won, the war was a godsend for the U.S., debilitating two states which, to this day, are reviled officially as outlaws. When the military balance shifted toward Iran after 1983, the U.S. tilted toward Iraq, understanding Iran as the more dangerous outlaw, but covertly supplied arms and maintained relations with the latter as well (for a slightly different slant on U.S. wartime relations with Iran and Iraq, see Foran 1993). If the United States tilted toward Iraq, the Soviets listed that way, invoking their "friendship treaty" and continuing as a major supplier of conventional weapons. Nonetheless, "at crucial moments both superpowers reached tacit understandings: firstly, to ensure that the Iran-Iraq War did not get drawn into the larger East-West conflict; and secondly, to guarantee free navigation to and from the Gulf ports" (Hiro 1991, 264). Overall, then, the 1980s afforded a certain respite for the United States, but it left Iraq with a crushing debt burden, a huge military machine, and a new start toward nuclear capability (Israel had taken out a major facility in a 1981 raid).

According to documentary evidence reviewed by Foran (1993, 12–15), the United States had, since 1985, been concerned about the threat posed by Iraq to both Gulf stability and Israeli security. Once the graver Iranian menace had been contained, Iraq could be confronted. Conversely, with the USSR reduced to a largely inward-turning Russia, the Iraqi regime was worried that the United States would monopolize power in the Gulf and attempted to rally Arab support for rebuffing the U.S. threat. We shall probably never know if the mixed signals sent by the Bush administration in the months leading up to the Kuwait invasion were intended to lure Iraq into an adventure that would serve as a pretext for smashing much of its damage potential, and indeed, consequences count more than intentions. In his careful, detailed analysis of the U.S. response to the invasion, Telhami (1994) attributed the October 1990 decision to double U.S. forces and resolve the situation militarily to a perception that the anti-Iraq coalition could not last long because of escalating Israeli- Palestinian tensions following the Temple Mount massacre earlier that month. It is a measure of hegemonic decline that, to carry out its military mission, the United States had to rely on UN sanctions and resolutions; on Japanese, German, Saudi, and Kuwaiti financing, and on deals with Egypt (massive debt forgiveness) and Syria ($1 billion and free rein in Lebanon) (Kienle 1994; Baker 1994). By the same token, it is a measure of hegemonic persistence, and of the lag of politico-military as compared to economic decline, that the United States was able to dominate and manipulate UN decisions, extract billions from its allies, and construct the coalition in the first place.

What of the postwar (post-slaughter?) settlement as it has taken shape over the last three years? From the standpoint of core domination and U.S. hegemony, a slightly new order prevails in the region, but it is a shaky one in which ideological heterogeneity and interstate rivalries complicate, and probably dampen, the radicalizing effects of tremendous intraregional inequalities. Small populations with large quantities of oil coexist uneasily with large impoverished populations, while political and sectarian creeds compete for mass allegiance. The two states with oil and people, Iran and Iraq, continue as "outlaws" in U.S. eyes, to be handled by a "dual containment" policy (Lake 1994). Accordingly to its critics, this policy is unworkable and unnecessary: the successful containment of Iraq requires Iranian cooperation, and Iran is on its way back toward respectability, anyway (Gause 1994). U.S. supplies are now prepositioned in Kuwait and Saudi Arabia in case trouble arises.

At the same time, steps toward an Israeli-Palestinian reconciliation may lead to the removal of a huge stumbling block for core domination: the identification of Israel as a militarized, aggressive outpost of Western colonialism and U.S. imperialism. Iraq itself may have become a laboratory for the new U.S./UN mode of policing the world, of which we are seeing variants in Somalia, Bosnia, and North Korea. Not every crisis involves one state's total eradication of another's sovereignty, so one would imagine that as crises depart from violations of that fundamental principle of the interstate system, they would become less amenable to UN consensus (even Yemen and Cuba did not oppose the first anti-Iraq resolutions). In the last few years, the UN peacekeeping budget has quite suddenly jumped from the millions to well over a billion dollars. A three-way policy debate has arisen in the United States, among neoisolationists, go-it-alone hegemonists, and international institutionalists who favor working through global and regional organizations.

This last policy will almost certainly prevail in the middle term, as U.S. hegemony gives way to what may be called core condominium. In the Gulf and the Middle East more generally, the U.S./West European/Japanese interest continues to lie in access to steady oil supplies at reasonable prices. However, realizing this interest will require devising a regional political framework that assuages mass anger and resentment without giving away the store—and that means coming to terms with semiperipheral turbulence.

IRAQ AND SEMIPERIPHERAL TURBULENCE

World-systems analysis has long held that semiperipheral states generate an outsized share of political turmoil, both internally, because of their economic, ethnic, and/or regional heterogeneity, and externally because their attempts at upward mobility sometimes involve their neighbors. In the recent global wave of struggles for democratization, semiperipheral states have been disproportionately prominent, in Latin America, in Central and Eastern Europe, in East Asia, and in Southern Africa. In the Middle East—which is so often omitted from analyses of development (e.g., Gereffi and Fonda 1992)—Israel, Iran, and Iraq have caused the most turmoil, although one should not forget Syria and Lebanon or the nearby hostile rivalry between North Atlantic Treaty Organization (NATO) members Turkey and Greece. We focus here on Iraq's trajectory, as the lessons of the Gulf Wars are particularly relevant to its ascent, decline, and possible stabilization.

At present, virtually all accounts of attempts at national development emphasize government economic policies, this or that model of growth. But it is worth noting that many of the most arresting semiperipheral ascents in modern history have included military conquest as a critical component, from the sixteenth-century expansion of England and the seventeenth-century rise of Sweden and Brandenburg-Prussia (Wallerstein [1974] 1980), to the nineteenth-century expansions of the United States, Russia, Australia, Chile, and the subsequent rise of Japan (Goldfrank 1981). In striking contrast to Iraq, however, none of those ascending states had to contend with significant core opposition, and although some were occasionally given a slap on the wrist (e.g., the War of 1812 for the United States and Crimea for the Russians) or ran into a semiperipheral rival, they were all protected by great geographical distances and/or core state sponsors. The world has indeed shrunk, and one lesson of the second Gulf War is that the military route to semiperipheral mobility may well be a relic.

Iraq's incorporation as a grain-exporting peripheral zone of the world economy occurred in the latter half of the nineteenth century, and it remained peripheral until the 1970s. During World War I, the British mandate took over from the Ottomans, leading to increased levels of agricultural exports and consolidation of the class power of landlords. (An oddity in Arrighi and Drangel's 1986 analytical survey of the semiperiphery is their classifying of Iraq as semiperipheral in the 1938–1950 period. They qualify this as deriving from a single data point in a single source [Morawetz 1977], without noting that another of their sources [Woytinsky and Woytinsky 1953, 390, 434] groups "all the Near East except Palestine and Turkey" in extreme poverty in 1938 and rates Iraq as a "prevailing subsistence economy" in 1948. Thirty-three percent of the population was undernourished in 1949, and 56 percent in 1957 [Darwish and Alexander 1991, 15].) After World War II, petroleum exports began to contribute growing proportions of GNP. In 1951, a fifty-fifty formula was negotiated for sharing oil revenues between the state and the British-owned Iraq Petroleum Company (IPC) (Penrose and Penrose 1978). However, most of the funds were invested in agriculture rather than industry (Gerke 1991), further enriching the rural bourgeoisie, though also making it more dependent on the state. In 1958, a military "revolution" overthrew the monarchy, dissolved the British-influenced Development Board, expropriated the landed elite, and upped the government's share of oil rents.

Economic disruption and political instability marked the ensuing decade. Petroleum output grew slowly and the agrarian reform was ill-prepared, leading to considerable urban migration. On the other hand, some import-substituting industrialization began, and landowners lost most of their power. State strength grew at the expense of the urban bourgeoisie under the so-called Arab Socialist regimes of the mid-1960s, while the brief Ba'th regime in 1963 had weakened the working class by eradicating the Iraqi Communist party. However, although the partial oil nationalization of 1964 increased state revenues, industrial nationalizations were poorly managed and agriculture continued to decline, leading to greater reliance on imported foodstuffs (McLachlan 1979). For a few years after the Ba'th return to power in a 1968 coup, Iraq was still a peripheral country: troubles with the Kurds in the north and Shiites, mostly in the south, marked the unfinished tasks of central government control, let alone national integration, even as its strengthened state and petroleum reserves prepared it for advancing.

Wallerstein (1979) described three modes of semiperipheral ascent: promotion by invitation, seizing the chance, and selfreliance. As a member of OPEC, Iraq seized the chance to nationalize oil in 1972 and then to use the phenomenal growth in its oil revenues after 1973 for upward movement in the world-system.[2] However, there were elements of "invitation" as well, since France, Italy, Japan, and the USSR contributed technology and loans to facilitate increased productive capacity. Already in 1974, state oil rents had mounted to $6.7 billion in contrast to $487 million in 1968 (Stork 1982). Throughout the rest of the decade, burgeoning revenues bought vast growth in the role of the state, which came to dwarf any social group in importance. Taxes were cut, freeing the state from dependence on civil society, and funds were allocated to services and education, job creation, and subsidized food. Ba'th party members penetrated the military and the civilian security apparatus, and in 1979 Saddam Hussein, until then formally number two, became president and commander-in-chief as well as secretary-general of the party. The regime bought acquiescence and some popular support by distributing benefits, while controlling potential dissidence through coercion and intimidation (al-Khalil 1989). A new private sector elite of contractors acquired considerable wealth through development projects, but they numbered only in the few thousands and could not form a "solid base for the regime" (Chaudhry 1991, 16), which drew its nucleus of support from the party-state bureaucracy itself. Important positions went overwhelmingly to Arab Sunnis (about 23 percent of the population), and specifically those with clan or local (Tikriti) ties to the ruler himself. Perhaps, due in part, to the Pan-Arabism of Ba'th nationalism—the post-1958 regime, in contrast, had instead stressed Iraqi nationalism (Greenfield and Chirot 1994)—Iraqi economic policy was dominated by military mobilization against both Zionism and, during the 1980s, Iranian/Shii expansionism.

As the examples of Brandenburg-Prussia in the seventeenth and eighteenth centuries and Japan from 1890 to 1940 suggest, in the past, military mobilization could indeed be part of a successful strategy of semiperipheral ascent. However, in spite of core-state support received during the war with Iran, both directly and through the lax enforcement of restrictions on advanced weapons exports, military mobilization has proved a self-defeating strategy for Iraq, both by generating overwhelming opposition and by diverting vast amounts of capital into unproductive investments and an enormous security apparatus. This is not to deny that the 1970s saw economic advances typical of import-substituting semiperipheral countries. Agricultural output in principal commodities showed overall increases (Mofid 1990), although improved diets and higher incomes meant that imported food ($1.4 billion worth in 1980) was necessary to meet the demand. The state-controlled service sector and state industries absorbed much of the displaced agricultural work force—Iraq was 68 percent urban by 1977—and about 70 percent of industrial output was produced by the 280 state firms, with dramatic increases in iron and steel, fertilizers, and petrochemicals (Gottheil 1981; Farouk-Sluglett and Sluglett 1990, 233).

With the wrinkle that petroleum accounted for the overwhelming majority of exports in all directions, Iraq's trade patterns over the decade also conformed to the standard semiperipheral pattern. Core-bound oil bought capital goods, sophisticated consumer products, and arms, while oil sold to the periphery bought minerals and low-wage manufactures.[3] Also typical of semiperipheral countries was the shift in the relationship between social classes and the state, with the latter gaining at the expense of the former. Furthermore, as controllers of a rentier state dependent on a commodity with low labor force requirements, the Ba'th party elite was unusually unconstrained by class pressures, a pattern very different from those semiperipheral states in which class forces are extremely heterogeneous and conflicting.[4] This meant that structurally, the individual ruler, Saddam Hussein, enjoyed a very wide range of autonomous decision making. His decision to invade Iran in 1980 ended up squandering many of the gains of the 1970s, reducing the state's autonomy vis-à-vis other states and domestic classes and stalling, if not reversing, Iraq's ascent in the world-system.

Earlier, we discussed this war from the perspective of hegemony. From that of Iraq's trajectory, it was a disaster: one analyst estimates its cost to have been $452.6 billion (Mofid 1990). Saddam Hussein had positioned himself as the most logical Arab standard-bearer after Egypt's deal at Camp David; a quick victory over the supposedly disorganized Iranians would remove the (misperceived) threat of revolt by Iraqi Shiites, liberate the Arabs and the oil of Khuzistan, and establish Iraq as the dominant regional power. However, this was not to be: after initial setbacks the Iranians rallied, and as the war came to be politically useful to the revolutionary regime, they insisted on armistice terms that Saddam Hussein could not accept. Iraq's pursuit of a guns and butter policy could not last, as foreign reserves dwindled and oil exports and prices dropped. Oil's contribution to GDP averaged only 30 percent a year during the war, down from 55 percent in 1979. Labor scarcity from military recruiting negatively affected both industrial and agricultural output. Yields declined and foodstuff imports grew, to $3 billion by 1987. The only way out was increased indebtedness, which reached $81 and $89 billion by the time the war ended (Hiro 1991), with much of it owed to the Gulf states, less than a third owed to the West and Japan, and between $6 and $9 billion owed to the USSR. Only in military capacity did the war strengthen Iraq, as the state built up a huge army and an enormous armaments industry (Eilts 1991).

The major economic policy reorientation toward the end of the war was the privatization of some commerce, industry, and agriculture. Designed to increase productive efficiency and, possibly, to impress Western lenders, privatization had negligible effects, aside perhaps from shifting some of the blame for shortages away from the government. The main beneficiaries were the contractor intermediaries, who remained dependent on the regime for preferment (al-Khafaji 1990). In no sense did they become a vibrant class by itself that might spearhead the next phase of Iraqi economic growth, similar, say, to the state-created industrial bourgeoisie of South Korea. Nor were they, or any other element of civil society, in a position to oppose the decisions to invade Kuwait and not to yield to U.S./UN diplomatic pressures.

Iraq's decline did not stop with the end of the Iranian war. Foreign debt continued to grow, and Western banks refused additional loans. Looting Kuwait and then controlling its oil and ports could reverse the decline and allow Iraq to resume its march toward unifying the Arab nation and attempting to undo the consequences of a colonial past. However, the global consequences of Iraq's annexation of Kuwait were too grave for the United States. As Farsoun (1991:3) put it, "Iraq's bid for regional hegemony threatened U.S. global hegemony in which oil, especially Middle Eastern oil, plays a pivotal role."

Beyond the obvious massive damage done by the United States and United Nations to its population, military machine, infrastructure, agriculture, industry, and oil-exporting activities, Iraq has shown other indications of regressing toward, if not all the way to, peripheral status. The power center was contracted to a very small group of Saddam Hussein's intimates and ultra-loyal officers in order to prevent a coup d'etat (Khalidi 1991). About 10 percent of the pre-1958 elite have resurfaced as elements of the bourgeoisie and as major contributors to the regime (al-Khafaji 1991), as state oil rents no longer enable it to exist above the other classes. In addition, traditional tribal chiefs have begun receiving large salaries in return for support ("Still There" 1992, 15), and foreign firms were invited to help develop new oil fields and increase yields from old ones during the economic crisis that followed the war with Iran.

On the other hand, the ability of the army to suppress the Kurdish revolt and to punish the southern Shiites for their rebellion—both groups, of course, having been cynically encouraged and then abandoned by the United States—suggests that Iraq was not bombed as severely as some first thought. Another indication is the rebuilding that has occurred in the last three years, in spite of considerable suffering and middle-class exodus. Ninety percent of oil export capacity has been rebuilt (Feuilherade 1992), and prewar levels of production could be reached in a year after the UN bans are lifted (Tanner 1992). Of course, 30 percent of oil revenues are owed to Kuwait as compensation, the massive foreign debt remains, and much infrastructure requires rebuilding. On balance, we think Iraq will survive as a semiperipheral country (albeit a weakened one), above all because Turkish fears of Kurdish autonomy and Saudi fears of the southern Shiites converge on the goal of a unitary, but hamstrung, Iraq. Moreover, with the second largest proven oil reserves in the world, Iraq should have the opportunity to undertake renewed upward mobility in the world-system by means other than military ones.

CONCLUSION

In the case we have examined, oil rents led to revolution in Iran and to a military strategy for advance in Iraq, two trends that neutralized one another at a fearsome cost in lives and livelihoods. The costs of Iraq's initial failure prompted it to try again, with even more disastrous results. Core power, in this instance under the leadership of a declining but still potent United States, thwarted a potential challenge, both to core domination of a critical region and to the precarious balance of power among competing semiperipheries. Quite possibly, the military path to semiperipheral advance is no longer a viable option.

NOTES

We thank Hal Aronson, Edmund Burke III, and Paul Lubeck for their advice and suggestions at several stages of this research.

1. Mahdavy (1970) first conceptualized the rentier state. According to subsequent state literature, the source of state revenues affects a country's political and socioeconomic conditions. Three tendencies are said to accompany the flow of external rents into the domestic realm. First, the state strengthens its relative position, as it is less constrained by class pressures, and political demands and

participation diminish in a state that is not dependent on taxes for revenues (Beblawi 1987). Second, state revenues will be independent of internal productive activities; state rents amount to locational gifts of nature. Only a small percentage of the population will be involved in the rent-generating process, however much the majority may benefit from it. Third, the model asserts that allocating economic and social benefits buys legitimacy for the rentier state. Weber posits that legitimacy exists insofar as people subscribe to institutional rules, but the rentier state paradigm associates legitimacy with popular expectations of economic entitlements.

2. Wallerstein (1979) asserts that semiperipheral states are more involved in political and market control than core or peripheral states, "since the semi-peripheral states can never depend on the market to maximize, 'in the short run,' their profit margins" (72). Rentier states differ somewhat; it is their long-run profits that are at risk. They seem to have a short-term window of opportunity in which to use their rents to invest in major transformations. In recent decades, political involvement in the market by oil rentier states has included both transnational syndicalism and various ambitious investment programs, of which Iraq's military-inclined variant is one. From this perspective, Beblawi (1984) may be right that in the long run, the oil states may return to the periphery though many have been promoted temporarily to the semiperiphery (or even the core).

3. Rentier states differ from other semiperipheral ones in that they exchange a no-wage commodity for high-wage commodities with the core and the same no-wage commodity for low-wage commodities with the periphery, thus achieving their intermediate position.

4. Prior rentier state analysts have looked at class either by disregarding it (which speaks volumes about the trend toward authoritarianism in these regimes) or by focusing on legitimation through entitlements. In the latter instance, class pressures may force benefit continuity. The model's claim of sufficient state autonomy to act without concern for dominant class or mass interests should give way to a more historical and interactive analysis that considers a changing balance of power in state and class structures.

REFERENCES

Arrighi, Giovanni, and Jessica Drangel. 1986. "The Stratification of the World-Economy: An Exploration of the Semiperipheral Zone." *Review* (Fernand Braudel Center) 10, no. 1 (Summer): 9–74.

Baker, Raymond. 1994. "Imagining Egypt in the New Age: Civil Society and the Leftist Critique." In T. Y. Ismael and J. S. Ismael, eds., *The Gulf War and the New World Order*. Gainesville: University Press of Florida, 399–434.

Beblawi, Hazem. 1984. *The Arab Gulf Economy in a Turbulent Age*. London: Croom Helm.

———. 1987. "The Rentier State in the Arab World." In H. Beblawi and G. Luciani, eds., *The Rentier State*, vol. 2. London: Croom Helm, 49–63.

Chaudhry, Kiren Aziz. 1991. "On the Way to Market: Economic Liberalization and Iraq's Invasion of Kuwait." *Middle East Report* 21 (May/June): 14–23.

Darwish, Adel, and Gregory Alexander. 1991. *Unholy Babylon*. London: Victor Gollancz.

Eilts, Hermann Frederick. 1991. "The Persian Gulf Crisis: Perspectives and Prospects." *Middle East Journal* 45 (Winter): 7–29.

Farouk-Sluglett, Marion, and Peter Sluglett. 1990. *Iraq since 1958*. New York: Tauris and Co.

Farsoun, Samih. 1991. "The Middle East in a Changing World Order." Paper presented at Taft Conference, University of Cincinnati, April.

Feuilherade, Peter. 1992. "A Brisk Trade in Recrimination." *Middle East* 208 (Feb.): 23.

Foran, John. 1993. "Development, Democracy, and the New World Order: Problems and Prospects for the Middle East in the 1990s." Unpublished paper, University of California, Santa Barbara.

Gause, F. Gregory, III. 1994. "The Illogic of Dual Containment." *Foreign Affairs* 73, no. 2 (March/April): 56–66.

Gereffi, Gary, and Stephanie Fonda. 1992. "Regional Paths of Development." *Annual Review of Sociology* 18:419–48.

Gerke, Gerwin. 1991. "The Iraq Development Board and British Policy, 1945–50." *Middle Eastern Studies* 27 (Apr.): 231–55.

Goldfrank, Walter L. 1981. "Silk and Steel: Italy and Japan between the Two World Wars." *Comparative Social Research* 4:297–315.

Gottheil, Fred. 1981. "Iraqi and Syrian Socialism: An Economic Appraisal." *World Development* 9 (Sept./Oct.): 825–37.

Greenfield, Liah, and Daniel Chirot. 1994. "Nationalism and Aggression." *Theory and Society* 23, no. 1 (Feb.): 79–130.

Hiro, Dilip. 1991. *The Longest War: The Iran-Iraq Military Conflict*. New York: Routledge.

al-Khafaji, 'Isam. 1990. "The Parasitic Base of the Ba'thist Regime." In Committee against Repression and for Democratic Rights in Iraq (CARDRI), ed., *Saddam's Iraq-Revolution or Reaction*. London: Zed Books, 73–88.

———. 1991. "The State and Infitah Bourgeoisie in the Arab Mashreq: The Case of Egypt and Iraq." Unpublished manuscript.

Khalidi, Walid. 1991. "The Gulf Crisis: Origins and Consequences." *Journal of Palestine Studies* 20 (Winter): 5–28.

al-Khalil, Samir. 1989. *Republic of Fear*. New York: Pantheon Books.

Kienle, Eberhard. 1994. "Syria, the Kuwait War, and the New World Order." In T. Y. Ismael and J. S. Ismael, eds., *The Gulf War and the New Order*. Gainesville: University Press of Florida, 383–98.

Lake, Anthony. 1994. "Confronting Backlash States." *Foreign Affairs* 73, no. 2 (Mar./Apr.): 45–55.

McLachlan, Keith. 1979. "Iraq: Problems of Regional Development." In A. Kelidar, ed., *The Integration of Modern Iraq*. London: Croom Helm, 135–49.

Mahdavy, Hossein. 1970. "Patterns and Problems of Economic Development in Rentier States: The Case of Iran." In M. A. Cook, ed., *Studies in the Economic History of the Middle East*. London: Oxford University Press, 428–67.

Mofid, Kamran. 1990. "Economic Reconstruction of Iraq." *Third World Quarterly* 12 (Jan.): 48–61.

Morawetz, David. 1977. *Twenty-five Years of Economic Development, 1950 to 1975*. Washington, DC: World Bank.

Penrose, Edith, and E. F. Penrose. 1978. *Iraq: International Relations and National Development*. Boulder, CO: Westview Press.

Peterson, Peter G. 1994. "Entitlement Reform: The Way to Eliminate the Deficit." *New York Review*, 41, no. 7 (Apr. 7): 39–47.

"Still There, Dividing and Ruling." 1992. *Middle East* 209 (Mar.): 13–15.

Stork, Joe. 1982. "State Power and Economic Structure: Class Determination and State Formation in Contemporary Iraq." In T. Niblock, ed., *Iraq: The Contemporary State*. New York: St. Martin's Press, 27–46.

Tanner, James. 1992. "Iraq Oil Industry Rapidly Recovers Export Potential." *Wall Street Journal*, 26 Mar.

Telhami, Shibley. 1994. "Between Theory and Fact: Explaining U.S. Behavior in the Gulf Crisis." In T. Y. Ismael and J. S. Ismael, eds., *The Gulf War and the New World Order*. Gainesville: University of Florida Press 153–83.

Timmerman, Kenneth R. 1991. *The Death Lobby*. Boston: Houghton Mifflin.

Wallerstein, Immanuel. (1974), 1980. *The Modern World-System. Vols. 1, 2*. New York: Academic Press.

———. 1979. *The Capitalist World-Economy*. New York: Cambridge University Press.

———. 1992. "The Collapse of Liberalism." In R. Miliband and L. Panitch, eds., *Socialist Register 1992*. London: Merlin, 96–110.

Woytinsky, W. S., and E. S. Woytinsky. 1953. *World Population and Production*. New York: Twentieth Century Fund.

5

Global Restructuring, Transnational Corporations and the "European Periphery": What Has Changed?

Denis O'Hearn

The economic state of the European Union (EU), formerly called the European Community (EC), has changed even more rapidly than its name since the 1970s. At the start of the 1980s, the EC suffered from "Eurosclerosis," a disease of inflexible markets and market responses that supposedly kept European firms from successfully competing with their Japanese and U.S. counterparts. By the end of the 1980s, economist Lester Thurow had declared Europe the likely winner in a head-to-head confrontation with the United States and Japan for global hegemony. Within a few years, however, the sclerosis seemingly returned. Despite these changes, the EU—or at least, its German-centered core—remains in a hegemonic struggle with the United States and Japan. Successful competition is the goal of the EU strategy of restructuring—centered around liberalizing policies that will open economies of scale and scope in the world's "largest market" while enabling the "leanest and meanest" European corporations and financial institutions to participate in markets that change with increasing rapidity.

However, the EU hegemonic project has a critical contradiction. Its central aim of increasing the competitiveness of the largest and most technologically advanced firms, sectors, and regions threatens to exacerbate uneven development among its regions and, in particular, to marginalize the so-called European periphery.[1]

In this analysis of the consequences of EU restructuring on the EU periphery, I will concentrate on how industrial policy affects semiperipheral economic activities.[2] As the EU periphery expands, I argue, it is becoming more marginal to the productive aspects of the "European project." It is an important buffer zone, or mediator, in the movement of capital and people into and out of Europe, but the social costs of maintaining such walls and gates around the European fortress may conflict with the competitiveness of the project itself.

REGIONAL INEQUALITY IN EUROPE AND THE PROBLEM OF CONVERGENCE

Some authors emphasize widening regional inequality within European states, implying that intrastate inequalities have become as important as those between EU countries (Dunford and Kafkalis 1992, 18). However, EU peripherality is still concentrated in a handful of countries and regions. Apart from Madrid, the richest regions of Spain, Greece, Ireland, and Portugal have lower incomes than the poorest regions of all other member states (except Wales and the Mezzogiorno in Italy; see Figure 5.1). The per capita incomes of the ten least developed EU regions are less than half those of the least developed core region.[3] At the top end, the wealthiest regions are in the "greater German coprosperity sphere" of parts of Germany, Denmark, the Netherlands, and Northern Italy—popularly called the "Eurobanana" because of its geographic shape (Perrons 1992, 171).

Figure 5.1
Distribution of GDP per Capita among EU Regions, 1990
(EU average = 100)

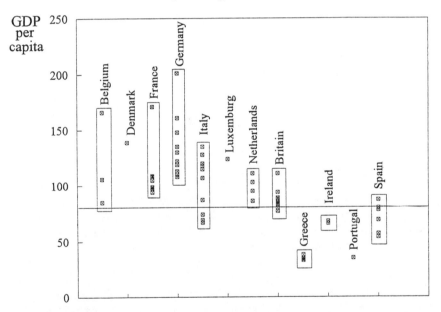

Source: Eurostat (1993)

Inequality between the core and periphery has increased since the early 1970s, after decreasing between World War II and the 1970s. Thus, some observers note a convergence in times of economic expansion (Perrons 1992, 173; Dunford and Kafkalis 1992, 21). However, the convergence of the 1960s may have been a result of large inward flows of foreign direct investment (FDI) in the periphery, while subsequent stagnation was partly related to the structural consequences of the resultant stock of TNC investments (Bornschier 1980; O'Hearn 1990).

Since the recession, Spain (1985–1988) and Ireland (1987–1990) briefly approached rates of growth necessary for convergence with the EU core, primarily due to inflows of FDI, which appear to be temporary. Skepticism about the long-term flow of FDI in Spain is confirmed by the concentration of recent inflows in a few sectors such as automobiles. Growth led by transnational corporations (TNCs) is also phantom to the extent that the incomes from regional economic activities accrue to core capitals through profit repatriation. This is reflected in an increasing gap between gross domestic product (GDP) and gross national product (GNP)—for instance, GNP (locally accruing income) is now 12 percent lower than GDP in Ireland.

However, the most important result of regional inequality since the 1980s is the record rates of unemployment and underemployment. Unemployment rates in Spain, Ireland, and Mezzogiorno reached 20 percent in the mid-1980s and, despite periodic growth upturns, they have remained high or even increased. Lower global unemployment rates in Greece and Portugal mask widespread rural underemployment, the replacement of full-time permanent employment with part-time and temporary employment, and high regional unemployment rates. One impact of restructuring is that even surges of investment in the Europeriphery do not induce significant new employment. The dependent industrialization of the 1960s and 1970s at least created substantial (if not sufficient) manufacturing employment to compensate for semiperipheral rural people migrating to cities, but TNC investments of the 1990s lack even this short-term compensation.

EUROPEAN STRUCTURE AND EUROPEAN RESTRUCTURING

European restructuring began in earnest in the early 1980s. Influential studies of the EC (Albert and Ball 1983) found that stagnation and unemployment in Europe were the result of inflexible market mechanisms that had been impaired by decades of government regulation, barriers to trade, subsidies to inefficient producers, high taxes, and centralized collective bargaining. Japanese and U.S. economic successes proved that a new economic model was necessary. The European answer is a liberal "big market" (Grahl and Teague 1990) in which the private sector can reorganize itself to face the challenges of rapidly changing demand and shortened product cycles. The creation of a Single European Market (SEM) is intended to provide the economies of scale and scope that reorganized corporations require in order to compete with the United States and Japan in research and development (R&D), design, and new production processes. National governments can no longer subsidize their uncompetitive industries but are expected to join the whole community in subsidizing the technological advancement of leading "European" firms and sectors.

Leading firms and sectors are expected to combine scale with flexibility. An accelerating pace of technological change has substantially increased the fixed costs of innovation (requiring large-scale organizations) while rapidly changing market conditions increase the need for flexibility in production (which is supposedly difficult to maintain in large-scale organizations). The answer is flexible intra- and interfirm relationships that combine economies of scale, scope, and versatility. This implies a return to place—increased locational proximity between agents in high-tech innovation-intensive corridors, industrial districts that specialize in high-quality goods, and flexible networks of large firms and local subcontractors (Amin 1992, 128). EU policy, therefore, (1) favors the corporate giants that are expected to compete successfully in global markets and (2) encourages locally agglomerated production complexes with close and flexible cooperation between producers and consumers. Corporate responses vary, but they generally take agglomerated forms (Coriat 1991; Lung 1992; see also Amin 1992 on flexible corporate structural forms).

While a common view of agglomeration is that restructuring involves the creation of global corporate networks that regionally concentrate R&D, production, and distribution in each of the major trading blocs (Europe, North America, and Asia), it is unclear whether these regional complexes will be located predominantly in the cores of each trading bloc or to what extent peripheral localities may participate in the new, flexible arrangements. EU "regional policy" (i.e., peripheral policy) presumes that the restructured periphery will participate in networks of small and medium-sized local firms. However, EU industrial policy centers on developing large global competitors, so its regional policy ignores the impact of large corporate restructuring on the periphery. Thus, Amin (1992, 128) noted a "policy tension" between perspectives on regional development that (1) emphasize local networks as indigenous solutions for regional problems and (2) assess local prospects in the context of contradictory globalizing and localizing trends in the location of activities. EC regional policy is framed in the context of the first perspective and basically oblivious of the second.

Just as small-scale local entrepreneurship was the EC answer to foreign disinvestment and peripheral deindustrialization in the 1980s, networks of small firms are the EU answer to the problem of rising inequality under the SEM. Liberal EU philosophy assumes that regional equality can be achieved if the "less-favored" regions become more competitive and self-reliant, thereby reducing "their" productivity gap behind the core regions. However, this apparently progressive "bottom-up" approach is unrealistic because its only policy for redirecting activities toward the periphery is a vague hope that improved transport, communications, and vocational training will attract investments.

To the limited degree that theories of restructuring consider noncore areas, they simply assume that core-like localization and innovation can occur everywhere. Nonetheless, compelling arguments predict that localized productive-research-marketing networks will concentrate in core localities. Although new technologies permit the arms-length TNC control of decentralized production structures, stronger forces appear to encourage concentration in core areas (van Tulder and Junne 1988). Perrons (1992, 189–90) argued that restructuring has increased the importance of white collar workers relative to direct-production workers, so economies of core agglomeration have become relatively more important than labor economies. Dunford and Kafkalis (1992–14) found that market forces attract "locally embedded" networks to the core because it offers more advanced technical, social, and institutional infrastructures for knowledge-intensive production. Activities increasingly concentrate even in cores of cores—for example, Paris has two-thirds of French R&D, management, and marketing jobs—while semiperipheral agglomerations are networked outward and upward to core TNCs.

The rules of the Single European Market strengthen the pull of the core by liberalizing trade and harmonizing standards to create economies of scale for a few "champion" firms. European industrial policies on mergers and technology aim to increase scale at the expense of smaller firms, creating a basic contradiction between the goal of competing with the United States and Japan and the stated (but clearly secondary) regional policy of convergence.

Article 85 of the EU Competition Policy prohibits transactions that "prevent restrict or distort competition, *except those which the Commission believes will contribute more to productive efficiency than they will detract from allocative efficiency through the acquisition of substantial market power*" (Frazer 1990, 616, emphasis added). EU Know-how Licence Regulation gives a block exemption from scrutiny to interfirm technology collaboration that will increase the firms' market power, arguing that the increased market competitiveness of collaborating firms will outweigh any negative impacts of their collusive market behavior on other EU firms. EU regulations are backed up by administrative decisions covering specific sectors, such as a decision by the Information Technology Directorate General to promote a strategy of mergers in electronics that would facilitate the growth of a handful of "Eurogiants" that could challenge US and Japanese competitors.

EC merger and technology policies undoubtedly favor large firms (which are overwhelmingly concentrated in the Eurocore) at the expense of the so-called small and medium enterprises (SMEs), which are concentrated in higher numbers in the periphery. The major result of EU restructuring, then, is less novel than the post-Fordist literature would indicate: it is simply the concentration and centralization of capital. The market share of the top one hundred European firms in manufacturing and energy rose from 14.8 percent in 1982 to 20 percent in 1988 (Amin 1992, 134).

Information and Communication Technologies (ICT) is a case in point. EU policy aims to provide a market that is large enough to improve the competitiveness of a few large ICT producers. An EC Commission report (quoted in Bornschier 1992, 15) found that digital communications systems are so complex that a company must capture 8 percent of the world market to cover its development costs. However, no EU state represents even 7 percent of the world market. Even with the SEM, the minimum efficient scale in these sectors will not allow diffusion to the EU periphery. Gerstenberger (1991) concluded that "mainly the jobs in Japan and East Asia would profit from a strategy of enforced ICT diffusion in Europe."

The concentration and centralization of capital incorporates the destruction of previously decentralized activities and their concentration in core agglomerations. However, Amin (1992, 137) also emphasized that TNC activities continue to cross national borders while local semiperipheral industries fail, so that the degree and kind of participation of local regions in the European project is increasingly dictated by strategies of the largest firms, rather than by local conditions within any "decentralized networks."

Since the rationale of the SEM is to enable large firms to acquire economies of scale by increasing the size of their potential market, larger firms benefit only by driving smaller ones out of the newly penetrated markets. A study by Bulges and Ilzkowitz (quoted in Perrons 1992) found that the forty sectors most likely to be affected by the removal of tariff barriers account for particularly high shares of semiperipheral manufacturing, reaching over 60 percent in Portugal and Greece. They concluded that trade will cause indigenous sectors to collapse as demand is supplied by TNCs. This has already happened in the British telecom market and throughout Irish industry after tariff barriers were removed in the early 1970s (O'Hearn 1989). More recently, former German Democratic Republic (GDR) firms that were not internationally competitive but did supply the local market were destroyed after their sudden exposure to West German competition. EU policies to increase competitiveness routinely conflict with policies for cohesion.

This conflict can be intensified by EU policies that chip away at the policy instruments of the semiperipheral states. Perrons (1992) argued that monetary union erodes the ability of states to use devaluation in order to create a "breathing space" for indigenous producers. Andrikopoulou (1992) discussed how the EU withheld structural funds to the Greek Panhellenic Socialist Movement (PASOK) government until it replaced its socialist development plan with a more liberal one. Moreover, the Maastricht treaty restricts semiperipheral policy options because it demands "convergence" in debt/GNP ratios, inflation, and interest rates—a process that can only be met by revenues generated by widescale privatization and austerity programs.

Finally, Dunford and Kafkalis (1992) examined the effects of EU decentralization of development promotion during the 1980s—which was supposedly a move to encourage indigenous development "from below." The Delors Plan (Committee for the Study of Economic and Monetary Union 1989, 13) favored local development strategies and agencies that could adapt to local conditions. However, the agencies' local understanding was matched neither by instruments to combat uneven development or by a community-level response to the issue of regional imbalance. Decentralization simply increased competition among local agencies to attract investments, and the TNCs benefited from the resulting upward bidding war. The problem worsened as the number of competing regions increased, while "core" areas, such as Britain and France, began to actively compete for TNC investments.

Jacques Delors (1989) insisted that the SEM will not intensify uneven development. However, the economies and flexibility derived from proximity to suppliers and consumers, access to a varied workforce, cheaper transport costs, and other factors not only favor the core but also large centers in the core. The European core will dominate the high-wage/high-tech/high-profit economic activities, while peripheral zones will perform lower-tech and labor-intensive activities. To the degree that restructuring increases the share of the former activities or that the latter are being brought into closer spatial proximity to the former, the periphery faces the likelihood of further marginalization within the European economy.

REGIONAL FUNDS: THE MISREPRESENTATION OF PERIPHERALITY?

The first principle of EU regional policies is that they must not interfere with overall European competitiveness, which is centered on the large core firms. In place of regional policies that cheapen labor or capital, Delors (1989) recommended policies that supposedly "reduce the peripherality" of poorer EU regions. However, the Eurospeak definition of peripherality is entirely spatial, ignoring logical distinctions between core and peripheral economic activities and the interdependence of core competitiveness and peripheral underdevelopment. Therefore, EU regional policy aims to "bring the periphery closer to the core" by improving its transport and communications infrastructures. There is no consideration that such programs might simply increase the peripherality of regions by increasing the degree to which they can be penetrated and controlled by the core.

The other central pillar of regional policy, job training, is of little use without a policy to create jobs for trainees. Spain, Ireland, Greece, and Portugal have the highest levels of education in Europe but the lowest levels of vocational training (Perrons 1992, 178–79). Nonetheless, Irish evidence shows that young men who undergo such training have no greater likelihood of being employed than the untrained (Breen 1991). As a result, a third of Irish youths emigrate within a year of leaving school (Begg and Mayes 1991, 70).

EU regional policy is funded by three "structural funds." Up to half are earmarked for infrastructure, a quarter is for aid to private investment (programs that "enhance entrepreneurship"), and a quarter is for tourism, agriculture, and "human resources." Although regional funds doubled in real terms during 1987–1993 to ECU 14 billion (approximately $28 billion), they still comprise only 25 percent of the EU budget and just 0.3 percent of the combined EU GDP. More important, the regional fund of ECU 14 billion compares to estimated gains of ECU 216 billion from the SEM, which will accrue mainly to the large core firms. Regional funds are much less important than the Common Agricultural Policy (CAP), which mainly aids the richer rural areas of the core.

Because of its spatial definition of peripherality, the EU deemphasizes the importance of technology in the semiperiphery. This is convenient for an industrial policy designed for the largest EU firms. The concentration of high-tech activities in the core is, therefore, one of the most important features of uneven development in the EU. In 1989, 75 percent of European R&D expenditures were concentrated in Germany, France, and the United Kingdom (UK). Within Italy in 1982, 72 percent of R&D was concentrated in the northwest and just 5 percent in the south. Clearly EU policy reproduces uneven technology development by committing the vast majority of funds to programs that are designed to enhance the competitiveness of the giant core firms.

EU technology policy began in 1981–1982 as a direct response to the perception that Europe was falling behind Japan and the United States in high-tech research and its application to new products. The first step was a joint initiative between the EC and twelve giant electronics companies. The resulting European Strategic Programme for Research in Information Technology (ESPRIT) was designed to unite national research programs. ESPRIT and subsequent programs were grouped together in 1986 in a single budget aimed at long-term, cross-national research collaboration. Another program, EUREKA, is intergovernmental rather than EU-funded. Established in 1985 in response to the U.S./Japanese threat, EUREKA promotes cross-border R&D collaboration. It is enterprise-driven and its funding is tied directly to the market potential of a project, which again concentrates the program in the EU core. Significantly, the budget of EUREKA is equivalent to the entire EU research budget.

Half the funds for these programs are devoted to supporting technologies such as information and communications technology and industrial and materials technology (Dunford and Kafkalis 1992, 14). They flow to giant corporations such as Siemens and Philips and to "centers of excellence" in the EU core, reinforcing the spatial concentration of high tech production. A recent report found that "some projects . . . can only be created once for the whole Community" and in these cases, "the Less Favoured Regions may not be the best location for such installations." Peripheral regions, says the report, can only participate in "small-scale" technology programs whereby a large number of research facilities can be established "and thus be located in a number of regions, including Less Favoured Regions." The report goes on to acknowledge "other limits" to funding research in the periphery, specifically, "the need for resources to be allocated to the most dynamic partners who are pushing forward the industrial competitiveness of Europe" Commission of the European Communities (1992, 8–9). As Grahl and Teague (1990, 177) noted, technology policy "could only work by privileging the very largest companies in the formation of policy, and has resulted in structures which continue to favor the strongest and most powerful economic agents."

The few existing technology programs for the periphery are miniscule, attracting only 9 percent of regional funds. They are structurally inferior because they only promote the development of small and medium-sized enterprises in nonleading sectors. This reflects EU the policy that semiperipheral competitiveness in the leading sectors weakens core competition against the United States and Japan.

PERIPHERY AND THE TNCS

The logic of restructuring and of European hegemonic competition leads one to expect economic activities to agglomerate in core poles, as economies of cheap peripheral labor become less important relative to economies provided by spatial centrality. On the other hand, the emphasis on networks of small local producers under SEM appears likely to reproduce core-periphery productive hierarchies or, worse, simply to cause the destruction of peripheral indigenous industry. However, these are largely theoretical conclusions, based on the analysis of EU structures and policies. The actual results of restructuring will take time to unfold.

To what extent, however, have core agglomeration and indigenous peripheral failures already occurred? What are the emerging patterns of investment and productive location? To what degree has restructuring and integration revived the EU periphery, again made it dependent on core investments, or simply marginalized it as activity moves to the core? Official EU hopes for convergence center on two factors: the attractiveness of the periphery to investors in the conditions of the SEM and the development of small, local industries to fill niches that are left empty by core firms. I will tentatively examine each of these developments in turn.

Dependence on TNCs has become more difficult as rationalization has cut back the number of foreign operations. The managing director of the pharmaceuticals firm Pfizer, for instance, claims that "what does not make sense is to manufacture on eight sites" (Abrahams 1993). In response, the company closed its Greek operation and expected to close more. Similar closures have been rampant in electronics. The cutbacks appear to have been greater in the EU periphery than in the core because of the decreasing advantages of low labor costs relative to other economies. In the predominantly foreign UK electronics industry, for instance, wages of unskilled and skilled manual workers make up only 13 percent of production costs (of which 4 percent are in computers; see Goodhart 1993).

Foreign investments come from external (mainly U.S. and Japanese) investors who gain access to the SEM by producing in the EU and EU firms that move to the periphery to exploit labor-cost advantages, receive state incentives, and (mainly in the Spanish case) move production close to an important market.

More than half of inward investment in the EU comes from the United States. Restructuring in the early 1980s brought a fall in net U.S. investments throughout the EU. After 1986, they began to rise again but their peripheral share remained low (United States [various years]). Thirty-six percent of the value of recent U.S. investments in the EU have gone to one recipient, Britain, which takes about 40 percent of all inward investments into Europe in value terms and houses 37 percent of non-European subsidiaries operating in Europe (Cassell 1993a). While the EU received over half of U.S. foreign electronics investments in 1991, most subsidiaries were located in Britain and Germany.[4] The OECD reported that the other major recipient of inward investment is France, due to its proximity to the EU core (Tucker 1993).

There is also an agglomeration of the small share of investments that go to the periphery. U.S. capital investments in Greece and Portugal decreased in real terms after 1989. They increased slowly in Ireland, but most new U.S. investments aggregated in Spain. In 1992 and 1993, however, half this investment was clumped in the spatially concentrated auto industry (United States [various years]).

Most worrisome is the fact that the recovery in U.S. capital investments since 1987 failed to create significant employment (Figure 5.2). Net employment in U.S. manufacturing subsidiaries rose by a mere 5,000 in Spain during 1989–1991, by 1,000 in Ireland, and by only 100 in Greece and Portugal. Gross new employment created by U.S. investments in Ireland during the period was less than that associated with smaller investment levels in the 1970s (O'Hearn 1993, 183).

Another mitigating factor is the rapid expansion of the EU periphery. Figure 5.3 compares the growth of capital expenditures by U.S. TNCs with the growth of the EU peripheral population (due to the accession of Greece in 1981 and Spain and Portugal in 1986 and the integration of the former GDR in 1991). The number of applicants who compete to attract inward investments has grown much more rapidly than the investments. The contrast in Figure 5.3 is even starker if one considers Britain's serious entry as a competitor for inward investments.

Extra pressure comes from Eastern Europe, which is attracting increasing numbers of investments because of its proximity to EU core markets and its cheap and disciplined labor force. East European competition for foreign investments increased rapidly after 1990 because of tariff reductions agreed by the EU in the Interim Europe Agreements and Copenhagen conclusions. The EU envisaged free trade with the five Central and East European countries by 1998. During 1991–1992, EU trade with Eastern Europe grew faster than with any other region of the world. The most important inward investments in Eastern Europe have been in motor vehicles and textiles/clothing.[5]

Japanese and Asian investments have had far less impact in Europe than U.S. investments. Nearly one-fourth of Japanese FDI goes to the EU, which housed 684 Japanese companies in 1991. However, this FDI is very agglomerated—Britain attracts 41 percent while only Spain attracts significant amounts to the periphery (Cassell 1993a). During 1951–1990, Japan invested $55.3 billion in the EU but only $2.7 billion (5 percent) in the periphery, including 1.9 billion (68 percent) in Spain (Japan External Trade Organization, personal communication June 2, 1994). Moreover, any influx of non-EU FDI after restructuring and the SEM seems to have already passed its peak. The head of the Invest in Britain Bureau (IBB) claimed that "the big US companies are already here" and future investments will be mainly small firms seeking market access. Instead of "mega-projects," Japan will concentrate on small supplier investments in Britain (Cassell 1993a).

In the absence of major inflows from outside of Europe, intra-EU and indigenous investments are the remaining possible sources of economic expansion.

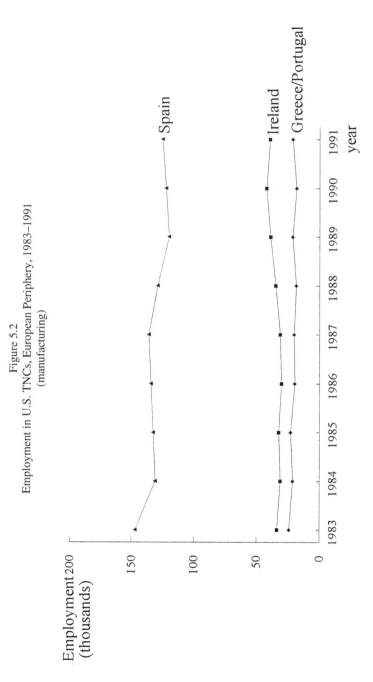

Figure 5.2
Employment in U.S. TNCs, European Periphery, 1983–1991
(manufacturing)

Source: U.S. Department of Commerce, various years.

Figure 5.3

Capital Expenditures by U.S. TNCs and Population of European Periphery, 1979–1993

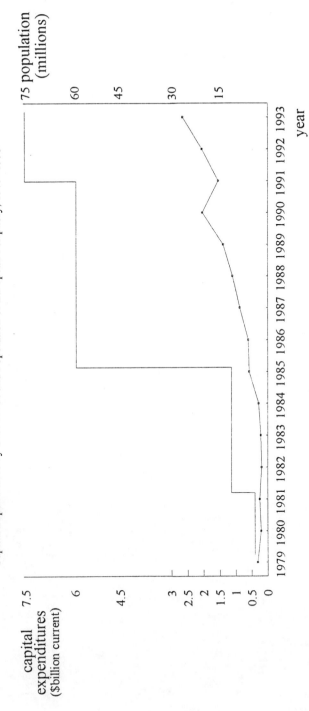

Source: U.S. Department of Commerce, various years.

The degree of intra-EU investments in the periphery are limited by tendencies toward agglomeration in the EU core. Into the mid-1990s, manufacturing companies were still being rationalized, with daily announcements of closures and downsizing. Moves by leading sector companies to consolidate their European operations shifted jobs from the periphery to the core, while other companies rationalized their labor-intensive operations by moving outside the EU to Eastern Europe or the former GDR.[6] Textiles produced in high-tech core factories, for example, are sent to labor-intensive East European factories to be made up into clothing. During 1988–1992, EU textile exports to Eastern Europe increased from 348 to 1,196 million ECU (344 percent) while return imports of clothing increased from 936 to 2,075 million ECU (222 percent) (communication from Eurostat).

Still, a great deal has been made of the flow of EU core capital into Portugal and (especially) Spain since the two nations joined the EC in 1986. About 70 percent of FDI in the Iberian peninsula during 1986–1992 was from the EU. However, this appears to have been only a speculative "bubble" of postaccession investments. FDI began to fall after 1991 in both countries. Manufacturing FDI in Spain fell by two-thirds in 1992 to its lowest level since 1987 and again fell in 1993 (Burns 1993b). Even these figures overstate the effects of FDI on the Spanish and Portuguese economies because of the low proportion that is invested in production. Only one-fifth of FDI in Portugal was in manufacturing; half was in finance, real estate, and business services; and the rest was in construction, hotels, and restaurants (Organization for Economic Cooperation and Development 1992). Moreover, manufacturing investments were concentrated—the Volkswagen-Fiat Autoeuropa project announced in 1991 was scheduled to invest more than 3 billion dollars, which is practically equal to the entire FDI flow for Portugal in an entire year. Two other projects by Pepsico and Neste dominated the rest of recent manufacturing FDI (Wise 1993).

The limitations of Eurocore investments in the EU periphery should come as no surprise. Surveys of locational decisions by large EU investors indicate, as the restructuring literature predicts, that proximity to markets is the most important factor in the location of production (Cassell 1993b). Such behavior is unfavorable for the periphery because most producers aim for core European markets. This helps explain the success of Britain and France in attracting inward investments despite their higher labor costs. Even where market proximity indicates location in the periphery, unstable peripheral markets can make the projects unstable. Renault, for example, halved its Portuguese auto production in the 1990s because of instability of the Spanish auto market (Wise 1993).

Indeed, the auto sector exemplifies many of the EU periphery's problems. While Lung (1992) argued that flexible processes such as just-in-time production are not common in the European industry, vertical structures have become more concentrated. Investments have been spatially concentrated—with Japanese plants in England (Sunderland, Burnaston, and Swindon) and European plants in Spain (Madrid), Portugal (Setubal), and (for Fiat) the Mezzogiorno. New assembly plants are increasingly located in Eastern Europe—such as Fiat and General Motors in

Poland, Volkswagen in Czechoslovakia, General Motors and Suzuki in Hungary. With the increased size of the Europeriphery, a few regions "win" the competition for FDI.

Labor-intensive auto parts production comprises most of the sector's semi-peripheral production. Japanese purchases remain highly concentrated in England. Of Nissan's 198 European component suppliers, 132 are in Britain, 29 in Germany, and 13 in France. Of Honda's 150 European suppliers, 70 percent are British (Way 1993). Ireland, an obvious semiperipheral supplier with a number of established part makers, supplied just $12 million of Nissan and Toyota's $2.25 billion components purchases in Europe in 1993. German car companies have shifted their purchases to East European suppliers—Ford in Hungary and General Motors in Turkey and Czechoslovakia (countries that have labor-cost advantages of up to 50 percent over Ireland). Thus, even where labor-cost advantages still attract FDI, the expanding EU periphery has marginalized many regions as new investments are concentrated.

Moreover, restructuring has concentrated some products themselves. The Swedish truck firm Scandia and the Dutch firm Iveco have attempted to increase their competitiveness by using fewer components. Iveco cut its workforce by more than 10 percent and reduced its number of suppliers from 2,000 to 700 (mostly in Spain and the United Kingdom) by producing modules instead of parts (Done 1993a). Auto companies are also drastically cutting their numbers of suppliers. Volkswagen/Audi, for instance, expected to cut its number of suppliers from more than 2,000 to 100–200 by the year 2000 (Done 1993b).

Finally, EU regional policy has failed to create vibrant networks of indigenous firms. Indigenous company failures reached record levels in Spain in the 1990s. Ten of thirty-one Spanish companies dropped out of the *Financial Times* group of 500 largest European companies in 1993 alone, and the remaining twenty-one were all in services. Foreign takeovers as well as failures left the auto and auto components sectors almost entirely in foreign hands, along with foreign domination in chemicals, cement, and other sectors (Burns 1993a).

Industrial centers such as the Basque country were particularly hard hit—in twenty years, this region went from a full-employment economy to an unemploy-ment rate of 23 percent. Its steel and ship sectors were destroyed by European competition and EU-imposed cutbacks, while its small supplier sectors such as car components also declined. In 1991 alone, Basque industrial production fell by 4.5 percent and 20,000 jobs were lost (Burns 1993c). Portuguese steel, fertilizer, textile, and clothing companies have collapsed. Even Setubal, Portugal's "success story" in attracting FDI, has become a high-unemployment region due to indigenous closures. Most of Ireland's indigenous industry was wiped out by free trade after accession to the EC in the 1970s, but failures continue. For example, employment in indigenous Irish firms fell from 156,000 in 1980 to 119,000 in 1991 (O'Hearn 1993).

THE MARGINALIZED PERIPHERY: WHAT ROLE?

Recent changes in the southern EU periphery look ominously familiar to anyone who knows the Irish economy. Irish industry, which was destroyed after EC accession in 1973 was only partly replaced by FDI. However, TNCs were unreliable engines of growth because of their short life span and their failure to expand, and also because they created a dependence on ever-increasing flows of FDI for economic expansion, which were not forthcoming. After investments in basic manufactures dried up, the Irish turned to electronics, then to pharmaceuticals and, most recently, to international services. The result—between indigenous closures, TNC cutbacks and restructures, and the difficulty in attracting new investments—was a steady decrease in manufacturing employment and a rising rate of unemployment. Increasing numbers of Irish people were marginalized at the periphery of the EU during the 1980s. Seventy percent of the unemployed are now long-term unemployed—and essentially unemployable.

The failures of Ireland—which had long been considered the most successful attractor of TNCs in the semiperiphery—exemplify a broad problem of marginalization of the European periphery. Restructuring, core agglomeration, and localization reduced the supply of FDI; new forms of production reduced the number of jobs that accompany a given investment; and a vastly enlarged European periphery increased the competition for the dwindling supply of investments. This brings to mind the old conundrum of whether the periphery suffers from core exploitation or from a lack thereof. Large regions of the European periphery have been marginalized as core firms lost interest in exploiting their labor while indigenous producers failed to compete in the SEM. Instead of exploitation, growing numbers of people face the economic oppression of long-term unemployment. Even core regions contemplate new forms of work organization—job sharing, a reduced workweek, and so on—to avoid unemployment. In such an environment, increasing marginalization appears to be the future of the EU periphery.

What has changed? Restructuring has changed the specificities of peripheral regions' structural relationship to the EU. There are important differences between Ireland's continuing role (now alongside Britain) as a point of entry for non-EU capital and the southern periphery's role as a buffer zone between "Fortress Europe" and African and Asian migrants. The latter role has created specific anomalies such as high unemployment regions that attract pools of migrant Third World labor. It has also created a role for the Southern periphery as policeman for Europe against the southern and eastern migrants (Bunyan 1993).

However, restructuring has also intensified existing trends. It increased the dependence of the widening EU periphery on dwindling supplies of FDI, while vastly increasing the difficulties of indigenous firms. The growing semiperipheral reserve army heightened the pressure on all European workers to increase their "flexibility" (to accept lower wages and reduced labor power). Restructuring has reduced the policy choices of regions as the EU demands privatization and free trade while presenting a Cuban-type isolation as the alternative to compliance.

The EU intensifies regional peripheralization by introducing communications and transport infrastructures that are not linked to local innovation. It trains peripheral workers and professionals without prospects of work, motivating them to traverse the new transport infrastructures to core labor markets. It increases competition among peripheral regions and states at the very time when solidarity and creative mobilization against the excesses of the EU model are most critical. Moreover, it proletarianizes labor without the likelihood of a job. Overall, it increases the disparity between the profitable high-tech, but still delinked, foreign sectors and the low-profit, unstable, indigenous ones.

NOTES

1. This "periphery," of course, is actually a semiperipheral zone, a term that usually refers to the semiperipheral regions that are members of the EU. Throughout this chapter, *EU periphery* refers to Ireland, Greece, Portugal, Spain, the Mezzogiorno, and the former German Democratic Republic (GDR). The *European periphery* refers also to Turkey and the former Soviet bloc of Eastern and Central Europe.

2. Although I will concentrate on peripheral members of the European Union, it is clear that the former East European bloc is now clearly integrated as a European peripheral zone. Competition between EU members and the former Soviet bloc for external investments is an important part of the process of marginalization of both zones.

3. This, of course, has changed since the accession of the former GDR to the EU. The GDR entered the EU at the income level of the other peripheral regions but has deteriorated since.

4. Britain has the fourth largest electronics industry in the world, but it is nearly all foreign owned (Cane 1993).

5. Despite the significance of competition for inward investments from Eastern Europe, even these countries report difficulties attracting investments. Hungary, for instance, attracted more than $5.5 billion during 1989–1993, which it claimed to be half of total inward investments in Eastern Europe. However, foreign investments, even in Hungary, peaked in 1991 at $1.7 billion, leading the minister for International Economic Relations to remark, "The beautiful days are over" (Denton 1993).

6. A large Singapore-based electronics firm, for instance, recently set up its European headquarters in Britain but intended to put its manufacturing operations in Eastern Europe. According to its chief executive, "The UK is OK cost-wise if you're employing hundreds of people, but if you're employing thousands you need to go somewhere cheaper" (Buxton 1993).

REFERENCES

Abrahams, Paul. 1993. "Drugs R&D Is at Risk, Says Pfizer," *Financial Times*, 13 Dec., 10.

Albert, M., and B. J. Ball. 1983. *Towards European Economic Recovery in the 1980s.* European Parliament Working Document. Luxembourg: European Parliament.

Amin, Ash. 1992. "Big firms versus the regions in the Single European Market." In M. Dunford and G. Kafkalis, eds., *Cities and Regions in the New Europe: The Global-Local Interplay and Spatial Development Strategies.* London: Belhaven Press, 127–49.

Andrikopolou, E. 1992. "Whither regional policy? Local development and the state in Greece." In M. Dunford and G. Kafkalis, eds., *Cities and Regions in the New Europe.* London: Belhaven Press, 195–212.

Begg, I., and D. Mayes. 1991. "Social and Economic Cohesion among the Regions of Europe in the 1990s." *National Institute Economic Review*, (Nov.), 63–74.

Bornschier, Volker. 1980. "Multinational Corporations and Economic Growth: a Cross-National Test of the Decapitalization Thesis." *Journal of Development Economics* 7:191–210.

———. 1992. "The European Community's Uprising: Grasping towards Hegemony or Therapy against National Decline in the World Political Economy." Paper delivered to European Conference of Sociology, Vienna, 26–29 Aug.

Breen, Richard. 1991. *Education, Employment and Training in the Youth Labor Market.* General Research Series paper no.152. Dublin: Economic and Social Research Institute.

Bunyan, Tony. 1993. *Statewatching in the New Europe.* London: Statewatch.

Burns, Tom. 1993a. "The FT500—Household Names among the Fallen." *Financial Times*, 10 Feb., xviii.

———. 1993b. "Spain Has a Head Start on Delors Jobs Plan." *Financial Times*, 10 Dec., 2.

———. 1993c. "Survey of the Basque Country: 'Complicated' Recovery Forecast," *Financial Times*, 24 Nov., 41.

Buxton, James. 1993. "Singapore Group Plans 300 High-Tech Jobs," *Financial Times*, 16 Nov., 11.

Cane, Alan. 1993. "Can Britain Make It? Foreign Ownership Handicaps Electronics." *Financial Times*, 1 Mar., 7.

Cassell, Michael. 1993a. "Survey of Business Locations in Europe: Britain Takes the Lion's Share." *Financial Times*, 11 Oct., 11.

———. 1993b. "Survey of Business Locations in Europe: The Deciding Factors." *Financial Times*, 11 Oct., iii.

Commission of the European Communities. 1992. *Evaluation of the Effects of the EC Framework Programme for Research and Technological Development on*

Economic and Social Cohesion in the Community. Commission of the European Communities Report no. 48. Luxembourg: Organization of Petroleum Exporting Countries.

Committee for the Study of Economic and Monetary Union, ed. 1989. *Report on Economic and Monetary Union in the European Community.* Luxembourg: Commission of the European Community.

Coriat, B. 1991. "Technical Flexibility and Mass Production." In G. Benko and M. Dunford, eds., *Industrial Change and Regional Development.* London: Belhaven, 134–58.

Delors, Jacques. 1989. "Regional Implications of Economic and Monetary Integration." In Committee for the Study of Economic and Monetary Union, ed., *Report on Economic and Monetary Union in the European Community.* Luxembourg: Commission of the European Community, 81–89.

Denton, Nicholas. 1993. "Hungary Sets Up Investment Promotion Agency," *Financial Times,* 6 Oct., 8.

Done, Kevin. 1993a. "International Company News—Iveco Gambles High Stakes on Future." *Financial Times,* 5 May, 25.

————. 1993b. "International Company News—Sharp Reduction in Number of Component Suppliers Planned." *Financial Times,* 10 June, 28.

Dunford, M., and G. Kafkalis. 1992. "The Global-Local Interplay, Corporate Geographies and Spatial Development Strategies in Europe." In M. Dunford and G. Kafkalis, eds., *Cities and Regions in the New Europe.* London: Belhaven, 3–38.

Eurostat. 1993. *Regions Statistical Yearbook.* Luxemburg: Office of Official Publications of the European Commission.

Frazer, T. 1990. "Competition after 1992: The Next Step." *Modern Law Review* 53, no. 5:609–23.

Gerstenberger, W. 1991. "Impact of Information Technologies on Future Employment in the European Community: Executive Summary." Paper delivered to European Community Conference, Brussels, 17–18 Oct.

Goodhart, David. 1993. "Numbers Crunch—Wage Costs are Important but Productivity Differences Mean That Their Net Effect on Competitiveness Is Hard to Calculate." *Financial Times,* 13 Oct., xxii.

Grahl, J., and Paul Teague. 1990. *1992: The Big Market: The Future of the European Community.* London: Lawrence and Wishart.

Lung, Y. 1992. "Global Competition and Transregional Strategy: Spatial Reorganisation of the European Car Industry." In M. Dunford and G. Kafkalis, eds., *Cities and Regions in the New Europe.* London: Belhaven, 68–85.

O'Hearn, Denis. 1989. "The Irish Case of Dependency: An Exception to the Exceptions?" *American Sociological Review* 54, no. 4 (Aug.):578–96.

————. 1990. "TNCs, Intervening Mechanisms and Economic Growth in Ireland: A Longitudinal Test and Extension of the Bornschier Model." *World Development* 18, no. 3:417–29.

————. 1993. "Global Competition, Europe and Irish Peripherality." *Economic and Social Review* 24, no. 2 (Jan.):169–97.

Organization for Economic Cooperation and Development. 1992. *Country Report: Portugal.* Paris: OECD.

Perrons, Diane. 1992. "The Regions and the Single Market." In M. Dunford and G. Kafkalis, eds., *Cities and Regions in the New Europe.* London: Belhaven, 170–94.

Tucker, Emma. 1993. "France Bucks Trend as Foreign Investment Rises." *Financial Times,* 1 Mar., 2.

United States Department of Commerce. [Various years.] *Survey of Current Business.* Washington, DC: U.S. Government Printing Office.

van Tulder, Rob, and Gerd Junne. 1988. *European Multinationals in Core Technologies.* New York: John Wiley and Sons.

Way, Arthur. 1993. "Survey of World Automotive Suppliers—Big Chance for Chosen Suppliers." *Financial Times,* 28 June, iv.

Wise, Peter. 1993. "Survey of European Finance and Investment—Portugal: Autoeuropa Proves a Magnet." *Financial Times,* 26 Apr., 26.

6

Product Cycles and International Divisions of Labor: Contrasts between the United States and Japan

Richard Child Hill and Kuniko Fujita

The postwar internationalization of the Japanese economy raises two anomalies from the vantage point of the American pattern. First, Japanese direct foreign investment has stimulated, rather than retarded, economic growth in less developed nations along the western Pacific Rim, and second, Japanese direct foreign investment has sustained, rather than weakened, Japan's own manufacturing base. Japan's globalization fits neither zero sum dependency models in its relationship to less developed East Asian nations nor deindustrialization arguments in relation to changes in its own domestic economy.

This chapter locates these anomalies in the contrasting ways in which Americans and Japanese link product cycles, international divisions of labor, and economic development. Americans believe in a laissez-faire philosophy but make trade and investment decisions based on oligopolistic bargaining and location strategies. The Japanese, by contrast, emphasize national comparative advantage and make trade and investment decisions in accord with market conforming state strategies. These differences help explain why, in contrast to the United States, Japanese postwar foreign investment has stimulated industrial development in neighboring East Asian nations but has not boomeranged to hollow out Japan's own manufacturing base.

JAPAN AND EAST ASIA IN THE WORLD SYSTEM

Bruce Cumings (1984) persuasively argued that Japan and its Northeast Asian neighbors, Korea and Taiwan, developed in this century through the special character of their interactions with one another and through their combined interactions with the world at large—economically, through product cycles, and politically, through the roles they played in two hegemonic systems: the Japanese Empire to 1945 and the American system of influence starting in the late 1940s.

Japanese colonialism created a Northeast Asian regional economy between 1900 and 1945. Japanese imperialism differed from the Western pattern in several ways. The Japanese colonized contiguous territory, allowing for tight integration of the colony to the metropole. They brought industry to the colonies rather than bringing colonial labor and raw materials to the imperial center. They colonized defensively, as a protection against their own conquest by more developed Western nations. Moreover, colonizing late, they planned their efforts in light of the past experiences of rival imperial powers.

Japan withdrew with her colonies from the world-system in the 1930s, attempting a go-it-alone regional path. At that time, it adopted many features of the development model that would prove so successful after World War II: product cycle–inspired domestic and foreign industrial policies, administrative guidance of the economy, big business conglomerates, and corporatism without labor.

The end of World War II brought a new hegemonic structure to the East Asia region. The Allied Powers settled on a containment policy vis à vis the Soviet Union and the Peoples' Republic of China (PRC), and they cast Japan in the role of a buffer state. Recognizing that resource-poor Japan could not play the desired part without access to a hinterland, the Americans created a triangular trade and investment structure, with the United States at the core, Japan in the semiperiphery, and Southeast Asia in the periphery.

The United States provided military and economic aid to Korea and Taiwan, which took on a perimeter role in the containment strategy. Mirroring Japan in the 1930s, these regimes possessed strong states, big business conglomerates, corporatism without labor, and limited social welfare. Directly dependent on the U.S. military in the 1950s, Korea and Taiwan became indirectly dependent on Japanese and American markets and technology starting in the 1970s.

Cumings wrote the seminal world-system analysis of Japanese and East Asian development but his argument now bears some reassessment. Cumings emphasized the historical and regional specificity of Northeast Asian development, but Japan's product-cycle relations with Korea and Taiwan now extend to Southeast Asia, the PRC, and indeed, to most of the eastern Pacific Rim. Korea and Taiwan have evidently taken more than Japan's domestic economic structure to heart; they have been emulating Japan in their foreign economic relations with their neighbors to the south, as well.[1]

Cumings saw little likelihood that Asian newly industrializing economics (NIEs) could achieve upward mobility in the world-system.[2] If upward mobility means one country moving ahead of another in rank order of wealth and the like, then Cumings's forecast mirrors contemporary reality. However, if upward mobility means narrowing the wealth gap among leader and follower countries, then many East Asian nations have been moving up the regional hierarchy.[3]

The end of the Cold War dissolved the Western containment strategy. As American hegemony declines, regionalization of the world political economy grows. Comparisons among rival core powers and world regions are particularly salient at the present moment. Our focus in this chapter is on contrasts between Japanese- and American-centered international divisions of labor.

PRODUCT CYCLES AND INDUSTRIAL DEVELOPMENT

At the turn of the century, Alfred Marshall foretold of England's inability to hold her own against other nations by the "mere sedulous practice of familiar processes." English and American ingenuity were reducing the nation's innovations "to a mechanical routine," thereby allowing energetic workers in less technically advanced nations to compete on a par with British labor. Sixty years earlier, "the finished commodities, and still more, the implements of production, to which [English] . . . manufacturers were giving their chief attention in any one year, were those which would be occupying the attention of the more progressive of Western nations two or three years later, and of the rest from five to twenty years later." France and, particularly, the United States were now threatening England's leadership.[4]

Marshall was depicting the interrelatedness of product cycles, business expansion and national power. Business enterprises are built upon discoveries. When an innovation displaces other products, the innovative firm enjoys a high rate of growth. The company can sell well above its costs of production so long as its innovation is not widely understood. However, the success of the innovation attracts competitors. As the inner workings of the new product become an open secret, production costs begin to dominate. The market becomes saturated, growth tapers off, and profitability is squeezed. Firms with lower costs or accepting a lower profit rate may then capture the innovator's market.

Companies attempt to prolong their product's life cycle by maintaining secrecy, controlling marketing outlets, and lowering costs.[5] Ultimately, however, a firm survives competition by developing new products. When the rate of growth in one product slows, the firm can switch to another and thereby sustain its profit rate. Since competition and technological change always threaten to wipe out an innovator's advantage, companies must reinvest profits to improve and expand production. Change is normal, and the existing state of affairs is never final. "The dialectic of the product cycle" propels capitalism onward (Hymer 1979, 79).

The Japanese take the product cycle axiom to heart, but they practice it in their own way. To understand how the Japanese think about the relationship between product cycles and development, it helps to contrast their view with the American experience.

THE U.S. PRODUCT CYCLE

Researchers attempting to explain the international division of labor emerging after World War II often rely on Raymond Vernon's (1971, 1979) rendering of product cycle theory. According to Vernon, the trade and investment patterns of U.S. corporations followed a predictable sequence of innovation, imitation, standardization and diffusion.

In the first phase of the product cycle, the U.S. firm *exported* the high-value product innovation. As the product stimulated foreign demand, foreign firms acquired an incentive to enter the market and were often assisted in doing so by their national governments. As foreign firms imitated the product and began producing it, U.S. exports slowed. In the second, *direct foreign investment* (DFI) phase, American corporations set up their own manufacturing plants in foreign countries to protect market share. In the third, *overseas sourcing* phase, technology had become standardized and widely disseminated and the limit of scale economies had been reached. Trade based on wage costs had commenced. American TNCs adopted a global outlook and set up production around the world wherever costs were lowest. By then, they were importing the product back home (Morris-Suzuki 1991).

Vernon's product cycle hypothesis relied upon the special conditions enjoyed by the American economy following World War II: huge corporations, mass production, scarce and well paid labor, high per capita income, large internal markets, and war devastated competitor nations. Under these circumstances, the U.S. market generated innovations that people in other countries came to desire as their own nations grew closer to American income levels and market conditions.

The U.S.-centered international division of labor created a dependency relationship for countries specializing in the later stages of the product cycle. American companies invested abroad to protect their hold on knowledge and assure their own continued growth. They brought capital, technology, and management to foreign countries but did so mainly to control that part of the product cycle taking place outside the United States. The American TNC thus sought a favorable business environment for its own survival, and not the development of the host society (Hymer 1979, 154).

In theory, the innovation advantages of U.S. firms over foreign competitors should have protected the jobs of American workers. As long as there was a technological gap between the United States and competing nations with respect to a given product, American firms should have produced the good at home and exported it abroad. U.S. workers would then have retained the comparative advantage of working in innovative industrial sectors and the technically advanced stages of the product cycle. In fact, however, U.S. companies transferred abroad industries in which they held a comparative advantage.[6] Moreover, the offshore movement of U.S. branch plants boomeranged to inflict damage on the U.S. industrial labor force (Bluestone and Harrison 1982).

As American companies expanded, they became more oligopolistic, "recognizing their mutual interdependence and striving to share in the pie without destroying it" (Hymer 1979, 82). Oligopoly blunted the dynamic of innovation in response to competition underlying the product cycle model. As the giant American companies' profits came to depend less on the home economy and more on the world economy, nation-centered competition among firms gave way to global market sharing and collusion. U.S. TNCs set up production behind Third World tariff walls to protect future market share. They could do this despite higher costs in less developed countries because they were subsidized by Third World governments and could draw upon their own oligopolistic advantages. Oligopolistic bargaining and location strategies thus displaced calculations about national comparative advantage.

In some industries and host countries, American TNCs exported from the beginning without engaging in import substitution. In segments of the garment industry, for example, TNCs imported capital, technology, packaged parts, and materials; used local labor for sewing and assembling; and exported goods abroad through their own distribution networks. Export expansion was possible from the beginning because TNC production technology was standardized and skilled labor, continuous learning, and the adoption of new technology were not required. Industrial development of this type provided host countries with employment and foreign exchange, but the education of local managers and workers and linkages with other industries were inherently limited.

U.S. companies attempted to prolong product cycles by controlling external markets and pursuing cheaper labor, as predicted by the product cycle model. However, instead of investing in new product development and upgrading technology at home, American companies diversified out of mobile manufacturing industries. U.S. imports from developing countries reversed trade flows in many manufacturing sectors and hollowed the nation's industrial base. Rising unemployment increased government expenditures at a time when tax revenues were falling. Disinvestment, unemployment, and fiscal crisis eroded the postwar social contract between American capital and labor (O'Connor 1973; Jenkins 1984).

THE JAPANESE PRODUCT CYCLE

Akamatsu Kaname, a Japanese economist, formulated a product cycle model of industrial development in the 1930s. Akamatsu's theory, however, was based upon the experience of a follower country, as Japan was at the time. The time-series curve for a developing country's product cycle—imports of a product followed by domestic production and later by exports—suggested to Akamatsu a pattern like "wild geese flying in orderly ranks forming an inverse V just as airplanes fly in formation" (Kojima 1977, 15). Such a product cycle took place for standardized, rather than new, products and in developing, rather than industrialized, countries.

The catching-up product cycle, when successfully pursued by firms in a developing country, evinces the following sequence: The developing country imports a new product. As local demand grows, companies begin domestic production. A learning process commences, assisted by imported knowledge and capital. As quality improves, local production expands. Expanding production allows for economies of scale and increased productivity. Costs are further reduced when locally produced intermediate inputs are substituted for imports. As costs and quality reach internationally competitive standards, foreign markets open up and further scale economies become possible. In this fashion, the import of a foreign good eventuates in industrial development via production for local and foreign markets.

The Japanese industrialized their nation through this kind of catching-up product cycle; to do so, they had to reduce production costs and raise product quality to the standards set by firms in advanced industrial countries. First World TNCs had attained economies of scale far more extensive than those prevailing in developing countries like Japan, they monopolized advanced technologies and made them available only under royalty or through DFI, they were able to integrate production and sales operations into global marketing and information networks, and they possessed a superior ability to differentiate and market products according to brand and design.

Japan developed by challenging Western capitalist nations on a new, competitive front and using a new, institutional framework, just as the United States had challenged Great Britain a century earlier. Japan industrialized on the basis of learning, that is, by borrowing foreign technology rather than by invention or innovation (Amsden 1989).[7]

The Japanese did not simply imitate foreign technologies; they emulated them. Japanese manufacturers assimilated foreign knowhow and then applied it to their own production organization with even greater efficiency. Lacking novel technologies, the Japanese built their competitive advantage, first by penetrating world markets on the basis of low unit costs (low wages in relation to productivity) and then by producing high-quality products efficiently and bringing new generations of the same product to market quickly. By successfully translating the "flying geese" product cycle model into strategic industrial practice, Japan brought a new developmental framework into play in the world economy.[8]

Japanese officialdom encouraged continuous learning and facilitated collective mobilization behind what had been learned. To a far greater degree than their western counterparts, Japanese development officials recognized that productivity is dependent upon institutions as well as investment (Johnson 1982). To overcome the penalties of lateness, the Japanese state intervened in the economy on behalf of business, but with the premise that business must be disciplined in the interests of the nation.[9]

To facilitate import substitution, Japanese state officials placed tariffs on imports, subsidized infant industries, and agreed to purchase domestic products that were still in the early stages of development. To promote exports, the central government reduced taxes on export earnings, lowered interest rates for export financing, and provided long-term export credits (Kojima 1977, 153).

The Japanese organized huge trading companies with hundreds of subsidiaries throughout the world to offset the economy of scale, marketing, and information advantages possessed by foreign transnational corporations. Japan's trading companies identified the nation's comparative advantages and helped small- and medium-sized companies engage in overseas trade and investment. The government also established the Japanese External Trade and Research Organization (JETRO) to promote international trade and information gathering.[10]

The Japanese also took a much more catholic approach to the comparative advantage thesis than was commonly set forth in Western development theory, particularly when it came to continually improving, rather than disengaging from, mature industries.[11] With the flying geese metaphor in mind, the Japanese persistently upgraded and diversified their manufacturing base: toward more technology-intensive products and production processes and a more skill-intensive labor force.

As Japanese firms adapted Western innovations to the special conditions of their own economies, they were able to initiate their own export and direct investment cycles. Their target was the markets of East Asian developing countries that were lagging behind them in the industrialized pecking order. Japan's early relations with the Asian NIEs and Association of Southeast Asian Nations (ASEAN) countries conformed to product cycle descriptions of a "middle country"—one that imported from developed countries and exported to developing countries (Morris-Suzuki 1991). Not yet prepared to compete on the world market for sophisticated, capital-intensive manufacturing, Japan occupied an intermediate position in a trans-Pacific triangle: it imported advanced manufacturing and raw materials from the United States and exported simpler manufacturing to East Asia. The United States helped maintain open and expanding Asian markets for Japan's exports in exchange for Japan's willingness to serve as a political buffer against neighboring communist states (Morris-Suzuki 1991, 138; Pyle 1992).

Japan's product cycle moved more into line with those of developed countries during the 1970s. Japanese wages rose rapidly and were no longer low by international standards by the end of the high growth period (1950–1965). A currency appreciation in 1971 forced Japan to open its markets wider to manufacturing imports and stiffened foreign competition against Japanese companies. The Asian NIEs began import substitution policies aimed at long-term industrial growth, including protective tariffs on a range of manufacturing imports combined with big incentives for manufacturing DFI.[12] As a consequence, Japanese DFI flowed into Southeast Asia to preserve established markets and take advantage of lower production costs in labor-intensive industries.

With the flying geese development model in mind, Japanese officials supported import substitution investment in Southeast Asia, viewing it as a stimulant and complement to the growth of heavy industry in Japan. They argued, for example, that Japanese investment in textile production in Southeast Asia would stimulate textile machinery production in Japan. Japan's exports of intermediate products did, in fact, soar as Japanese TNC textile and electronics subsidiaries in the Asian NIEs and ASEAN purchased substantial semiprocessed inputs from Japan (Morris-Suzuki 1991, 141).

Japanese learners eventually became innovators through habitually scanning the world for new technologies, mastering them at home, and investing heavily in research and development. Today, as Japanese industry concentrates on knowledge intensive, high value end products and high-tech parts, an innovation centered product cycle is increasingly evident (Yamada 1990, 4–5; Kiyonari 1993). Factories are networking automation equipment for efficient, small-lot production to create high-value-added products for a diversified domestic marketplace. Vast funds are being expended on research to strengthen technological capabilities (Burderi, et al. 1992).

CONTRASTS BETWEEN THE UNITED STATES AND JAPAN

Japanese thinking about product cycle industrialization contrasts with the American thinking in several ways. Believing in the liberal creed, U.S. officialdom equates the individual pursuit of profit with the national interest. However, the Japanese developed within the framework of defensive nationalism and see the world differently. They think that a firm's quest to maximize profits through territorial expansion can conflict with national development objectives. Because a nation's labor force cannot move across borders with the ease of capital, the interests of a nation's citizens are not identical with the interests of a multinational firm. Governments must monitor and guide corporate investment decisions in the interests of workers, communities, and the state (Kojima 1977, 117; Amsden 1989).

Proponents of the flying geese development model (Kojima 1977; Shinohara 1982; Yamazawa 1990, 1992) believe DFI to developing countries should be trade-oriented; that is, aimed at complementing and strengthening comparative advantage in investing and receiving countries alike.[13] The potential conflict between direct foreign investment and national development is circumvented when investment upgrades the industrial structure in host *and* investing nations and accelerates trade between them.

Manufacturing DFI is of mutual benefit when the industries are those in which investing nations are losing comparative advantage while recipient countries are gaining it, or are expected to gain it. DFI from a comparatively disadvantaged industry in the investing country that is a potentially advantageous industry in the host country promotes mutual interest because "comparative profitabilities in trade oriented DFI conform to the direction of potential comparative costs" (Kojima 1977, 76–77). Manufacturing investment should be export-oriented, so as not to merely serve the privileged in the recipient countries, and industries should be transferred, step by step, from advanced to developing countries.

Kiyoshi Kojima, a development economist who has influenced Japanese trade policy, has argued that American DFI often has not conformed to the comparative profitabilities formula, has not complemented the host economy, and therefore has not been trade oriented. Instead, U.S. firms transferred abroad industries ranked at the top of America's comparative advantage. Postwar U.S. manufacturing DFI was mainly undertaken by industries, like chemicals, machinery, transportation, and scientific instruments, that devoted a relatively high proportion of resources to research and advertising and tended to be dominated by large firms (Vernon 1971, ch. 3; Hymer 1979, ch. 9).

Oligopoly accounts for American investment behavior. Under competitive conditions, the profit rate from DFI in an advanced industry ought to be lower than domestic returns thereby precluding overseas investment in that industry. However, under oligopolistic conditions, including the advantages in technology, product differentiation, and marketing possessed by the giant firm, comparative profitabilities are divorced from comparative advantages and DFI can be more profitable than domestic investment. Moreover, when a less-developed country levies a high tariff to protect its own industry, an oligopolist can readily relocate production, sell behind the tariff wall, and remain profitable.

Japanese policy analysts who adhere to the flying geese model argue that DFI should complement capital, technology, and managerial knowledge that are in short supply in recipient nations. Foreign investors should play a tutor role: they should teach technical, managerial, and marketing knowledge to local people while maintaining competitive advantage by shifting to the production of more sophisticated, intermediate goods. However, the giant American firm seeks instead to maximize its profits from its initial advantage and consolidate itself against further attack. American TNCs control marketing through advertising and dealer networks and maintain entry barriers against smaller firms based on their ability to plan and coordinate over the whole product cycle (Hymer 1979, 229). U.S. TNC subsidiaries therefore stay in place rather than opening up production spaces by moving to new products. Moreover, by emphasizing export oriented transplants with high productivity and low wages, U.S.-style DFI promotes manufacturing enclaves with weak links to the host economy.

Japanese industry is also oligopolistic, but in contrast to the Americans, Japanese oligopolists heatedly compete with each other, even in protected markets. Unlike their American counterparts, Japanese industrialists have always been export oriented and, as late developers, they have continually been under competitive pressure from foreign companies in the world market. In order to improve their international competitiveness, they have had to achieve technological improvements and acquire new technology imports (Kohama 1990, 15).

As Japanese firms develop new products, they are shifting domestic production capacity to the higher-value-added innovations in order to maintain a leading market position. Japanese parent companies have traditionally turned over the production of more standardized, but still viable, product lines to their domestic subcontractors. However, as cost differences among segments of the workforce and regions have narrowed in Japan, companies have transferred mature technologies to the Asian NIEs and the ASEAN countries. Japan's domestic demand for the products of transferred technology are met by imports. This division of labor is promoting industrialization in the Asian NIEs and ASEAN countries while enabling Japan to maintain a leading economic position in the region (Yamada 1990).[14]

Some believe, with Walden Bello (1993), that the flying geese theory is simply the Japanese rationale for their dominant position in East Asia. We agree with Bello that East Asian regional integration is based upon a Japan-led technological pecking order and an unequal division of labor among nations. However, we favor the hypothesis that the late industrializing Japanese—having themselves experienced the necessity of catching up, been motivated by defensive nationalism, and depended for the ingredients for their manufactures on other nations in the region—have been more willing than Western capitalists to transfer appropriate technology, accept minority equity relations and generally operate within the framework of developing country industrial policies (Kojima 1977; Doner 1991; Aoki 1992; Hill and Lee 1994).

Bello (1993, 35) argued that thirty years after export industrialization began, South Korea and Taiwan are still mainly labor-intensive assembly sites for foreign, and mostly Japanese, components; they are, in his view, more technologically dependent on Japan than ever. However, on balance, the evidence suggests to us that South Korea and Taiwan possess more dynamic economies with wider margins for maneuver than Bello allowed.

We cannot treat this issue systematically here but will take, as one salient example, Japan's role in the development of the Korean steel industry, as detailed by Alice Amsden (1989, ch. 12). Korea's state-run steel operation, Pohang Iron and Steel Company, Ltd. (POSCO), was originally a turnkey operation put together by a consortium of Japanese steelmakers. However, Koreans participated in all phases of the original project. After start-up, POSCO narrowed the gap in labor productivity between the Korean and Japanese steel industries, progressively import-substituted all elements and executed all tasks initially supplied by the Japan Group, financed two-thirds of its second mill with retained earnings from its first mill's operations, sent personnel to Japan to learn about quality control, and subsequently established its own research and development center and moved into new product development. POSCO's purchases from suppliers progressively rose in local content, and with each capacity expansion local firms supplied more complex capital goods. Amsden concluded that POSCO learned enough from Nippon Steel and earned enough from its initial investment to reproduce itself and then go on to dynamic learning.[15]

In contrast to the United States, Japanese manufacturing DFI has not boomeranged to hollow out Japan's manufacturing base. Japanese DFI has been accompanied by a "conscious and concerted policy of upgrading the industrial and technological structure of Japan's economy" (Morris-Suzuki 1991, 146). The Japanese have played the game of catching up with the more advanced industrial countries, and they are acutely aware of their own vulnerability to competition from the Asian NIEs. Unlike their American counterparts, Japanese development officials take it for granted that the transfer of capital and technology overseas must be connected to a strategy of industrial restructuring at home.

From the Japanese perspective, if American companies were conscious of the U.S. national interest, they would strengthen their exports rather than set up foreign subsidiaries, which cut off U.S. comparative advantage by increasing imports of those products from abroad. Rather than shifting from old, comparatively disadvantaged industries to new ones, American workers are absorbed in comparatively disadvantaged older industries and the service sector. The loss of markets and reverse imports results in difficulties in U.S. balance of payments, the export of job opportunities, the hindrance of structural adjustment, and the promotion of a protectionist national outlook.

Japan's Ministry of International Trade and Industry (MITI) has introduced a wide range of upgrade incentives, including assistance for computers, robotics, and software and facilitating DFI for small- and medium-sized firms to help them survive and accelerate internal structural adjustment. MITI also manages redeployment in sunset industries (Dore 1986). Moreover, Japanese industrialists consciously link their foreign investments abroad to the production of higher-value, more specialized products at home.[16] Because new employment in expanding sectors has steadily replaced job losses in contracting ones, Japan's high-technology supplier relationship with the Asian NIEs and ASEAN Four encountered little labor opposition.

Because Japanese investment in Asian NIE and ASEAN production networks continues to create demand for Japanese goods and services, Japan's DFI and international trade are mutually reinforcing. However, as long as Japan's role as a supplier of inputs to East Asia continues to exceed its role as a market for East Asian goods, this complementary relationship between foreign investment and trade also depends on continued Asian NIE and ASEAN access to American and European markets.[17]

Innovation and domestic market expansion are also more closely correlated in Japan than in the United States. Technological innovation has two aspects—new products and new production processes. Advances in product technology can stimulate consumer demand and economic growth by enhancing the utility and quality of products. However, if the cost of product innovations is not offset by rising productivity, supply and demand will be limited and there will be little growth in the market. When advances in product and production technology go together, technological innovation expands markets. Accustomed to being in the lead, U.S. capitalists came to neglect the shop floor. Accustomed to catching up, Japanese capitalists attempted to continuously improve production organization. As Japanese product innovations broaden the range of consumer choice, rising productivity from process innovations also keeps prices in check, spurs domestic demand, and opens up new export markets (Yamada 1990).

Chen (1989) related telling differences between Japanese and American TNC competitive strategies in the consumer electronics industry. In radios, when U.S. producers faced competition from the Japanese, they did not attempt to move up in the market by investing in process and product innovations; instead, they abandoned radio production altogether and moved to other product lines in which they had a better comparative advantage. On the other hand, when the Japanese encountered radio competition from Hong Kong, they further automated domestic production, shifted to higher-value radios through improving technology and design, and located some production offshore.

U.S. manufacturers moved the monochrome television industry offshore in the late 1960s, mainly to Taiwan, and subsequently shifted all color TV production to the same offshore locations in the 1970s. When the Japanese encountered color TV competition from Taiwan and South Korea, they did not move production wholesale offshore but rather they rejuvenated their domestic industry by increasing automation and improving technology and design. They succeeded in making their products more price competitive and yet more sophisticated and of higher quality than those offered by their competitors. Thus, Japan emerged as a leader in television technology and innovative design. The United States responded to Japanese competition by imposing trade restrictions on Asian TV exports. Japan then shifted production of color TVS for the American market to the United States. Soon after, Taiwanese and South Korean TV manufacturers also set up production in North America.[18]

CONCLUSION

The American product cycle model focuses on location theory and the oligopolistic firm, while the Japanese emphasize comparative advantage. The former model is firm based, while the latter is nation based. The Japanese think that investment policy should be subordinated to trade policy. American TNC decisions may be rational where profit maximization for the firm is concerned, but antitrade investment conflicts with national development objectives. Given the relative immobility of labor in comparison to capital, economic development and welfare should be framed in national economic terms.

The United States seeks trade liberalization from foreign countries but has to increase its own protection of traditional industries. As oligopolistic firms interpenetrate each other's markets, competition turns to collusion and the dualistic American structure threatens to spread to the entire world economy. From the Japanese perspective, the United States should increase domestic instead of foreign investment in order to strengthen the competitiveness of traditional industries and create new products for export.

The flying geese hypothesis suggests that Japan and East Asian countries are now linked together by innovation and catching up product cycles and by stages of specialization among and within product sectors (see Figure 6.1). Japan is now the center of product and process innovation in sophisticated, capital intensive manufacturing; the Asian NIEs are middle countries in a catching up product cycle importing advanced manufacturing from Japan and exporting simpler manufacturing to the ASEAN Four; and the ASEAN Four are lower-rung players in a catching-up product cycle whereby they import capital intensive manufacturing from Japan and the Asian NIEs and exporting primary commodities and light manufacturing.

Figure 6.1
Economic Development and Trade:
Japan, Asian NIEs and ASEAN

	1950s	1960s	1970s	1980s	1990s
Japan Industrial structure	Labor intensive light manufacturing industry	Capital intensive heavy industry	Knowledge intensive processing and assembly industry	High value added industy (informationalized industry)	High value added industry (flexible industry)
Trade	textile	steel machinery	cars consumer electronic products	high value added products (VTRs)	high value added products (high definition TVs, laser printers, surface treatment steel)
Asian NIEs Industrial structure			Labor intensive industry	Capital intensive industry	Knowledge intensive processing and assembly industry
Trade			consumer goods	standardized parts and machinery	color TVs, VTRs, ingot and semi-product steel
ASEAN Industrial structure				Labor intensive industry	Capital intensive industry
Trade				consumer goods	standardized parts (printers)

Source: Ministry of International Trade and Industry, Tsusho Hfakusho (White Paper on International Trade), pp. 107-158; Nisennen no sangyo kozo (Industrial Structure in 2000), Tokyo, 1990.

Product cycle sequences and developmental stages are guided by potential as well as actual comparative advantage (Amsden 1989). National governments intervene in the market to guide production through indirect (e.g., taxes and subsidies) and direct (e.g., public enterprises and local content legislation) mechanisms, and they learn from each other's industrial policy experiences (Chen 1989).

Flying geese industrialization is premised on unequal technological capacities among nations. The critical issue is whether, as some Japanese government economists claim, the flying geese approach offers the best hope for negotiating competing national interests and stabilizing relations among economies that are unequal in size and stage of development. The Japanese view is premised on a strong state in relation to transnational corporations and "selective control over direct investment outflow to eliminate anti-trade investments" (Kojima 1977, 115).

Ironically, Americans tout laissez-faire and practice oligopoly; the Japanese, on the other hand, privilege state intervention while conforming more closely than Americans to competitive market behavior.

NOTES

We wish to thank Sakurai Kimihito, John Walton, and David A. Smith for their critical comments on earlier versions of this paper.

1. Today's leading foreign investors in the ASEAN Four countries (Malaysia, Thailand, Indonesia, Philippines) for example, are not Western capitalist powers nor even Japan (save for Thailand) but the Asian NIEs (South Korea, Taiwan, Hong Kong, and Singapore) (Chen 1993).

2. Cumings (1984) argued that Korea and Taiwan are dependent on core TNCs for all factors of production except cheap labor and they find even their labor advantage eroded by competition from poorer less-developed countries (LDCs). They are also constrained in moving to second stage industrialization by small domestic markets, a limited resource base, and core country protection of their own markets. For a discussion of how Korea moved to second stage industrialization, see Amsden (1989); for Taiwan, see Wade (1990). For evidence on the developmental impact of Japanese direct foreign investment on the East Asian NIEs, see Yamada (1990) and Hill and Lee (1994).

3. Trends in GNP per capita ratios between Japan and other East Asian nations suggest a narrowing of the wealth gap in recent years; see Hill and Fujita (1994).

4. Marshall's statements are quoted in Hymer (1979, 230).

5. These competitive strategies are not mutually exclusive and the Japanese have developed others as well, including continuous improvement and shortened product cycles.

6. It was not the more routinized industries that accounted for the lion's share of U.S. investment abroad, as one might expect from product cycle theory, but those

characterized by high capital intensity, advanced technology and differentiated products (Vernon 1971, ch. 3).

7. Where invention refers to a new idea, and innovation to the application of the idea to commercial use (Amsden 1989, 6).

8. Amsden (1989) argued that Japanese development institutions are not unique but rather are present in a larger set of late industrializing countries—nations that began the twentieth century in an economically backward state and dramatically raised their national income per capita by selectively investing in industry. Culture and history determine how well these institutional traits operate in individual countries. For example, the catching up paradigm operates particularly well in Japan and Korea because the state in both countries was able to exact performance standards from big business in exchange for trade protection and subsidies.

9. As Amsden (1989) has argued, this is just the reverse of Western liberalism, which assumes that business best serves the interests of society in the absence of state intervention.

10. Japan's emulation development model also encouraged the growth of salaried managers rather than private entrepreneurs, the integration of workers into the enterprise to facilitate workplace learning, and a preoccupation with shop floor organization to optimize technology transfer (Amsden 1989).

11. The comparative advantage thesis states that countries are better off specializing in a limited number of industries, depending on their resource endowment.

12. For example, these include tax holidays in priority industries, accelerated depreciation, tariff exemptions in machinery and equipment, export-processing zones, and willingness to accept polluting industries.

13. We are referring here to the view put forward by the Institute for Developing Economies in Tokyo and its *Journal of Developing Economies*, a perspective that seems to be largely shared by Japan's Ministry of International Trade and Industry.

14. Japan's economy grew at an average annual rate of 11.1 percent during the 1960s but fell to 5.2 percent during the 1970s and 4.2 percent during the 1980s. The Asian NIEs, ASEAN Four, and PRC economies grew at rates that were often 50 percent to 100 percent higher than those of Japan during the 1970s and 1980s (Duesterberg 1994).

15. Bello (1993) also argued that instead of transferring state-of-the-art high technology, Japanese companies transfer less-advanced technologies to integrate Taiwanese and Korean firms as subordinate elements within an Asian Pacific–wide division of labor. Regional integration is thus the regionalization of the Japanese economy, and not the creation of a regional economy with centers of accumulation. There is truth in this, but it should also be noted that technology can only be transferred if the host nation possesses the capacity to absorb and utilize it effectively. American TNCs may, on average, ship more sophisticated technology abroad than the Japanese, but they also seem more prone to create isolated economic enclaves in host economies. As for the absence of growth poles in East

Asia, it merits repeating (refer to note 1) that the Asian NIEs, taken together, now invest more in Indonesia, Malaysia and the Philippines than does Japan (Chen 1993).

16. Kojima (1977, 141–45) described a mid-1970s debate between MITI's Economic Structure Council and Japan's big business federation, the Keidanren, over the direction structural change should take in Japan's economy in relation to the 1973–1974 energy crisis. The issue was MITI's proposal to transfer energy-intensive intermediate materials and heavy industries abroad and to develop knowledge intensive industries at home. Keidanren officials argued that knowledge intensification should not be seen simply as a separate sector but as something to do across all industries. Heavy and chemical industries would remain the mainstay of Japan's world industrial base, the Keidanren argued, and should be located mainly in Japan. It is hard to imagine this kind of discussion taking place in the United States, contrasting as it does with the lack of American corporate consciousness of a national interest and the predisposition toward disinvestment among big American manufacturers.

17. For example, a high percent of Asian NIE and ASEAN electronics and automobile manufacturing exports are produced by Japanese TNC subsidiaries. The bulk of their purchases are made in Japan, but the bulk of their export sales go to industrial countries other than Japan, and particularly to the United States (UNTNC 1991, 49–50). The United States now runs big deficits with Japan and southeast Asia. Between 1982 and 1987, for example, the U.S. trade deficit with Asian NIEs increased 4.6 times while the deficit with ASEAN rose 3.2 times (Morris-Suzuki 1991, 149). The boomerang has thus, to some extent, been deflected from Japan to strike less adaptive industrial economies, like the United States. The North American Free Trade Agreement (NAFTA) is, among other things, meant to counter the deflected boomerang effect. At the same time, however, East Asian countries are progressively relying more on their own internal markets and those of their neighbors and less on the West (Duesterberg 1994).

18. In semiconductors, U.S. manufacturers moved the labor intensive assembly stage to Asia early on and eventually came to assemble most semiconductors in Asia. Japan set a maximum limit of 5 percent for its offshore semiconductor production and at the same time automated the assembly process and improved technology and design. Japan also invested heavily in semiconductor plants in the United States and Europe in the early 1980s in anticipation of protectionist measures (Chen 1989).

REFERENCES

Amsden, Alice. 1989. *Asia's Next Giant: South Korea and Late Industrialization.* New York: Oxford.

Aoki, Takeshi. 1992. "Japanese FDI and the Forming of Networks in the Asia-Pacific Region: Experience in Malaysia and Its Implications." In Shojiro

Tokunaga, ed., *Japan's Foreign Investment and Asian Economic Interdependence*. Tokyo: University of Tokyo Press, 73–110.

Bello, Walden. 1993. "The Asia-Pacific: Trouble in paradise." *World Policy Journal* 10, no. 2 (Summer): 33–40.

Burderi, Robert, et al. 1992. "Global Innovation: Who's in the Lead?" *Fortune*, 3 Aug., 68–73.

Chen, Edward K. Y. 1989. "National Economic Policies for Industrial Development: Complementarity and Incompatibility among Countries in the Asian Pacific Region." In Prem Vashishtha, ed., *Complementarities and Cooperation: Asia Pacific Region*. New Delhi: National Council of Applied Economic Research, 152–86.

Chen, Edward K. Y. 1993. "Foreign Direct Investment in East Asia." *Asia Development Review* 11, no. 1:24–59.

Cumings, Bruce. 1984. "The Origins and Development of the Northeast Asian Political Economy: Industrial Sectors, Product Cycles, and Political Consequences. *International Organization* 38, no. 1:1–40.

Doner, Richard F. 1991. *Driving a Bargain: Automobile Industrialization and Japanese Firms in Southeast Asia*. Berkeley: University of California Press.

Dore, Ronald. 1986. *Flexible Rigidities*. London: Athlone Press.

Duesterberg, Thomas J. 1994. "Trade, Investment, and Engagement in the U.S.—East Asian Relationship." *Washington Quarterly* 17, no. 1:73–90.

Hill, Richard Child, and Kuniko Fujita. 1994. "Osaka's Asia Linkages Strategy: Regional Integration and Local Development in Japan." Paper presented at the 13th World Congress of Sociology, Bielefeld, Germany, 18–24 July.

Hill, Richard Child, and Yong Joo Lee. 1994. "Japanese Multinationals and East Asian Development: The Case of the Automobile Industry." In L. Sklair, ed., *Capitalism and Development*. London: Routledge, 289–315.

Hymer, Stephen. 1979. *The Multinational Corporation: A Radical Approach*. New York: Cambridge University Press.

Japan Ministry of International Trade and Industry. 1990. *Nisennen no Sagyo Kozo* (Industrial structure in 2000). Tokyo: Ministry of International Trade and Industry.

———. 1992. *Tsusho Hakusho*. White paper on International Trade. Tokyo: Ministry of International Trade and Industry.

Jenkins, Rhys. 1984. "Divisions over the International Division of Labor." *Capital and Class* 2:28–57.

Johnson, Chalmers. 1982. *MITI and the Japanese Miracle: The Growth of Industrial Policy 1925–1975*. Stanford, CA: Stanford University Press.

Kiyonari, Tadao. 1993. "Restructuring Urban-Industrial Links in Greater Tokyo: Small Producers' Responses to Changing World Markets." In K. Fujita and R. C. Hill, eds., *Japanese Cities in the World Economy*. Philadelphia: Temple University Press, 141–58.

Kohama, Hirohisa. 1990. "Japan's Economic Development and Foreign Trade." In Chung Lee and Ippei Yamazawa, eds., *The Economic Development of Japan and Korea*. New York: Praeger, 3–18.

Kojima, Kiyoshi. 1977. *Japan and a New World Economic Order*. Boulder, CO: Westview Press.

Lee, Chung H., and Ippei Yamazawa. 1990. In Chung H. Lee and Ippei Yamazawa, eds., *The Economic Development of Japan and Korea*. New York: Praeger.

Morris-Suzuki, Tessa. 1991. "Reshaping the International Division of Labor: Japanese Manufacturing Investment in South-East Asia." In J. Morris, ed., *Japan and the Global Economy*. London: Routledge, 135–53.

O'Connor, James. 1973. *The Fiscal Crisis of the State*. New York: St. Martin's Press.

Pyle, Kenneth B. 1992. *The Japanese Question: Power and Purpose in a New Era*. Washington, DC: AEI Press.

Shinohara, Miyohei. 1982. *Industrial Growth, Trade, and Dynamic Patterns in the Japanese Economy*. Tokyo: University of Tokyo Press.

Tokunaga, Shojiro. 1992. *Japan's Foreign Investment and Asian Economic Interdependence*. Tokyo: University of Tokyo Press.

United Nations Centre On Transnational Corporations (UNCTNC). 1991. *World Investment Report 1991: The Triad in Direct Foreign Investment*. New York: United Nations.

Vernon, Raymond. 1971. *Sovereignty at Bay: The Multinational Spread of U.S. Enterprises*. New York: Basic Books.

———. 1979. "The Product Cycle Hypothesis in a New International Environment." *Oxford Bulletin of Economics and Statistics* 41, no. 4:255–69.

Wade, Robert. 1990. *Governing the Market: Economic Theory and the Role of Government in East Asian Industrialization*. Princeton, NJ: Princeton University Press.

Yamada, Bundo. 1990. *International Strategies of Japanese Electronics Companies; Implications for Asian Newly Industrializing Economies*. Paris: Organization for Economic Cooperation and Development.

Yamazawa, Ippei. 1990. *Economic Development and International Trade: The Japanese Model*. Honolulu: East-West Center.

———. 1992. "Gearing Economic Policy to International Harmony." In Glenn D. Hook and Michael A. Weiner, eds., *The Internationalization of Japan*. London: Routledge, 119–30.

7

Restructuring Space, Time, and Competitive Advantage in the Capitalist World-Economy: Japan and Raw Materials Transport after World War II

Stephen G. Bunker and Paul S. Ciccantell

Stable, secure access to relatively cheap raw materials is essential to sustained economic growth. All nations rising to dominant core positions have needed to obtain some, and in many cases most, of their raw materials from beyond their territorial boundaries. This requirement has obliged them to subordinate social formations where critical natural resources occur sufficiently (a) to assure stable supplies and (b) to protect the capital investments required to extract and transport the natural resources. Such subordination is costly, and to the extent possible core nations have reduced these costs by procuring acquiescence and collaboration from states and dominant classes in resource rich areas and by manipulating markets to establish dependent or tied trade and financial relations. Because transport constitutes a major share of raw materials costs in the core and because capital sunk in transport infrastructure for raw materials is costly, often specific to particular natural resources, and isolated from other economies that could shares its costs, the access strategies of core states and firms have often revolved around control over transport. In this chapter, we argue that raw materials access has been primary to hegemonic strategies, that aspiring hegemons will attempt to establish transport infrastructure in ways that lower the costs of their own imports, and that these hegemons will try to devolve as much of the cost of this infrastructure as possible on resource-exporting economies. We also argue that the construction of transport infrastructure has created important linkages and spread effects in all rising hegemons. We focus our argument on post–World War II Japan, with reference to the Netherlands, Great Britain, and the United States, rising hegemons of earlier periods.

HEGEMONY AND RAW MATERIALS

Hegemony is one of the most abstract terms in the social sciences. Its referents become increasingly amorphous as the scale of the social units thought to be exercising it expands. In international relations it is invoked to explain phenomena that resemble simple economic dominance, but it also serves to grapple with complex, nearly intangible, systems of agreement and acquiescence that facilitate certain patterns of trade, ranging from the conduct of individual states to the use of international currencies. We approach this evanescent abstraction from a radically concrete perspective: we propose that in many cases, we can understand the creation and exercise of hegemony best as we consider directly the physical characteristics of its most frequent object—raw materials that are critical to the continued economic or military power of industrial nations we sometimes call hegemonic and that simultaneously define the economies of the regions from which they are extracted.

This focus on raw materials is not simply strategic or arbitrary. Most of the sustained discussions of hegemony take access to raw materials in international trade as either their point of departure (McMichael 1984) or their arena of evidence (Keohane 1984; Krasner 1978). None of these writers, however, incorporate into their analysis the fundamental dependence of industry on a broad and constantly expanding array of raw materials and the consequent imperative for firms and states of nations that become hegemonic to secure access to cheap and reliable supplies.

As we discussed elsewhere (Bunker and Ciccantell 1994b), Christopher Chase-Dunn's (1989, 166–200) comprehensive review of the concept of hegemony in world-system analysis best exemplifies this oversight. Chase-Dunn has it backward when he catalogues efficient technologies, cheaper mass production, and investment capital first as conditions for the "determination of which country becomes a hegemon" and only then states that they "have eventually developed access to cheap inputs of some staple foods and raw materials, most often produced in the periphery, which have been important inputs to industry" (1989, 174). None of the first conditions he lists are possible without the last, but the last cannot be developed without some of the capacities created by the first. The timing and development of Britain's search for timber in the seventeenth and eighteenth centuries (Albion 1926), in comparison with its nineteenth-century extension into Latin American politics and trade for very different commodities, makes this point fairly clear. Brockway's (1979) account of coordinated diplomatic, scientific, commercial, and colonial endeavors as British firms and the British state assured stable supplies of rubber, quinine, and sisal makes the point even more clearly.

Chase-Dunn's focus on technology, industrial organization, and investment capital as determining which nations become hegemons, as well as the relegation of access to raw materials to a secondary plane, in fact *reverses* the historical sequence characteristic of rising hegemons. Transport is a critical part of capitalist production. The early period of the development of the capitalist world economy, typically termed mercantile capitalism, has been seriously mislabeled. This period was not characterized by a different form of capitalism; it was instead a period of capitalism in which the value created in transport was predominant.

Transport was the leading sector of production at critical moments in national industrial development in Holland, Britain, and the United States prior to the Industrial Revolution. The seaborne transport industries (shipbuilding and shipping) had a range of developmental effects that were widely recognized as critical to industrial development. These industries created vertically integrated industries from raw materials extraction to relatively technologically and organizationally sophisticated and relatively capital intensive industries in all three nations. These vertically integrated industries also had a wide variety of linkage effects into other industries, both in other raw materials–extracting industries and in industrial activities such as ironmaking.

The shipping and shipbuilding industries of these nations were also technological leading sectors, since the tremendous opportunity for savings in raw materials costs that could be derived by reducing transport costs of bulk raw materials created huge economic incentives for investment in developing technological innovations which reduced transport construction and operating costs.

These technological innovations in construction and operation brought with them an increase in the capital-intensivity of these industries, as illustrated by the introduction of cranes and other equipment for moving heavy burdens in Dutch shipyards, which reduced labor requirements for construction and made the construction of larger ships feasible, and as the development of larger ships requiring fewer sailors per ton transported similarly shows. These technological innovations in construction also required innovations in industrial organization, often via the migration of skilled shipwrights and of shipbuilding and shipping capitalists from an established hegemon to a rising hegemon in search of economic opportunities; the introduction of advanced modes of industrial organization with a highly developed division of labor into these rising hegemons would then serve as a template for the organization of new industries. In short, as Wallerstein (1980) argued in the case of the Dutch and as we will argue for the case of Japan, the most important sector in which transport costs can be reduced is in the bulk transport of raw materials, which creates tremendous incentives for technological and organizational innovation and for capital investment in shipbuilding and shipping.

Raw materials acquisition needs have thus historically driven the development of these industries as leading sectors in rising hegemons, both in the early history of the capitalist world-economy in Holland, Britain, and the United States and in the post–World War II era as Japan confronted a globally built environment structured to serve the needs of the United States and Europe but that could not provide sufficient quantities of raw materials to Japan at sufficiently low prices to make Japanese industrial production cost-competitive with industries in the core nations. Japan's rise to challenge U.S. hegemony during the last forty years, is in large part, a story of raw materials access via Japanese shipping and shipbuilding which made possible the development of the Japanese steel industry and of a diversified industrial economy based on low cost-imported raw materials.

In the following sections, we will consider how Japan has manipulated transport in the post–World War II world economy. Because the volume of raw materials in transmaritime trade has at least quadrupled since 1960, the available economies of scale have increased proportionately. Capturing economies of scale in transport requires the construction of massive port systems, which must be capable not only of accommodating large boats but also of loading them and unloading them quickly enough to prevent incurring the huge costs of tying up the capital intensive ships too long in harbor. The costs of building such ports have enhanced a feature of all constructed transport systems; that is, to the extent that exporting and importing systems must be physically compatible to take advantage of cost-saving technologies, importers can tie exporting nations to their markets by fomenting mutually compatible port systems at both ends of the voyage. One of the clearest indications of the increasing power of Japan and the European Community (EC) in the world system is their unusually rapid construction of such systems, both at home and in selected parts of the periphery and semiperiphery. Japan's topography favors such port systems, but the state and heavy industrial firms have collaborated in building the domestic and the international environment in such a way as to maximize these advantages.

THE RAW MATERIALS TRANSPORT REVOLUTION AND JAPAN AS A RISING HEGEMON IN THE POST–WORLD WAR II ERA

Just as the two transport revolutions of the nineteenth century, the introduction of railroads for land transport and the replacement of sailing ships with steamships for ocean transport, were key elements in the expansion of the capitalist world economy that encompassed virtually every location on the face of the earth, an ocean-shipping revolution in the second half of the twentieth century has also been a central element in the physical and economic restructuring of the world system (Mandel 1975). The transport revolutions of the nineteenth century served to more tightly and much more cheaply link the core nations of Western Europe to raw materials supplies and markets for finished products in distant nations, as well as to promote trade in two other nations rising to core status during the second half of the nineteenth century, the United States and Japan. The United States rose to a hegemonic position in the world-system based largely on domestic raw materials, its domestic railroad network for raw materials transport, its international railroad links with Canada and Mexico (giving the United States access to raw materials in these nations), and its militarily secure position, which was relatively distant from other core nations.

U.S. hegemony was quickly challenged after World War II by the reconstruction of Japan and Western Europe, particularly Germany, largely funded by U.S. aid. Access to adequate supplies of raw materials quickly became a central issue in resource-poor Japan as industrial production increased during the 1950s; for Germany and the rest of Western Europe, depletion of domestic raw materials during the industrial growth in the 1950s and 1960s also led to a similar concern with raw materials supplies. The central elements of this concern were efforts to diversify sources of raw materials imports and to lower the costs of transporting these raw materials because of the increasing distance between the sources and these industrial nations. The increasing distance between sources of raw materials and the industrial nations that consume them resulted from a common problem encountered by raw materials consumers: consumers first utilize resources located nearest consuming centers until, over time, the quantity and quality of these resources become depleted, forcing the consumers to search for new sources in more distant regions. The result of this diversification of raw materials supply sources, which are typically in very distant areas because of the relationship between depletion and distance, and also of investments to lower the cost of raw materials transport, was the revolution in raw-materials ocean shipping of the second half of the twentieth century.

The ever-increasing volume of raw materials required for industrial production in the capitalist world economy has meant that the raw-materials access strategies of states and firms have increasingly focused on transport. Transport innovations, particularly newer and larger ships and ports, have tended to link increasing numbers of raw materials–extracting regions with only a relatively small number of industrial centers. At the same time, the dramatic increases in the scale of industrial production in the post–World War II period would have simply been impossible without transport innovations that could reduce, or at least prevent a dramatic increase in, raw materials costs. Japan had only small domestic resources of a few raw materials initially and had rapidly exhausted these resources after World War II; moreover, the nation was far from most raw materials–producing regions after World War II, except for those controlled by China and the USSR, which were therefore politically unattractive sources. As the result of these factors, Japan has been particularly dependent on increasing raw materials inputs through new transport systems linking its industrial centers to many distant parts of the world. Japan has responded by taking the global lead in developing, building, operating, and utilizing larger and more efficient ships, promoting the development of large ports; promoting the exploitation of scale-accessible deposits; and locating domestic heavy industry around large ports to allow raw materials imports to be unloaded directly to consuming plants, thus eliminating the need for internal transport of these large volumes of raw materials.

The tremendous increase in raw materials extraction in a growing number of countries since World War II has resulted in a large increase in the absolute volume of raw materials entering international trade, as Table 7.1 shows.

Table 7.1.
Volume of International Seaborne Raw Materials Trade (Thousands of Metric Tons)

	Petroleum	Coal	Iron Ore	Bauxite and Alumina
1960	*366,000	46,000	101,000	17,000
1970	995,000	101,000	247,000	34,000
1980	1,320,000	188,000	314,000	48,000
1990	1,190,000	342,000	347,000	52,000

Sources: Fearnleys, *World Bulk Trades* (various years); Fearnleys, *Review* (various years); United States Bureau of Mining, *Minerals Yearbooks* (various years); Drewry Shipping Consultants (1972a, 8; 1980, 35).
*Figure is for 1962.

The increasing role of relatively remote raw materials–extracting regions (especially Australia) and the rapidly growing imports of raw materials by the relatively most remote industrial processing and consuming nations (Japan and, in recent years, the newly industrialized countries of Southeast Asia) have resulted in a significant increase in the average distance traveled in the seaborne raw materials trade, as Table 7.2 shows.

Table 7.2.
Average Distance Traveled in the Seaborne Raw Materials Trade
(Total Ton-miles Divided by Tons Transported)

	Petroleum	Coal	Iron Ore	Bauxite
1960	*4,508	3,152	2,614	2,000
1970	5,625	4,762	4,425	2,918
1980	6,227	5,090	5,258	3,917
1990	5,267	5,406	5,700	3,942

Sources: Fearnleys, *World Bulk Trades* (various years); Fearnleys, *Review* (various years).
*Figure is for 1962.

The combination of the increasing volume of international trade in raw materials and the increase in the average distance traveled by each ton of seaborne raw materials trade have resulted in a major increase in the key metric of transport as part of the production process—the volume of ton-miles of raw materials transported—as Table 7.3 shows.

Table 7.3.
Total Ton-miles of Transported Raw Materials (Billions of Ton-miles)

	Petroleum (Crude)	Petroleum Products	Coal	Iron Ore	Bauxite and Alumina
1960	1,650	145	264	34	
1970	5,597	890	481	1,093	99
1980	8,219	1,020	957	1,651	188
1990	6,261	1,560	1,849	1,978	205
1991	6,500	1,500	1,905	1,965	

Sources: Fearnleys, *World Bulk Trades* (various years); Fearnleys, *Review* (various years).

The combination of these changes in raw materials extraction and changes in transport created a tremendous incentive for a major technological revolution in transport, since a major increase in raw materials transport capacity was essential for industrial growth to take place on this scale, which is a central dimension of position in the world-system. The shape of these transport patterns (systems) depends on the built environment, which influences access capacity and cost for different nations and regions within them. The central element of this transport revolution in ocean shipping of raw materials in the second half of the twentieth century has been the tremendous expansion of the size of ships as well as the capacities of the ports and inland transport systems that serve these transport systems.

The key to taking advantage of the increasing economies of scale made available by technological advances in ship construction in the post–World War II era is the careful matching of all of the stages of the transport system in order to minimize the total cost of transport (Kendall 1972; Jansson and Shneerson 1982; Garrod and Miklius 1985). By tailoring transport systems from the mine to the consumer to take advantage of these economies of scale, the cost to the importer of the raw materials of each ton is dramatically reduced. However, this careful matching of the various components of raw-materials transport systems carries important risks for the sellers of raw materials, since, by tailoring their mines, inland transport systems, and port facilities to those of their customers' ships, importing ports, and processing plants, the number of potential buyers of their raw materials is also sharply limited, placing raw materials producers in a disadvantaged position in bargaining with buyers. Selling to other potential customers whose shipping and importing facilities do not match the characteristics of the exporter may result in increased storage costs, underutilization of inland transport systems and ports (with resulting higher-per-ton operating costs), and lower prices because these potential customers require lower prices to offset higher ocean transport costs per ton. The careful tailoring of mines and export transport infrastructure in many raw materials industries in Australia, Brazil, Canada, and other nations to the shipping and import infrastructure of Japanese firms has given these firms important advantages in bargaining over the prices of raw materials purchased from these nations.

The initial impetus for this transport revolution came from the rapidly growing volume of seaborne petroleum trade. Soon after the commercial production of petroleum began in 1859, the volume of petroleum in international trade, in combination with the cost and dangers of shipping it in barrels, led to the development of petroleum tankers in 1886 (Stopford 1988, 220). The rapid growth in the volume of crude petroleum trade, a commodity that is critical for industrial production and very easy to handle in bulk, created a tremendous incentive for increasing the size of oil tankers because of the economies of scale in shipping, which reduce the cost per ton-mile rapidly as ship size increases.

While during the nineteenth century, steel plants (the major consumers of both iron ore and metallurgical coal) had been located near raw materials supplies, by the early twentieth century, bulk shipping had eliminated the cost advantage of locating next to raw materials supplies. Steel plants increasingly were located on the coasts, reducing the cost of imports of iron ore and coal, which were replacing depleted domestic sources of these raw materials in core nations. The Bethlehem Steel plant at Sparrow's Point near Baltimore, Maryland, which was built in the early 1920s, was the prototype of this new pattern of steel mill location based on imported iron ore, in this case from Cruz Grande in Chile via the newly opened Panama Canal. Steel plants in Western Europe and Japan during the post–World War II period have followed similar patterns of coastal location and dependence on imported raw materials (Stopford 1988, 230–31).

A variety of factors combined to produce an increase in the size of ships carrying other major raw materials, especially iron ore and coal: the development of increasingly larger oil tankers; the increasing size of shipyards and experience, especially in Japan, in building larger ships; the growing volume of other raw materials trades, especially iron ore and coal due to demand for the growing world steel industry; the recognition that economies of scale also existed for other raw materials shipping; and the increasing average distance traveled by each ton of iron ore and coal. The result of this combination of factors has been a major increase in the average and maximum size of dry bulk carriers since the mid-1960s. The number of dry bulk carriers (ships specially built to carry cargoes of minerals and grains) increased by a factor of ten between 1961 and 1992, from 471 to 4,846, while the average size of each dry bulk carrier increased from 18,495 to 44,552 deadweight tons (dwt). The cumulative result was an increase in total available tonnage for shipping minerals and grains from 8.7 to 215.9 million deadweight tons during these three decades (Fearnleys [various years]; United Nations 1969), commensurate with the tremendous increase in minerals transport during the period.

Tremendous economies of scale in the cost of building ships have resulted from the increasing size of ships, which makes it far cheaper on a per ton basis to purchase a larger ship than a smaller one. However, even though the cost per ton is lower, the tremendous size of larger ships means that the total capital investment is much larger in larger ships, placing a premium on efficient operation and quick turnaround times in port in order to maximize the revenue earned by the ship so that the owner can repay the huge investments and loans required to buy the ship. This high capital cost makes it imperative for shipowners to employ their ships in tightly integrated transport systems to maximize revenues. In addition to economies of scale in building costs, these larger ships also have significant economies of scale in operating costs, with larger ships costing far less to operate on a per-ton basis than smaller ships. An important part of these operating economies of scale have resulted from technological advances which have reduced the amount of labor needed per ton transported on newer, larger ships.

The most important limitation on taking advantage of these tremendous economies of scale is the depth of harbors at the importing and exporting ends of a voyage. While 55 percent of world ports are accessible to ships of 23,600 dwt, only 19 percent are accessible to ships of 123,000 dwt (Stopford 1988, 278). Taking advantage of the economies of scale resulting from the technological development of ocean shipping in the post–World War II period thus requires either a great deal of naturally produced luck (the coincidence of large deposits of raw materials with existing or potential port sites with deep water drafts) or, far more commonly, a high degree of social manipulation of water depth on coastlines relatively near to important raw materials deposits. The vast majority of the 19 percent of world ports that are accessible to 123,000 dwt bulk carriers are only accessible because hundreds of millions of dollars have been spent (typically by the governments of extractive regions for export ports and the governments of raw materials–importing nations for import ports) to dredge channels or construct artificial islands for port facilities and industrial-processing plants. Governments, especially those in extractive regions, must assume huge debt burdens to make possible the appropriation of nature by private firms (often foreign raw materials TNCs) for sale to core consumers, mainly in Japan and Western Europe.

PORT FACILITIES AND JAPANESE RAW MATERIALS IMPORTS

One essential complement of increasing ship size was a corresponding increase in port size. The size of ports and the efficiency of loading and unloading processes have become increasingly important as ship size has increased, since larger ships mean that larger amounts of capital are tied up in the vessels, raising the cost of each day in port. In addition, the scale of port (and the mine-to-port inland transport system) is inseparable from the scale of extraction at the mine, even if the mine is near the port; the increasing scale of extraction at new mines has meant that ports and inland transport systems must increase in scale as well. The solution has been to reduce the labor required in ports through the introduction of relatively simple, but costly, mechanical equipment in order to speed up the turnaround time of large bulk carriers.

The high cost of terminal facilities makes it crucial to match the demand for the terminal's services with the terminal's capacity in order to minimize inefficiencies and costs to exporters and shippers. Since raw materials are typically shipped FOB (free on board, which indicates that the buyer pays shipping charges) from the exporting port, the responsibility for, and cost of building and operating, a terminal falls to the exporting firm, while the risk of wasted ships' time falls on the consumer of the raw material. The very costly construction of terminals to accommodate large bulk carriers has required large investments by exporting firms and governments, while the benefits of these terminals have fallen to importers who are able to make use of lower cost large-scale ocean transport.

The development of these large ports required tremendous capital investments. The success of raw materials–importing nations in transforming the construction of these raw materials export transport infrastructures into "development efforts" on the part of noncore nations has been striking. During the 1970s, for example, the World Bank provided over $1 billion for port development in the noncore nations, while the Asian Development Bank provided an additional $221 million dollars (United Nations 1982, 29). The responsibility for repaying these loans is borne by the raw materials-exporting states and not by raw materials importers, a major subsidy to importers of core raw materials.

The need for inland transport systems in exporting regions is dictated by the naturally produced location of raw materials relative to naturally produced locations suitable for port development, which may or may not have already been developed. Inland transportation of raw materials often constitutes a very large share of the total cost of developing mines, while port construction in remote regions also can contribute significantly to costs. The inland transportation of raw materials in industrial processing and consuming countries is, however, much more susceptible to human manipulation. Preexisting industrial and consuming centers located inland from ports, and often near former sites of domestic raw materials extraction, may force firms and states to invest heavily in railroad, water, and road transport facilities to link processing and consuming sites; when the depletion of domestic resources forces a shift to dependence on imported raw materials, the cost of moving these raw materials to existing inland processing plants is likely to be prohibitive. A much less expensive alternative for nations that become dependent on imported raw materials from both societal and governmental perspectives is the relocation of raw materials industries through the construction of new processing plants in port areas.

Since states are often the major source of funding for constructing inland transport facilities, governments in Japan and Western Europe have offered significant incentives to promote the relocation of raw-materials import-dependent processing plants to port areas through Maritime Industrial Development Area (MIDA) programs since the 1950s. The iron and steel industry, oil refineries, petrochemical complexes, aluminum smelters, and power plants have been the major raw materials–consuming plants that have been relocated to MIDAs (Hanappe and Savy 1981, 13). Large ships using firm- or government-financed ports that have been expanded or newly built can then unload directly into stocking yards at plants in the port area, eliminating inland transport costs in the importing area. The first examples of MIDAs in the capitalist world economy were the Botlek Scheme in Rotterdam in the Netherlands, which began operating in 1958 and was followed in the 1960s by the Europoort project and the Maasvlakte project (since the 1970s), all in the Rotterdam area; as well as other projects in the Rhine Delta at Antwerp, Amsterdam and Ijmuiden in the Netherlands, and the Weser ports, Wilhelmshaven, and Hamburg in West Germany; and in Japan, at the Tokyo, Ise, and Osaka-Kobe areas and in Kashima (Vigarie 1981, 24–25).

MIDAs are, in effect, a human-produced change in topography created by reclaiming land, digging new ocean and river channels, and making other modifications in port areas to provide both location and transport facilities for industrial plants. MIDAs are a restructuring both of nature and of the national economy through state policies and investment, done in combination with private firms, in order to manipulate nature, space, topography, and existing economic and social structures in search of private profits.

THE SHIPBUILDING INDUSTRY

An obvious essential complement to the shipping industry is the shipbuilding industry. The cyclical nature of the shipping industry has made shipbuilding extremely cyclical as well. This cyclicality derives from the capital-intensive nature of shipping and the resulting long payback period of large investments in each ship, making shipowners reluctant to temporarily or permanently reduce capacity in order to raise freight rates. The only measure usually taken by shipping firms in response to low freight rates is to put off the replacement of obsolete ships and delay planned capacity expansion. The consequences for shipbuilders are periods of extremely low demand with huge amounts of excess capacity and low prices for ships, followed by periods of high demand and capacity shortage accompanied by very high prices for ships. The large capital investment in shipyards forces firms to compete during periods of low demand for orders for ships, even selling ships below the cost of production in order to utilize some of their capacity and earn revenues that can be used to repay the loans and capital invested in the shipyard.

The single most important change in the shipbuilding industry in the post–World War II era has been the rise of Japan to worldwide predominance as the world's largest shipbuilding nation. Following a path laid out by Holland, Great Britain, and the United States. in their early rises to challenge existing hegemons, shipbuilding was targeted as a leading sector by the Japanese government soon after World War II. Japan's rise as a shipbuilding and shipping nation is examined in the following section.

TRANSPORT AS A JAPANESE RAW MATERIALS ACCESS AND DEVELOPMENT STRATEGY

Transport has played a variety of roles as a component of Japan's post–World War II raw materials access strategy and of its broader economic development strategy, which have been critical factors in Japan's rise to challenge U.S. hegemony during this period. By 1984, Japan accounted for 17 percent of total world seaborne imports in terms of volume because of the huge volume of raw materials imports, making that nation by far the world's most significant importing nation. Japanese exports, because they consist of industrial products of much lower volume and much higher value, were only 3 percent of world total exports in terms of volume in 1984 (Stopford 1988, 141); however, Japan's share of world exports in terms of value is much greater: 8.9 percent in 1984 (Chida and Davies 1990, 184). The key reason for the rapid growth of Japan's raw materials imports during the post–World War II era, which totaled 491.66 million tons in 1986, including 115.2 million tons of iron ore and concentrates, 91.4 million tons of coal, 157.4 million tons of crude oil, and 59 million tons of refined petroleum products (United States 1987, 509–14), has been Japan's rapid rate of economic growth.

The transport dimension of Japan's raw materials access strategy has focused on making possible the tremendous expansion of raw materials imports at competitive cost levels necessary for Japan's industrial expansion since World War II; petroleum, iron ore, and coal have been the most important imports in terms of volume, although bauxite, alumina, aluminum, copper concentrates, liquefied natural gas, and a host of other minerals were also imported in increasing volumes during the period. Transport as a raw materials access strategy has included research and development on the construction of larger petroleum tankers and bulk carriers in order to capture economies of scale in construction and operating, resulting in the development of large shipyards capable of building such ships. This led to the development of a Japanese shipbuilding industry that became the world's leading builder and exporter of ships, as well as a major consumer for the steel industry, which was targeted by the Japanese government as the key leading sector of the Japanese economy in the post–World War II era, both as an exporter of steel and as the provider of steel for infrastructure and industrial production for export. The ownership and operation of such large ships by Japanese shipping firms associated with the major industrial groups allowed these firms to free themselves from dependence on foreign shipping for imports and exports, giving them greater control over their production costs and their costs of supplying goods to foreign markets. The control over ocean shipping by Japanese consumers of raw materials on the basis of an FOB raw materials–exporting port has meant that any reductions in transport costs caused by technological improvements or changes in world-shipping market conditions can be captured by Japanese importers. The construction of large scale port and railroad infrastructures in raw materials-exporting regions paid for by extractive region governments or raw materials transnational corporations (TNCs), which was based on long-term contracts for raw materials supply with Japanese importing firms, allowed the efficient use of these large ships at no cost to Japanese firms or the state. Government subsidies for the construction of MIDAs in Japanese ports eliminated the need for the internal transshipment of raw materials imports, reducing raw materials import costs and allowing the government to redirect industrial development to new areas of the nation.

Japanese government and firm efforts to reduce transport cost were of particular importance given the tremendous distances that Japanese raw materials imports had to travel. Japan had a tremendous disadvantage relative to Europe and North America in iron ore and coal, which are the second and third most important raw materials traded in terms of volume (behind petroleum), with Japan's average shipping distance for iron ore being 6,140 nautical miles, in comparison with 4,300 miles for Europe and 2,970 miles for the United States, and with a Japanese shipping distance for coal imports of 6,240 miles, in comparison with Europe's 3,020 miles and North America's virtually entirely domestic supply (Drewry Shipping Consultants 1978, 1). This differential created a tremendous incentive for the Japanese government and firms to reduce transport costs, since these long distances would have made Japan uncompetitive in raw materials–based industries without reductions in transport costs.

Transport as a component of economic development strategy has been a major factor in Japan since the Meiji Restoration. The Japanese government's response to these problems resulting from dependence on foreign owned shipping was to subsidize and protect Japanese-owned coastal and international shipping companies competing with the foreign–owned lines, a policy that has continued in a variety of forms up until the present time. The high cost and foreign exchange drain of importing ships that were built in Europe also led the Japanese government to provide support for Japanese shipbuilders, another policy that has been maintained ever since.

After the end of World War II, initial Allied plans for Japan's post–war reconstruction imposed strict limits on the Japanese shipping and shipbuilding industries. The shift in U.S. policy in the late 1940s to favoring the reconstruction of Japan as a geopolitical bulwark in Asia led to the elimination of externally imposed restrictions on Japan's shipping and shipbuilding industries (Chida and Davies 1990, 62–65).

As the Allied restrictions were being eliminated, the Japanese government was developing its strategies for the reconstruction of the nation. The Priority Production System regulation of December 1946, for example, identified several key industries as the leading sectors in which resources should be concentrated, including coal and steel. A variety of laws dealing specifically with the encourage-ment of shipping and shipbuilding were also introduced in the late 1940s, including the Programmed Shipbuilding Scheme of 1947 (to support the growth of both shipping and shipbuilding), a program that has remained in operation. The goal of the program was to speed the construction of shipping to ease the severe post–war shortage based on government provision of low cost financing to private shipping firms (initially from the Rehabilitation Finance Bank and then, after 1953, from the Development Bank of Japan). The Korean War provided important benefits to Japanese shipowners and, especially, to Japanese shipyards because of the increased freight rates and demand for ships during the period (Chida and Davies 1990, 66–86).

The Programmed Shipbuilding Scheme has been the critical mechanism in the growth of Japan's shipbuilding industry. The program provides low cost partial financing to shipping firms, based on government estimates of the need for various types of new ships. These Japanese shipping firms then order ships from Japanese shipyards using this subsidized financing, which is supplemented by loans from commercial banks. The Japanese government was thus able to oversee the development of a domestic shipping fleet that could supply required transportation by subsidizing shipping firms and, indirectly, shipyards and steel mills in Japan (Chida and Davies 1990, 89–90).

This government direction and subsidization reflects the importance of transport as a strategic component of both raw materials access and economic development efforts on the part of the Japanese government. Japanese government policies during the 1950s favored the development of a Japanese-owned liner fleet to carry its light industrial exports, while government policies in the 1960s shifted to emphasize the construction of oil tankers and ore carriers, to transport the nation's rapidly growing imports of raw materials, and to containerships (at the end of the 1960s) (Goto 1984, 8). This government direction was critical to guaranteeing large volumes of raw materials at low cost to Japanese firms.

In addition to government support through financing, government support for research and development on ship construction also played a critical role in the post–World War II era. The single most important aspect of government support for the technological development of shipbuilding in Japan was the agreement signed between that Japanese government and a U.S. shipping firm, National Bulk Carriers (NBC), in 1951. The booming ship construction market had led NBC (owned by U.S. shipping magnate D. K. Ludwig) to search for a former naval shipyard that could be utilized for civilian shipbuilding, especially for large scale petroleum tankers (Todd 1991, 13). NBC investigated a number of former naval shipyards in Germany and Japan and selected the Kure naval shipyard in Japan. The terms of the agreement between NBC and the Japanese government on the ten-year lease (which was later renewed until 1962) were that "while NBC was to construct ships for its own purposes as and how it wished, as much Japanese steel as possible was to be utilized. Of even greater long-term significance was the insistence that all types of Japanese shipbuilders and engineers were to have free access to the establishment and were to be permitted to examine all aspects of its building system" (Chida and Davies 1990, 112). It was at this new shipyard that the technological and organizational developments that were to make Japan the world's leading shipbuilder were developed under what may be a set of unique lease terms intended to transfer advanced technology to Japan and to train Japanese engineers and managers at no cost to that country's firms or government.

Beginning in the early 1960s, other Japanese shipyards began introducing a number of technological innovations of their own based on the experience and technology introduced to Japan by NBC, including the replacement of labor with machines in the hull construction and fitting-out departments. The designing of ships was also rationalized and production control methods were improved, including the introduction of "section" or "block" building and welding, allowing the development of new larger shipyards with more efficient layouts to permit the construction of larger ships. All these improvements increased labor productivity and reduced the amount of labor required to build each ship, increasing the competitiveness of Japanese shipbuilding relative to the more labor-intensive methods that remained in use much longer in other nations (Chida and Davies 1990, 91–91). Japan has remained a world leader in shipbuilding technology, particularly in the reduction of labor requirements per ship through the introduction of capital-intensive mechanization and improved management.

These technological and organizational improvements in Japanese shipyards during the 1950s and especially the 1960s gave Japanese "shipbuilders sufficient economies of scale that they could lead the world in the new technology" of building increasingly larger oil tankers which were in increasing demand after the closing of the Suez Canal and as the distance between oil extracting regions and their customers increased (Chida and Davies 1990, 98–99). The rise of general freight rates during the closure of the Suez Canal included an increase in the cost of shipping other bulk materials, including iron ore. In the case of iron ore, this increase resulted in the share of ocean freight costs rising to more than half of the CIF price (Cash, Insurance, Freight, which indicates that the costs of shipping and insurance are paid by the seller) of iron ore imported to Japan, thus supplying a tremendous incentive for the creation of a large fleet of Japanese ore carriers. Although the Japanese steel firms initially intended to build their own fleets of ore carriers, the Japanese government's control over concessionary financing and the government's refusal to supply financing to firms other than the major shipping lines forced the Japanese steel firms to invest in shipping firms in order to secure partial ownership of bulk shipping. The tremendous expansion of the size of bulk carriers and of the number of Japanese-owned bulk carriers from the 1960s onward resulted from this government policy of linking the steel and shipbuilding industries (Chida and Davies 1990, 119). As the result of these technological innovations and the tremendous demand in Japan for bulk shipping, "Japan then emerged as the world leader in the production of very large vessels and subsequently dominated the market for oil tankers and ore-carriers. The timing of this development was particularly fortuitous for Japan as it occurred just as a boom began which required substantial numbers of large tankers" (Chida and Davies 1990, 133).

The Japanese government also provided financing on concessionary terms for the export of Japanese-built ships through the Export-Import Bank of Japan. Additionally, during the 1950s the government provided funding for the modernization of the Japanese steel industry, with one important result being the reduction in the cost of steel plate used in shipbuilding, which made Japanese ship exports much more cost competitive (Chida and Davies 1990, 108–9).

With this support from the Japanese government, the Japanese shipbuilding industry became the largest in the world in 1956 and has produced about half of total world output from the mid-1960s onward. Shipbuilding was also Japan's most important export industry between 1956 and 1960 (when the steel industry surpassed it in exports), and it remained one of Japan's three major export industries until recently (Chida and Davies 1990, 106).

The trend toward larger ships, which greatly benefitted Japanese shipbuilders, was a serious problem for the Japanese shipping industry, as well as for established shipping firms in other nations. The tremendous cost reductions presented by the economies of scale of larger ships made existing ships obsolete and forced down freight rates, requiring Japanese shipowners to replace older ships with new, larger ones in order to survive in the low freight-rate markets (Chida and Davies 1990, 133). Japanese shipbuilders and importers of raw materials greatly benefited from these investments in new ships, but Japanese shipping firms were forced to bear the high cost and risk of these investments (although the costs were at least partially offset by concessionary government funding).

The prosperity of Japanese shipping and shipbuilding during the 1960s and early 1970s came to an abrupt end after the "Nixon shock" of 1971 (impeachment), the oil crisis of 1973, and the ending of fixed foreign exchange rates. Both industries have been in a period of depression since the mid-1970s (Chida and Davies 1990, 138–39). The crisis for Japanese shipbuilders has been so severe that shipyard capacity was cut in two stages (the first in 1980 and the second in 1988), from 9.8 million gross tons per year in 1975 to 4.6 million gross tons per year in 1988, in order to improve the profitability of each firm and end the tremendous losses that had resulted from shipyards' competing with one another in a situation of excess capacity and low demand to the extent that ships were being sold below their costs of production (Nagatsuka 1989, 8–9). The crisis in shipbuilding also reduced the shipbuilding labor force from its peak of 273,900 in 1974 to only 84,600 in 1988 (Nagatsuka 1989, 24).

The decline in world trade after the oil crisis, especially in petroleum, left Japanese shippers with a great deal of excess capacity (too much tonnage) and Japanese shipyards with excess capacity (the ability to build too many ships per year) in the context of lower demand for shipping services and ships. Since freight rates are typically quoted in U.S. dollars, the appreciation of the yen since 1971 against the dollar has led to a steady fall in the yen income of shipping, a major factor in the shifting of the registry of Japanese-owned ships from Japan to flag-of-convenience nations (Chida and Davies 1990, 152–54).

The major response of Japanese shipping firms to the crisis since the mid-1970s has been to take advantage of the lower costs resulting from registration under flags of convenience through two mechanisms: tie-in ships built by Japanese shipyards for sale to nominally "foreign" companies (usually subsidiaries of Japanese firms legally registered in flag-of-convenience nations), which then lease the ships to Japanese shipping firms on long term contracts; and ships sold by Japanese shipping firms to these subsidiaries and then leased back. These nominally "export" sales also qualify for subsidized funding from the Export-Import Bank of Japan (Chida and Davies 1990, 177).

Ironically, flag-of-convenience registry was originated in Panama and Liberia during the late 1940s as the result of efforts by U.S. raw materials TNCs to reduce the cost of importing raw materials. U.S. raw materials TNCs lobbied their government to support the creation of open registries for flag-of-convenience registries in the two nations to escape their dependence on high-cost European-controlled shipping firms and on high-labor cost U.S. shipping (the result of the long tradition of labor militancy in U.S. maritime unions) (Cafruny 1987, 91–97). This mechanism created by U.S. raw materials TNCs and the U.S. government later came to serve Japanese raw materials firms quite well as they similarly sought to reduce transport costs through the use of flag-of-convenience registration for Japanese-owned ships.

At the Japanese end of these raw materials–import voyages, MIDAs have played an important role in the restructuring of Japan's port and industrial structures. New MIDA ports greatly reduced the concentration of imports and exports through a small number of ports. Between 1960 and 1975, the concentration of Japan's imports through its five largest ports fell from 64.9 percent to 40.4 percent, while exports from the five largest ports fell from 86.5 percent to 61.5 percent (Rimmer 1984, 120). This deconcentration of shipments through the five largest ports reflects the deconcentration of industrial production through the development of MIDAs. Government policies used MIDAs as growth poles in order to produce more balanced and decentralized regional development (Rimmer 1984:12). Steel firms, dependent on huge volumes of imported iron ore and coal, have been among the principal beneficiaries of MIDAs and related ports.

Japanese MIDAs are typically built on reclaimed land because of the lack of available land along the Japanese coast. Between 1954 and 1970, a total of 33,200 hectares was reclaimed, while another 42,700 hectares were reclaimed between 1971 and 1975 for MIDA development, with more reclamation planned. The reclamation is carried out by excavating deep channels leading to the new port, by hydraulically moving sand and mud from river deltas, and by disposing of urban garbage in the area to be reclaimed. The land is reclaimed by the government and then sold to private firms to repay the cost of reclamation. Reclaimed areas used for MIDAs include Port Island (4.3 square kilometers) and Rokko Island (5.8 square kilometers) in the port of Kobe, several piers and islands in Yokohama Bay, and in Tokyo Bay, Kawasaki, Tokyo, Chiba (36 square kilometers), Kisarazu, and Yokosuka (Karmon 1980, 285–97).

CONCLUSION

These Japanese transport strategies for raw materials access have been strikingly successful at guaranteeing long-term access at low cost to huge volumes of imported raw materials. During the 1960s alone, Sasaki (1976) estimated that Japanese government efforts to reduce the 20 to 30 percent share of freight charges in the total cost of imported raw materials through transport subsidies had the result that "the freight costs for both crude oil and iron ore were reduced by 40 percent . . . .. The effects of this reduction were significant and the consequent reductions in the price of electricity, petrol, iron and steel and many other products have made an immeasurable contribution to the national economy" (Sasaki 1976, 7).

The success of Japanese shipping and shipbuilding industries in lowering the cost of importing raw materials to Japan has often raised suspicions on the part of their competitors in the shipping and shipbuilding industries, as Drewry Shipping Consultants (1972a) noted:

> Japan has to import the majority of her raw materials and therefore it is to her advantage that bulk commodities should be carried in the cheapest possible way. This has led to many Europeans being of the opinion that over-capacity in world shipbuilding is to the advantage of the Japanese economy as it will continue to depress freight rates and therefore new building prices. It is argued that in Japan shipbuilders, shipowners, steelmakers, banks and the Government are all dedicated in working together to ensure continuing Japanese domination in the shipping and shipbuilding field (Drewry 21).

Flag-of-convenience registry has also been attacked by UNCTAD as a major cause for the continuing crisis in the world shipping and shipbuilding industries, on the grounds that the fiscal policies of the United States, Japan, and other core nations encourage shipowners to reinvest profits in buying new ships and registering them under flags of convenience, thus exacerbating the problem of excess capacity (Cafruny 1987, 252). As this chapter and our larger work on Japanese raw materials access strategies demonstrate, these concerns, expressed more than twenty years ago, were on the mark. Japanese state and firm strategies have used their domestic shipbuilding and shipping industries as mechanisms for reducing raw materials import costs.

The Japanese state and Japanese firms created a development strategy after World War II that focused on three closely linked industries: shipbuilding, shipping, and steel. Much of the steel sold in domestic markets was consumed by shipbuilding, eliminating the need for steel imports, while steel also became a major export product and was carried in Japanese-built and -owned ships. The ships provided by the shipbuilding industry to the shipping industry reduced foreign exchange costs of Japanese exports, and especially its huge volume of raw materials imports for the steel and other industries, while the export of ships and sale of shipping services to foreign customers earned huge volumes of foreign exchange. These industries were leading sectors for capital accumulation, technological improvement and adoption, and organizational innovations that were adopted by other industrial sectors.

This carefully planned multitude of interindustry linkages was closely tied to Japan's strategy for gaining access to new sources of raw materials, particularly in Australia, Brazil, and Canada. By creating transport links between Japan's industrial centers and the remote extractive peripheries of the Australian Outback, the Brazilian Amazon, and western Canada, Japan was assured of the huge volumes of raw materials at low cost that were essential to its industrial development. However, the tremendous cost of building inland transport infrastructure and exporting ports was not borne by the Japanese raw materials importers who benefited from the scale economies of ocean shipping permitted by the construction of these transport facilities. National and state governments in Australia, Brazil, Canada, and other nations; state-owned and capitalist firms; and the World Bank funded these massive transport projects to make it possible for Japan to import huge volumes of raw materials at low cost.

The case of Japan in the post–World War II era is the latest example of the critical role of transport, both as a leading industrial sector and as a key ingredient in raw materials access strategies, in the development of rising hegemons. This recurrent historical relationship between raw materials access, transport, and the hegemonic sequences in Holland, Great Britain, the United States, and Japan highlights the critical importance of the material dimension of the capitalist world economy and of the industries and technologies that link raw materials peripheries to rising core hegemons and their industrial centers. The creation of these bilateral links between the sites of particular raw materials in particular extractive peripheries and industrial plants in a rising hegemon's industrial centers provides the essential basis for the restructuring of the capitalist world economy in ways that support these core powers' efforts to challenge existing hegemons. Japan's construction of bilateral raw materials supply links have created a major portion of Japan's competitive advantage in the post-World War II era by restructuring global raw materials industries and transport systems to supply the nation with huge volumes of low-cost raw materials.

REFERENCES

Albion, R. 1926. *Forests and Sea Power: The Timber Problem of the Royal Navy, 1652–1862.* Cambridge, MA: Harvard University Press.

Brockway, L. 1979. *Science and Colonial Expansion: The Role of the British Royal Botanic Gardens.* New York: Academic Press.

Bunker, S., and P. Ciccantell. 1994a. "Nature, Transport and Hegemony in the Capitalist World Economy: The Cases of Holland and Japan."

———. 1994b. *Reorganizing Markets/Restructuring Nature: The Economy and Ecology of Japan's Global Search for Raw Materials.*

Cafruny, A. 1987. *Ruling the Waves: The Political Economy of International Shipping*. Berkeley: University of California Press.

Chase-Dunn, C. 1989. *Global Formation: Structures of the World-Economy*. Cambridge: Basil Blackwell.

Chida, T., and P. Davies. 1990. *The Japanese Shipping and Shipbuilding Industries*. London: Athlone Press.

Drewry Shipping Consultants. 1972a. *The Cost of Ships*. London: Drewry Shipping Consultants.

———. 1972b. *The Prospects for Bulk Carriers of "Panamax" Size Plus*. London: Drewry Shipping Consultants.

———. 1978. *Trends in Japanese Dry Bulk Shipping and Trade*. London: Drewry Shipping Consultants.

———. 1980. *Changing Ship Type/Size Preferences in the Dry Bulk Market*. London: Drewry Shipping Consultants.

Fearnleys. Various years. *Fearnleys Review*. Oslo: Fearnleys.

Fearnleys. Various years. *World Bulk Trades*. Oslo: Fearnleys.

Garrod, P., and W. Miklius. 1985. "The Optimal Ship Size: A Comment." *Journal of Transport Economics and Policy* 19, no. 1:83–89.

Goto, S. 1984. *Japan's Shipping Policy*. Tokyo: Japan Maritime Research Institute.

Hanappe, P., and M. Savy. 1981. "Industrial Port Areas and the Kondratieff Cycle." In B. Hoyle and D. Pinder, eds., *Cityport Industrialization and Regional Development*. Oxford: Pergamon Press, 11–22.

Jansson, J., and D. Shneerson. 1982. "The Optimal Ship Size." *Journal of Transport Economics and Policy* 16, no. 3:217–38.

Karmon, Y. 1980. *Ports around the World*. New York: Crown Publishers.

Kendall, P. 1972. "A Theory of Optimum Ship Size." *Journal of Transport Economics and Policy* 6, no. 1:128–46.

Keohane, R. 1984. *After Hegemony*. Princeton, NJ: Princeton University Press.

Krasner, S. 1978. *Defending the National Interest: Raw Materials Investments and U.S. Foreign Policy*. Princeton, NJ: Princeton University Press.

McMichael, P. 1984. *Settlers and the Agrarian Question: Foundations of Capitalism in Colonial Australia*. Cambridge: Cambridge University Press.

Mandel, E. 1975. *Late Capitalism*. London: New Left Books.

Nagatsuka, S. 1989. *Outlook for Demand-Supply of World Shipbuilding in the 1990s*. Tokyo: Japan Maritime Research Institute.

Rimmer, P. 1984. "Japanese Seaports: Economic Development and State Intervention." In B. Hoyle and D. Hilling, eds., *Seaport Systems and Spatial Change*. Chichester, UK: John Wiley and Sons, 99–133.

Sasaki, H. 1976. *The Shipping Industry in Japan*. London: International Institute for Labour Studies.

Stopford, M. 1988. *Maritime Economics*. London: Unwin Hyman.

Todd, D. 1991. *Industrial Dislocation: The Case of Global Shipbuilding*. London: Routledge.

United Nations Conference on Trade and Development. Various years. *Review of Maritime Transport* (New York: United Nations).

United States Bureau of Mines. 1987. "The Minerals Industries of Japan." In *Minerals Yearbook 1987*. Washington, DC: U.S. Bureau of Mines, 499–528.

———. Various years. *Minerals Yearbook*. Washington, DC: United States Bureau of Mines.

Vigarie, A. 1981. "Maritime Industrial Development Areas: Structural Evolution and Implications for Regional Development." In B. Hoyle and D. Pinder, eds., *Cityport Industrialization and Regional Development*. Oxford: Pergamon Press, 23–36.

Wallerstein, I. 1980. *The Modern World-System II: Mercantilism and the Consolidation of the European World-Economy, 1600–1750*. New York: Academic Press.

8

Capital, Labor, and State in Thai Industrial Restructuring: The Impact of Global Economic Transformations

Frederic C. Deyo

The remarkable economic successes of a number of East Asian countries, including South Korea, Taiwan, Hong Kong, Singapore, and, more recently, Thailand and Malaysia, were based in large measure on the exploitation of low labor costs to produce manufactured goods for world markets. As rising labor costs made such a strategy increasingly vulnerable to market inroads by countries like China and Indonesia, with their large pools of low-wage workers, these countries sought to restructure into higher-value-added market niches where competitiveness derives as much from process efficiencies, product flexibility, and quality as from cheap labor.

Such restructuring, understood here as a socially contested process in which states, corporate managers, and workers/unions seek to shape competitive strategies and industrial structures in ways that meet their own requirements and goals, has become increasingly problematic during recent years. First, beginning in the mid-1980s, emergent global pressures from the World Bank, the U.S. government, the International Labor Organization (ILO), the General Agreement on Tariffs and Trade (GATT), and other international and foreign sources have forced a gradual destatization of developing economies, including trade liberalization, privatization, and reduced developmental regulation and support for industry. As consequences of these changes, firms faced both intensified competition in domestic and international markets and reduced state developmental assistance and protection. At the same time, in many industries an increased volatility and segmentation in global markets, along with ever more rapid technological change necessitated a shift away from Fordist, standardized production in favor of improved organizational flexibility and innovation as a condition for survival under liberalized trade regimes.

In response to the competitive challenges posed by the globalization of neoliberal economic policies, on the one hand, and post-Fordist industrial organization, on the other, enterprises everywhere have sought to institute new competitive strategies to enhance efficiency and flexibility. This chapter explores the nature of these managerial strategies and their implications for workers through a case study of industrial restructuring in Thailand. It then assesses the role of the labor movements and the state in shaping or contesting these competitive strategies as well as the implications of the strategies for long-term development. Throughout the discussion, emphasis is placed on the labor and human resource aspects of industrial restructuring.

INDUSTRIAL RESTRUCTURING IN THAILAND

The Thai economy has expanded rapidly over recent years, based in large measure on growth in the export of textiles, wearing apparel, jewelry, toys, electronics assemblies, and other products in light-industry manufacturing sectors whose competitive advantage in world markets centers on abundant, cheap labor. This development strategy, however, has been jeopardized by rising wages. Between 1980 and 1988, the real earnings of manufacturing employees increased by 6.4 percent per year, with continuing rapid gains in the 1990s (World Bank 1991, cited in Brown and Frenkel 1993).

Wage escalation has been accompanied by economic liberalization, which has further magnified the impact of rising labor costs by dramatically boosting Thailand's trade dependency and competitive vulnerability. Between 1986 and 1991, trade as a percentage of gross domestic product rose from 60 to 80 percent (*Nation* 9/29/92). As a result, Thai industries are caught in a "sandwich trap," facing upward cost competition from industries in less-developed countries, but partially excluded from higher-value-added market niches by well-established producers in more advanced countries like South Korea and Taiwan.

Finally, neoliberal structural reforms diminished the possibilities for extensive reliance on state-led industrial restructuring through selective trade protection, promotional industrial targeting, labor market intervention, state enterprise, and other instruments of state strategy which had played important roles in the older NICs. This diminution in state developmental capacity occurred at precisely a time when new pressures for industrial restructuring impose new tasks on states to encourage increased industrial flexibility and technology transfer.

In seeking to meet heightened competitive pressures, Thai employers most often adopted cost-cutting measures that continue to lock firms into direct cost competition with lower-tier producers, in lieu of longer-term programs to restructure into higher-value-added, skill- and technology-intensive activities. To the extent that these short-term measures enhanced organizational flexibility, they sought not only to reduce production costs, but also to increase cost flexibility and reduce excess capacity and overhead during market downturns through "external" or "numerical" flexibility (Standing 1989). This form of "static" flexibility fosters quick adjustments in employment levels, skill mixes, and production through hiring and firing of workers, employment of temporary and contract workers, and reliance on short-term subcontracting, measures that replace fixed with variable labor and other costs even as they foster product flexibility. While useful in the short term, such measures may undercut longer-term investments in employee skills, technological innovation, and supplier capabilities, which are essential for dynamic flexibility, the critical basis for movement upward into higher-value-added market niches.

Short-term cost-cutting strategies have been encouraged by several managerial considerations. These include the immediate cost disadvantage facing firms that take on long-term investments in training, research and development, work reorganization, and other areas in contrast to other firms that do not, the possibility of appropriation of the benefits of these investments by competing firms which, for example, hire away newly trained workers and thus acquire not only their training but the technological innovations they have learned as well, and the difficulties in adopting participatory shop-floor practices necessary for flexible production in the context of low trust and confrontational labor-management relations.

RESTRUCTURING AND LABOR WELFARE

The social consequences of cost-cutting strategies are seen most immediately in trends toward labor casualization, sweatshop subcontracting, and widespread violation of minimum wage and social security laws, especially in light, labor-intensive export industries (Sussangkarn 1990; Yosamornsunton 1986). There are indications that both casualization and subcontracting have increased in recent years (Arom Pongpa-ngan Foundation 1988, 1991; Suesongham and Charoenloet 1993; Brown and Frenkel 1993). Survey data collected for the Thai Development Research Institute show that the ratio of temporary and contract workers outside the Bangkok area increased significantly in the 1980s (Charsombut 1990, 19). A 1988 labor survey in the Bangkok area found that about 19 percent of factory workers were employed on a temporary basis (Samakkitham 1990, 32). A more focused survey of four industrial areas near Bangkok showed a rapid increase in the number of firms employing at least 20 percent of their workforce on a temporary basis between 1983 and 1988. In one industrial area, over 60 percent of all workers held temporary employment status in thirty-one surveyed factories (Piriyarangsan and Poonpanich 1992). In many cases, the decision to make increased use of temporary workers followed labor disputes or worker efforts to establish labor unions.

THE ALTERNATIVE RESPONSE: DYNAMIC, FLEXIBLE PRODUCTION

It is clear that the short-term cost-cutting responses of most Thai firms to global competition compromise their prospects for long-term economic success. For this reason, it is important to look at cases where industry has invested in longer-term competitive restructuring supportive of dynamic internal flexibility. How successful have such efforts been? What are their limits under economic deregulation?

Finally, what are their consequences for workers and unions? The experiences of two automobile assemblers, Toyota and Mitsubishi, provide partial answers to these questions.

The expansion and development of automobile and other engineering-based industries plays an important role in industrial restructuring. In the past, these industries have not been directly supportive of export development. Indeed, they often required continuing import protection, a carry-over from earlier import-substitution periods. Rather, their importance derived from their multiple beneficial linkages to a large number of other industries, their attractiveness to foreign investors, and their capacity to act as conduits for foreign technology with subsequent spin-offs to local supplier and other firms.

In addition, regional trade liberalization led to a growing realization of the potential role of automotive exports as part of more general industrial restructuring. Thai-Hino Industry Co., an assembler and distributor of buses and trucks, sought to export vehicle components to ASEAN countries by the mid-1990s (*Nation* 2/17/93), while Opel, Toyota, and Mitsubishi planned to increase auto exports to other countries in the region (*Bangkok Post* 8/28/93; 9/11/92; 2/18/93). For these varied reasons, the Thai government has promoted the vehicle industry, which now employs tens of thousands of people in assembly and supplier plants.

Under liberalization, the Thai auto industry has faced growing international competition in both export and domestic markets. Beginning in 1991, auto import tariffs were substantially reduced. Similar tariff reductions were effected for completely knocked down units (CKDs), and a previous decision to incrementally increase required domestic content for locally assembled cars was rescinded, although suppliers of auto parts continue to enjoy moderate protection under existing domestic-content regulation. As a result, both auto assemblers and suppliers faced increased trade pressure during recent years, as seen in rising imports and declining exports (*Nation* 10/31/92; 12/7/92; *Asia Week* 2/24/93, 58).

Trade liberalization pushed local auto companies into head-on regional competition to attract or retain high-value-added production (Doner 1991). While assemblers sought to meet foreign competition through organizational and operational upgrading, including human resource innovations in the areas of worker training and shop-floor problem solving and improvement, such reforms have been uneven in depth and effectiveness.

Toyota Motor Company (Thailand) is perhaps the most aggressive of the Thai auto assemblers in upgrading domestic operations, both to maintain its premier position in the domestic auto market and to expand exports. Such upgrading has been especially evident in the company's human resource policy, the heart of "Toyotaism." A close look at personnel policy at a progressive company like Toyota suggests what may be the upper limit to near-term restructuring in Thai industry in the context of neoliberal reforms.

As Toyota sought aggressively to improve production efficiency and quality, it has continued to develop many of the human resource practices utilized by the parent company in Japan. Like several other auto assemblers, Toyota helps fund public and community educational and training programs. Toyota's most visible commitment in this regard is its support for a large training program for automotive engineering and research at Chulalongkorn University's Engineering School. In addition, the company established an Automotive Vocational Development Center to train workers in production processes and auto technology. Within the company's plants themselves, shop-floor quality circles meet at least weekly to deal with production problems. A very active suggestion program, buttressed by a generous award system, produces about 200 usable ideas per month. Worker appraisals, the basis for year-end bonus determination, give 30 percent weight to *kaizen* activities (the continual resetting of production and quality targets at ever higher levels). Workers are responsible for in-process inspection and are expected to stop the line if problems cannot be resolved immediately. Toyota regularly rotates workers among jobs and production lines as requirements dictate, although the requisite multiskilling for such flexible deployment is greatly reduced under Toyota's continuing efforts at job simplification.

The literature on flexible production suggests that dynamic shop-floor flexibility of the sort found at Toyota requires substantial workforce commitment, cooperation, and involvement, and that these, in turn, presuppose progressive, trust-engendering employment practices and harmonious industrial relations (Kochan and Katz 1988; Streeck 1991). In part, Toyota conforms to the expected pattern. Once part of the "Toyota Team," regular workers and skilled workers above them enjoy at least limited promotional opportunities. For these workers, wages and benefits are substantially better than those enjoyed in other companies. Moreover, the company provides a wide range of recreational, educational, and other facilities and programs offered at the parent company in Japan.

However, this is not to say labor relations at Toyota are entirely harmonious. Indeed, rather serious problems arise from other employment practices at this company. Toyota, like most other firms, uses temporary contract workers for a large number of entry-level production jobs. These workers, who usually have some experience in the industry (often with suppliers), are hired for a fixed term to do specific jobs and receive little on-the-job training. At the end of their contract, they may or may not be hired as permanent Toyota workers. A reliance on contract labor accomplishes several things. First, it reduces labor costs. Contract workers are obtained from an independent placement company through which Toyota pays referred workers. This company provides inferior work benefits and pays contract workers less than regular Toyota workers. Second, the use of contract labor fosters external flexibility to meet market fluctuations. Third, however, contract labor supports internal flexibility as well, insofar as it permits careful selection of regular workers, creates strong motivation to work hard to earn permanent status, and yields moderately strong skills among entry-level workers without requiring substantial company training. This is an important consideration in view of relatively high rates of labor turnover and corresponding high training costs.

The use of contract workers, who account for around 25 percent of the workers on most lines, has produced conflict and divisions in the workforce as they sought wage and benefit parity with regular workers. Furthermore, it has been opposed by regular workers and their union as a threat to their own job security and wages. A further problem is that rapid company growth forced Toyota to resort to external hiring of large numbers of workers at the technical, engineering, and managerial levels, thus compromising the motivational benefits of internal labor markets and corporate socialization.

Finally, the preservation of payroll flexibility through the use of large, variable bonuses creates a continuing potential for labor conflict and mistrust. Given Toyota's somewhat acrimonious relations with its union, which it fought strenuously to avoid recognizing at the outset of the initial unionization drive, this potential is further increased.

Given these various morale-compromising problems, it is not surprising that Toyota's workforce turnover rate, although low by Thai standards, is still relatively high. While much of this instability is accounted for by temporary and contract workers, quit rates among engineers and middle-level management have become a concern as well.

However, having said all this, it is important to note that despite an industrial relations climate marked by some degree of conflict and mistrust, Toyota has achieved national and regional recognition for its high-quality, flexible production. We will return to this unanticipated finding.

MITSUBISHI

Perhaps more typical of the difficult transition to flexible, high-quality production among Thai auto assemblers is the case of MSC Sittipol (hereafter referred to as Mitsubishi), a manufacturer of Mitsubishi cars and trucks. With the exception of the Lancer, which is exported to Canada as the Colt, Mitsubishi's vehicles are sold primarily in the domestic market. Like Toyota, Mitsubishi tried to become more productive in domestic and export markets through improved quality and productivity and has sought to introduce new training programs, quality circles, suggestion systems, and other supportive human resource practices.

The company's successes have been mixed. On the one hand, Toyota now views Mitsubishi as a credible threat to its own fledgling export program, given Mitsubishi's diversified and integrated Thai operations, and indeed, the Lancer/Colt is Thailand's most successful export model. On the other hand, Mitsubishi has faced some important problems in its upgrading efforts. At the Lat Krabang plant outside Bangkok, where Galants, pickups, and large trucks are assembled, large numbers of vehicles are routinely diverted from production lines for the correction of paint and trim defects. Indeed, at a second Thai Mitsubishi plant, quality problems forced a recent halt in Colt exports to Canada. Quality circles have been instituted in the truck plant but have been abandoned in the auto and pickup plant because of lack of worker cooperation. Moreover, an extensive training program for new engineers is undermined by very high quit rates among engineers, a large percentage of whom leave the company within two years.

In part, these problems are attributable to Mitsubishi's personnel practices, which are more traditional than those found at Toyota. A somewhat larger proportion of production workers are contract workers, who are hired "on loan" from suppliers. More middle-level staff are externally hired, with a corresponding deemphasis on internal promotions. Status distinctions, displayed by elaborate hat and uniform color coding, are especially sharp and tend to inhibit joint problem solving in quality circles. Beyond midday meals, transportation, and uniforms, few nonmandatory employee benefits or social programs are provided.

The experiences at Toyota and Mitsubishi suggest several tentative conclusions. First, major assembly firms have made substantial efforts to meet new competitive pressures through improved quality, efficiency, and flexibility. As part of their efforts to achieve these goals, they introduced corresponding reforms in human resource management. More uneven and less successful, however, were efforts to introduce employment practices in areas of worker welfare and security that are often assumed to be important for flexibility reforms. However, it is important to note that the resulting morale problems, union conflict, and even high turnover rates have not seriously undercut efforts to enhance flexibility and quality. Toyota, after all, is internationally recognized for quality and efficiency, and for its part, Mitsubishi is relatively successful in exporting economy cars to North America. At Mitsubishi, however, conflict and low morale, eventuating in somewhat higher quit rates than at Toyota, undercut efforts to improve flexibility and quality. It may be that in this case a critical threshold was reached beyond which lack of trust and low morale do begin to compromise flexibility.

CONTENDING COMPETITIVE DEMANDS AND MIXED STRATEGIES

Competition places multiple demands on companies, and these demands sometimes push in very different directions. Immediate pressures encourage short-term cost cutting through casualization, labor-law evasion, efforts to cut wages and benefits, and sweat-shop outsourcing. Pressures for internal flexibility and improved quality highlight the need for increased investments in human resource, technology, and organizational reforms, along with technology assistance to suppliers. Such reforms may be appropriate, and even superior in the long-term, but they are costly and risky in the short-run.

It is clear that firms in fact must and do simultaneously pursue several seemingly discordant strategies in meeting the diverse competitive pressures they face. But do these strategies conflict? More specifically, do not cost-cutting strategies which create conflict and mistrust undermine dynamic flexibility-enhancing measures through their negative consequences for cooperation and organizational morale?

Two alternative explanations may be offered for the coexistence of diverse, seemingly incompatible, competitive strategies. First, it should not be immediately assumed that these different strategies cannot be combined in mutually complementary ways. The use of skilled contract labor, for example, provides a temporary workforce with experience and skills in the industry, thus enhancing both internal and external flexibilities.

This same example also suggests a second alternative: that reliance on seemingly incompatible competitive strategies may be facilitated by processes of institutional segregation which permit their simultaneous pursuit. Toyota and Mitsubishi utilize multiple labor systems insofar as casual, contract, and regular employees work together on the shop floor under quite different employment conditions. At the outset of employment, new workers are made aware of the tenure, conditions, and security of their employment as well as differences among the three categories of employment. Demarcations among the categories are further reinforced by differences in cap color codes, extent of participation in quality circles and other work activities, and types of assigned duties. Whether this instance of institutional segregation has been entirely successful, given the morale problems associated with multiple labor systems at both Toyota and Mitsubishi, is uncertain.

AUTOCRATIC DYNAMIC FLEXIBILITY AND INDUSTRIAL ASCENT

A further paradox is suggested by the coexistence of harsh, autocratic labor practices on the one hand, and the apparent success of internally flexible production systems, on the other. The very fact that Toyota and Mitsubishi have successfully implemented internal flexibility reforms in their efforts to become internationally competitive, and despite trust-evading and morale-deflating autocratic labor practices, suggests that internal flexibility may not, in fact, place as stringent demands on industrial relations systems and employment practices as one might infer from the literature on Japanese and European industry. It also raises the possibility of subtypes or hybrids of internal flexibilization, which have not been noted in a flexible production literature centering largely on Japan, Europe, and North America but are likely to occur in more authoritarian political systems, such as those in East and Southeast Asia.

Work reforms in the auto industries of Germany and Sweden fostered high levels of high-quality, shop-floor innovation and product flexibility (see Streeck 1991; Turner 1991). In many cases, such flexibility was accompanied by substantial proactive shop-floor participation on the part of workers and unions in production decisions and trouble-shooting, extending even to direct business dealings with suppliers. In the case of Japan, more circumscribed forms of participation flowed from managerial success in containing worker militancy in the 1950s and in encouraging the subsequent emergence of more enterprise-focused company unions. In both cases, the early political need for management to accommodate labor demands in developing competitive strategies precluded simple cost-cutting responses and pushed companies toward progressive human resource strategies and participative forms of flexible production.

However, what of Thailand and other developing countries that lacked the democratic traditions and strong unions that encouraged participative flexibility in the industrialized countries? Union density in Thailand is very low, at roughly 6 percent overall, and it is even lower in the private sector (Brown and Frenkel 1993). Where private sector unions do exist, as at major auto assemblers like Toyota, their weakness and exclusion from participation in decision making render them unable to play the role of Japanese enterprise unions in supporting participatory, flexible production systems (Poonpanich 1991). To the extent that internal flexibility and innovation-fostering subcontracting have been instituted, their form was determined less by labor politics than by the competitive requirements themselves. Consequentially, the inclusion of workers in decision making and in the sharing of material benefits has been far more limited. In the case of the auto industry, workers participate in quality circles and other deliberative fora for improving quality and productivity. However, an observation of the discussion that occurs in these meetings suggests more a question-and-answer process than one of joint problem solving. Similarly, the wage and benefits gap separating production workers and managers in these firms is far wider than that obtaining in European or Japanese firms.

The rather top-down model of flexibility found in Thai auto firms shares with its more participatory counterparts in Europe and Japan multiskilling, in-process inspection, just-in-time production and delivery, and constant improvement in process and product. It differs substantially however, in its internal politics in that the exclusionary internal flexibility of Thai firms favors management autocracy over worker participation in "flexibly" organizing work and deploying labor.

Is such exclusionary, autocratic internal flexibility less competitive than more participatory forms found elsewhere? Perhaps not: first, it may well be that managerially imposed, flexible production systems that attend mainly to the dictates of market competition, and only minimally to social and political considerations, are highly competitive. This possibility strongly suggests itself in the context of increasing economic pressures and Japanese competition in European automobile markets, where employers are now seeking to rescind some of their earlier concessions in matters of employment security, worker participation, and human-centered work organization (*Wall Street Journal* 11/4/93).

A second consideration relates more specifically to developing countries like Thailand. Following Amsden (1989), one may distinguish between cases of industrial advance based on continued product and process innovation in industrially advanced countries and firms and other cases in which such advance is rooted in local adaptation and the implementation of technologies and processes developed elsewhere. While Amsden argued that the latter case centers competitive success on shop-floor implementation, she suggested that the major role is played by engineers, rather than by production workers per se. Indeed, it may well be that the international transfer and adoption of already debugged product and process technology is less dependent on proactive problem solving and involvement on the part of production workers than would be the case for innovation in new products and processes. From this, it follows that factories in developing countries relying mainly on technologies developed abroad, say in Japan, may require less of their shop-floor workers and, for this reason, find it less necessary to institute the sorts of trust and commitment-supporting employment practices associated with more innovative flexible-production systems found elsewhere.

Of course, there may well be a critical threshold beyond which autocracy, mistrust, and conflict vitiate efforts to introduce the degree of participation and job involvement required by all variants of internal flexible production, as seen especially in the failure of quality circles and the continuing loss of trained engineers at Mitsubishi. Short of this threshold, however, autocratic, low-trust internal flexibility may provide an adequate basis for competitive success in the second-tier, technology-dependent automotive industries of developing countries.

STATE AND LABOR IN INDUSTRIAL RESTRUCTURING

The earlier experience of economic development in South Korea, Singapore, and Taiwan during the 1970s and early 1980s suggests the importance of strong proactive state involvement in industrial restructuring, particularly in such areas as education and training, infrastructure, export promotion, research and development, and the creation of a strong supplier base for major industries. Under liberal economic restructuring, the destatization, marketization, and privatization of the economy have greatly reduced the role of the Thai government in these necessary support roles.

An equally serious a problem is a state labor regime that encourages short-term cost-cutting strategies in preference to longer-term competitive investments in most Thai firms. Internal flexibility in German, Swedish, and Japanese industrial firms stemmed, in part, from need to accommodate the demands of strong, militant trade unions which, in Germany and Sweden, enjoyed subsequent coalitional inclusion in, and support from, the state. Quite different is the situation in Thailand and most other developing countries where, even under democratization, labor movements have been marginalized in political arenas and places of employment. With a few exceptions, such as the effective blocking of privatization efforts by state enterprise workers during the late 1980s, Thai labor failed to resist either the negative consequences of cost-cutting competitive strategies adopted by most Thai employers or the loss of union independence under the highly autocratic reforms and enterprise unionism instituted in the few companies that adopted more far-sighted competitive strategies.

Labor's continuing marginalization and weak response are somewhat surprising given an increasingly well-educated workforce, a continuing democratic transition from the mid-1980s (briefly interrupted by martial rule), and active involvement in labor education and training programs on the part of international and domestic nongovernmental organizations (NGOs). Why has labor remained a politically marginal force in national development?

First, economic structural reforms both reflected and reinforced a weakened bargaining position on the part of labor. As elsewhere, competitive pressures created a credible threat of shutdowns, retrenchments, and relocation of production to cheaper labor sites in the absence of wage and benefit restraints. Conversely, the competitive strategies of managers, including especially an increased use of temporary and contract labor and outsourcing of production, themselves directly undercut labor's bargaining power.

Second, labor regime liberalization accompanying the democratic transition has been partial and selective, at best. The state retains an important role in creating and preserving a political context within which a liberalized market economy and an exclusionary democracy can safely function. Where unions have been able to preserve previously won gains and security through resistance to privatization, outsourcing, flexibilization, and so forth, they evoke continued coercive state controls. Thus, for example, Thai labor repression has been sustained in the state enterprise sector, where unions effectively blocked privatization efforts and provided national leadership in labor's successful struggle to force the passage of expanded social security legislation in 1990 (Voravidh 1993).

In addition, the deradicalization of labor has necessitated a fuller institutional separation of economic from political conflict through the proscribing of political unionism other than that still permitted within state-sponsored corporatist structures. Such depoliticization assures labor's continued political exclusion during democratization and its corresponding inability to effectively contest economic reforms that disempower them.

Third, under labor market deregulation, the state has failed even to enforce existing legislation guaranteeing fair labor standards, adequate work conditions, job security, or minimum wages. This further encourages employers to avoid or undercut unions, evade labor legislation, increase reliance on outsourcing and temporary labor, and engage in a variety aggressive anti-labor practices.

More generally, to the extent that there has been an attenuation of coercive state labor controls in the context of political liberalization and democratization, labor market deregulation has not implied a general relaxation of labor controls. Rather, it signals a devolution of those controls from the state to the enterprises, as economic and industrial restructuring strengthens the hand of management to contain and disorganize, or, alternately, to co-opt labor at the enterprise level. It is, in part, for this reason that labor regime liberalization has not posed a threat to governments, local business, or international investors. Thus, business elites, including multinational investors, are less prone than earlier to urge the government repression of labor and increasingly likely to institute progressive labor policies internally, especially in large organizations requiring skilled labor.

In part as a consequence of a general lack of state support for industrial restructuring, internal flexibility reforms have thus far been confined primarily to large, resourceful, and mainly foreign companies like Toyota, Thai-Hino, Sony, and Mitsubishi (see Siengthai 1988). These companies, along with a few exceptional domestic firms such as those in the Siam Cement group, are able to absorb the short-term competitive disadvantages of increased expenditures in training, research and development, and work reorganization. Indeed, in some instances, as in the case of Toyota's funding of the automotive engineering program at Chulalongkorn University, these firms have taken a lead role in investing in an industrially supportive public infrastructure. The very exceptionality of these programs points to the inability of most firms to assume the burden of such public investments and to the corresponding need for far greater government assistance.

CONCLUSION

In the Thai context, neoliberal reforms of trade, industry, and labor policy have discouraged enterprise reforms supportive of industrial upgrading. Additionally, they have encouraged enterprise-level labor systems characterized either by "market-depotism" or, alternately, autocratic internal flexibilization; imposed increased hardships on labor; and undercut the capacity of organized labor to contest new managerial strategies. In the short run, the Thai economy continues to grow quite rapidly as managers reduce costs and increase external flexibility. In the longer term, however, growing social tensions and a progressively reduced ability to compete with lower-cost producers will likely force a reconsideration of economic strategy.

NOTES

This research was supported by grants from the Thailand-U.S. Educational Foundation (The Fulbright Program) and from the Social Science Research Council. The chapter has benefited from helpful suggestions by Jószef Böröcz, Rick Doner, Steve Frenkel, and David A. Smith.

REFERENCES

Amsden, Alice. 1989. *Asia's New Giant: South Korea and Late Industrialization.* New York: Oxford University Press.
Arom Pongpa-ngan Foundation. 1988. "Labor Relations Strategies and Short-term Employment." Unpublished manuscript.
———. 1991. "Temporary Employment after the Ministry of Interior Decrees No. 11" (in Thai). Unpublished manuscript.
Asia Week. (Hong Kong). Various years.
Bangkok Post. (Bangkok, Thailand). Various years.

Brown, Andrew, and Steve Frenkel. 1993. "Union Unevenness and Insecurity in Thailand." In S. Frenkel, ed., *Organized Labor in the Asia-Pacific Region: A Comparative Analysis of Trade Unionism in Nine Countries*. Ithaca, NY: ILR Press, 82–106.

Charsombut, Pradit. 1990. *Provincial Industry Labor Market*. Bangkok: Thailand Development Research Institute Foundation.

Doner, Richard. 1991. *Driving a Bargain: Automobile Industrialization and Japanese Firms in Southeast Asia*. Berkeley: University of California Press.

Kochan, Thomas A., and Harry C. Katz. 1988. *Collective Bargaining and Industrial Relations: From Theory to Practice*. Homewood, IL: Irwin Publishers.

Nation. (Bangkok, Thailand). Various issues.

Piriyarangsan, Sangsit, and Kanchada Poonpanich. 1992. "Labor Institutions in an Export-Oriented Country: A Case Study of Thailand." Paper presented at the International Workshop on Labor Institutions and Economic Development in Asia, Bali, Indonesia, 4–6 Feb.

Poonpanich, Kanchada. 1991. "Employment Promotion and Workers' Participation."

Samakkhitham, Somsak. 1990. *Economic Life of Low-Level Workers* (in Thai). Bangkok: Arom Pongpa-ngan Foundation.

Siengthai, Sununta. 1988. "Thai-Hino Industry Co., Ltd." In *Case Studies in Labor-Management Cooperation for Productivity Improvement*. Bangkok: ILO, 265–308.

Standing, Guy. 1989. *The Growth of External Labor Flexibility in a Nascent NIC: Malaysian Labor Flexibility Survey (MLFS)*. World Employment Programme Research Working Paper No. 35 (November). Geneva: ILO.

Streeck, Wolfgang. 1991. "On the Institutional Conditions of Diversified Quality Production." In Egon Matzner and Wolfgang Streeck, eds., *Beyond Keynesianism: The Socio-Economies of Production and Full Employment*. Brookfield, VT: Edward Elgar.

Suesongham, Sakool. 1993. "Trade Union Struggle in Thailand: A Cycle of Defeat." In Arnold Wehmborner, ed., *NIC's in Asia: A Challenge to Trade Unions*. Singapore: Friedrich-Ebert-Stiftung, 17–23.

Suesongham, Sakool, and Voravidh Charoenloet. 1993. "Fragmentation of the Trade Unions: Inevitably or Not?" Paper presented at a conference organized by the Friedrich-Ebert-Stiftung [foundation] on NICs in Asia: A Challenge to Trade Unions," Singapore, 30 March-1 April.

Sussangkarn, Chalongphob. 1990. *Labor Markets in an Era of Adjustment: A Study of Thailand*. Bangkok: Thailand Development Research Institute Foundation.

Turner, Lowell. 1991. *Democracy at Work: Changing World Markets and the Future of Labor Unions*. Ithaca, NY: Cornell University Press.

Voravidh, Charoenloet. 1993. "Export-Oriented Industry in Thailand: Implications for Employment and Labor." In Arnold Wehmborner, ed., *NIC's in Asia: A Challenge to Trade Unions*. Singapore: Friedrich-Ebert-Stiftung.

Wall Street Journal. (New York). Various years.

World Bank. 1991. *The Challenge of Development*. Oxford: Oxford University Press.

Yosamornsunton, Amphan. 1986. "Wages and Working Conditions in the Garment Industry." Master's thesis in Economics, Thammasat University.

Part II

NEW SOCIAL MOVEMENTS AND POSSIBILITIES FOR RESISTANCE

9

Globalization, India, and the Struggle for Justice

Timothy J. Scrase

The axis of the new world conjecture is Western capitalist aggression against the
Third World peoples, with the aim of subordinating their further evolution to the
demands of redeployment of transnational capital.   —Amin (1990, 48)

It might be said that, again in varying degrees, all of international politics is
cultural—that we are . . . in a period of globewide *cultural* politics.
                                                        —Robertson (1992, 5)

In this chapter I provide a critique of the most recent shift in global analysis—the
shift to theoretically account for the increasing trend toward *globalization*—a term
that describes the intensification of social and cultural interconnectedness across the
globe. In particular, I argue that the view of globalization, as formulated by writers
like Robertson (1992), has the tendency to relegate the political-economic analysis
of global social change to a secondary status and, as an outcome, plays down the
significance of inherent inequalities in the capitalist world-system, as espoused by
theorists like Wallerstein, Frank and many others. In the context of analyzing
sociocultural change in the Third World, I argue that culture should neither be seen
as an epiphenomenon in analyses of the world-system nor be privileged over and
above the political-economic realm. By privileging culture and cultural analysis,
"culture" is rendered both static and, as an abstract analytical category, it is
divorced from the social, historical, and political processes that lead to its formation
and reproduction. What is required in the analysis of the political economy of
social change is an approach that treats culture and class as central and dynamic.
Moreover, I contend that there is an essential cultural logic to the globalization of
capitalism, yet the way in which this logic is manifested in advanced capitalist
societies is fundamentally distinct from that in peripheral states. This becomes
significant when one considers the various agendas for social justice that are raised
in peripheral states such as India. In fact, by focusing on groups in India who are,
in various ways, continuing to encounter the economic and cultural logic of

globalization, I attempt to demonstrate the significance of a political-economic analysis in accounting for the ways in which disparate groups deal with the vagaries of the capitalist world-system. I therefore argue that the emergence of new social movements in the Third World today, such as those found in India, can be seen as a continuing response and challenge to, rather than a divergence from, increasing economic marginalization and impoverishment manifest in the world capitalist system.

My argument in this chapter, therefore, is presented with two pleas in mind. The first is a plea for caution in staking too much faith in the idea of the autonomy of culture in the globalization process, and the second is a plea for a reconsideration of the complex issues, politics, and processes of social change in so-called Third World, peripheral or developing societies as they constitute the dominant, although seemingly near-forgotten, "other side" of the claimed success and growth of core capitalist societies. Thus, in the context of the proceeding discussion, we can ask: within the context of the Third World, how are we to read global social change? Is it an extension merely of the global accumulation of capital or is there something inherently new to the process? Finally, what can we make of the various Third World (localized) political struggles over justice and human rights—are these merely cultural spectacles or do they, in reality, have an equally political economic and historical genesis?

DEFINING GLOBALIZATION

There have been, and continues to be, numerous definitions in the recent sociological literature to describe the process of globalization. In a foreword to their edited collection, *Globalization, Knowledge and Society*, Albrow and King (1990, 1) wrote:

> If we already lived in a single world society then all the talk about globalisation would be in the past tense. Instead, globalisation is the present process of becoming global: globality itself lies in the future, but the very near future. Each major aspect of social reality (the structure, culture and personality of traditional terminology) is simultaneously undergoing globalisation, as witnessed by the emergence of the world economy, a cosmopolitan culture and international social movements.

Anthony King came straight to the point when he wrote that "globalization is a process and the world system is a structure" (1991, 1). Roland Robertson went one step further by providing a number of definitions emanating from a theoretical position in which he claims *engagement* with globalization, and not merely citing a theoretical position that involves reactions to, or a product of, the globalization process (1992, 49). Additionally, in his recent book (1992) he often interchangeably uses "globalization" and "global unicity" and also speaks of "worldism." In any event, globalization describes the shrinking of the world—whereby the local becomes global and the global determines the local.

McGrew (1992) summarized many of the central outcomes and processes of late twentieth-century globalization. These included:

> the tremendous expansion of transnational corporate activity; the existence of global communications and media networks; the global production and dissemination of knowledge, combined with (amongst other factors) the escalating significance of transnational religious and ethnic ties; the enormous flows of people across national boundaries; and the emerging authority of institutions and communities above the nation state (1992, 63).

Drawing on the writings of Giddens (1990) and Harvey (1989), McGrew further pointed to one key aspect of globalization: that globalization consists of both scope (or "stretching") and intensity (or "deepening") (1992, 68). In other words, there is both a stretching across the globe of social, political, and economic activity and an accompanying intensification of the effects of these social, political, and economic decisions to the point where individuals are made to feel "truly global."[1] To my mind, therefore, globalization describes the process of the consolidation of the world capitalist system by an unprecedented emphasis on economic and cultural flows across national borders and mediated by the increasing global power of both transnational corporations and international agencies.[2]

In general, the literature on globalization speaks of two great although, I would argue, not necessarily divergent, perspectives. Using the well-known metaphor of core and periphery, one perspective focuses on the rise and spread of the capitalist world-system—a system that, as it evolves and consolidates, draws peripheral nations into the fray of economic and social competition. Within this perspective, and particularly in the approach developed by Immanuel Wallerstein (e.g., 1974, 1980), it is the major issues of class and economic domination that are initially highlighted, while secondary importance is given to derivative concerns of culture.[3] This perspective is persuasive because, despite one of the most serious economic recessions in recent history, we are witnessing a strengthening and reaffirmation of the power of Western monopoly capitalism, coupled with an enormous level of manufacturing and industrial output from many semiperipheral states, and a massive turn, worldwide, to a consumer- and consumption-based society. Indeed, numerous large national and transnational corporations are maintaining or increasing their profit levels, particularly at the expense, it would seem, of the medium- to small-scale companies and family-owned small businesses.

Standing opposed to world-system theory is that which privileges the realm of culture in globalization. The main protagonist, Roland Robertson, pointed out that world-system analysis cannot be equated with globalization and, moreover, argued, "Even though they have a few important things in common, globalization analysis and world systems analysis are rival perspectives" (1992, 15). Interestingly, while criticizing Wallerstein for seemingly forwarding an economic deterministic analysis of the link between the growth of the capitalist world economy and the subsequent domination of peripheral nations, Robertson's own work (which stresses, among other things, a concern with global order) is, Arnason observed, "unmistakably indicative of a Parsonian approach, transferred from an artificially isolated and unified society to a global condition" (1990, 222).

In *Globalization*, Robertson proceeded to present a comprehensive analysis of global social change, an account constructed around the idea of the relative autonomy of culture (an approach that, as I will point out, remains contradictory and problematic). Additionally, his work stresses the significance of the reality of the "nationally constituted society" and the need "to see where individuals and constructions of the individual, as well as humankind, fit into the picture" of global change (1992, 5). He continually stressed that he wished to analyze the world as a whole and to show how globalization is a contested process.

Indicative of Robertson's "culturalist" approach is his outline of the origins of globalization. For him, globalization can be traced by analyzing a number of distinct stages, or phases. Phase one he terms the germinal phase (from the fifteenth to the mid-eighteenth century in Europe). Phase two is the incipient phase (the mid-eighteenth century to the 1870s), which saw in Europe the rise of unitary state, the idea of formalized international relations, sharp increases in legal conventions, and so forth. Phase three he termed the "take-off" phase (1870s to mid-1920s), which is cited as the preeminant phase for the process of globalization:

> "Take-off" here refers to a period during which the increasingly manifest globalizing tendencies of previous periods and places gave way to a single, inexorable form centered upon the four reference points, and thus constraints, of national societies, generic individuals (but with a masculine bias), a single "international society," and an increasingly singular, but not unified conception of humankind . . . . [It is characterized by the following:] Very sharp increase in number of global forms of communication. Development of global forms of competitions—for example the Olympics and Nobel prizes. Implementation of world time and the near-global adoption of Gregorian calendar. First *world* war (1992, 59; original emphasis).

Interestingly, in these and in the final two phases, which he terms the struggle for hegemony phase (1920s to late 1960s) and the uncertainty phase (late 1960s to present), Robertson made no connection between the global cultural changes he described in all five phases and worldwide trends in the development and spread of international capitalism. Surprisingly, at least in the model he provided, no direct mention is made of the rise of transnational enterprises, nor is there any link made between the growth of global media and cultural and economic imperialism.[4] In his attempts to privilege culture and, consequently, downplay significant economic change, Robertson's model of the "wholeness" of the globalization process looks, to put it mildly, somewhat askew. His at times outwardly antimaterialist position could thus serve to underplay the significance, for example, of various Third World struggles for social and economic justice fought out at the politicocultural level.

Despite my reservations with Robertson's account of globalization, he, along with others such as Eric Wolf (1982), Peter Worsley (1984), John Tomlinson (1991), and several papers in Albrow and King (1990), Featherstone (1990), and Anthony D. King (1991), have, in various empirical and diverse theoretical ways, raised to significance the issue of culture in global analysis. International tourism, rapid transport, global telecommunications, and the electronic mass media are but some of the assorted ways in which cultural contact, both within and between nations, has been facilitated. Moreover, as a response to the increasing global, social, and cultural homogenization, oppressed and marginalized groups are finding the necessary space in which to promote various social and political claims for justice and liberation, be it through the cause of tribalism, environmentalism, or indigenization. Thus, paradoxically, a degree of cultural heterogeneity, borne out of resistance, emerges from the mire of what often is, to employ a somewhat unfashionable term, economic and cultural imperialism. However, as Sklair (1991, 42) reminded us:

> Global capitalism does not permit cultural neutrality. Those cultural practices that cannot be incorporated into the culture-ideology of consumerism become oppositional counter-hegemonic forces, to be harnessed or marginalized, and if that fails, destroyed physically. Ordinary so-called "counter-cultures" are regularly incorporated and commercialized and pose no threat, [and] indeed, through the process of differentiation (illusory variety and choice), [they] are a source of great strength to the global capitalist system.

How autonomous these various cultural manifestations of resistance and rebellion are in terms of the shoring-up of the capitalist economy obviously remains problematic. It is to this issue that I will shortly turn.

GLOBALIZATION—THE POSSIBILITIES OF JUSTICE

It is argued in the literature that globalization has led to a broadly defined conception of justice in the late twentieth century. Indeed, in much of the world-systems literature (especially in the writings of André Gunder Frank) there is an overriding concern for understanding how injustice is perpetuated by the world-economic system (see Lauderdale [forthcoming]). In particular, a sense of group and individual justice is seen as emanating from a number of new social movements centered around themes such as *creolization* (whereby marginal, diasporic cultures are recognized as constituting a significant part in the overall dominant culture), *indigenization* (whereby social movements promote the rights and identities of native peoples), and *environmentalism* (in which disparate groups, mostly from the political left and center, are challenging the ravages of industrial capitalism).

Notwithstanding the laudable aims of many of the groups involved in staking claims for indigenization, environmentalism, and the like, I would argue that we must be wary of instances whereby claims for cultural recognition are subsumed under the weight of the commodification of such cultures. Documentaries such as *Millennium*, which was recently shown on Australian television and sponsored by the Body Shop and the ever-popular Christmas catalogues produced by Community Aid Abroad (CAA) not only raise awareness of the rights and concerns of indigenous peoples, but do so by promoting the acquisition of various Third World consumer goods purchased at the Body Shop, in the case of the former, or ordered from the CAA catalogue, for the latter.[5] While both groups broadly adhere to the theme of "think globally, act locally," what remains is a recognition of "indigenousness" and indigenous "justice" (a fair price for commodities) mediated by the market. To highlight the complexity of this problem, a spokesperson from the British-based organization Third World First recently, on Radio Australia, critiqued the position of the Body Shop for its promotion of petty commodity capitalism among Brazilian forest peoples, whereby it encourages them to harvest and process brazil nuts for the production of brazil nut oil (used in soaps and creams sold through the Body Shop). He pointed out that farmers in neighboring countries are already taking advantage of the current high international price for these nuts and, as a result, a saturated market will cause the price to eventually collapse. Thus, it is likely that the Brazilian forest dwellers will be only marginally better off despite the tremendous amount of labor involved in tending the plantations.

While we in the core celebrate difference and the glories that the market offers (by "discovering" Brazil nut oil soap; by feelings of empathy with the "earthy" qualities of the products), where does that leave the producers? The modern world-system was partly founded upon the unbridled exploitation of plantation economies. Their reemergence, especially for reasons of supposed good will, must be viewed with a degree of skepticism. Just as cultures can be readily commodified ("Aussie" being the latest trend in the United States), culture also has a material basis grounded in economic livelihoods and social arrangements based on class, race, and gender. For those on the margins of the Third World (on the "periphery of the periphery," so to speak), celebrations of "otherness," of marginality, must transcend mere media spectacles and the type of "get-rich-quick schemes" so eagerly promoted by transnational organizations such as the Body Shop.[6] In other words, if we want a just global society, indigenous cultures should not become the "fanciful playthings" of Western consumer capitalism.

In a recent critique of the process of globalization, which in particular addressed the question of a new dependency in the late twentieth century, Fernando Henrique Cardoso (1993) implored the reader to reconsider the ties between the First and Third Worlds—between the North and the South. In relation to the question of "a global justice," he wrote:

> The "new humanism," the "global village," and "spaceship earth"—all these
> fine-sounding phrases become cynical slogans when they do not include poverty,

backwardness, illiteracy, in short, the problems of the old Third World, as matters
to be discussed and faced at the global level. This "globalization" of Third World
problems cannot be approached as a unit since, as we know, the South is not
homogeneous. The term "new humanism" may mean, for many countries,
something like: "renegotiation of the foreign debt in terms compatible with
development, plus technology transfer, plus access to world markets." For other
countries it may mean nothing less than the direct transfer of food, health care, and
schooling (1993, 158–59).

In other words, Cardoso was pointing to the dangers inherent in a sociology of
globalization that seeks to define the process in macro terms and thus subsume the
interests of all countries, and all groups within these countries, to such an all
encompassing definition. I would also add the significance of the historical
dimension to the globalization process, to the extent that any consideration of
justice be seen in the context of historically determined processes of impoverishment and marginalization of classes and groups within the South. McGrew (1992,
79) put it this way:

With [global capitalism] has come an increasing penetration and consolidation of
capitalist social relations on a global scale. However, those excluded from or
resisting this transformation have become ever more marginalised. Thus, within
this world capitalist system there exists simultaneous processes of transnational
integration and national disintegration, as some communities are incorporated into
the system and others organized out.

In light of this argument, I am persuaded by the view of justice that was
developed by Young (1990) in her book *Justice and the Politics of Difference*:

Justice should refer not only to distribution, but also to the institutional conditions
necessary for the development and exercise of individual capacities and collective
communication and cooperation. Under this conception of justice, injustice refers
primarily to two forms of disabling constraints, oppression and domination.
While these constraints include distributive patterns, they also involve matters
which cannot easily be assimilated to the logic of distribution: decisionmaking
procedures, division of labor, and culture (1990, 39).

Thus, "justice" within the global system must not only include a consideration of
historical-economic and social forces (such as colonialism) of each specific social
formation, but must also be broad enough to encompass the variety of contemporary
forms of domination and oppression, be they mediated by class, institutional,
political, or cultural forms.

GLOBALIZATION, JUSTICE, AND INDIA

I was reminded, when preparing this chapter, of the occasion I had nearly five years ago to attend a Communist Party of India (Marxist) (CPM) victory rally in Calcutta, the capital of the state of West Bengal. They had again been elected to govern the state with a comfortable majority of seats, and on this occasion more than 1 million people were in attendance to join in the celebrations for democracy, justice, and equality, as well as to celebrate the defeat of divisionist politics of the opposition Congress party. This event struck me as a powerful signifier of the strength of participatory democracy and reaffirmed my skepticism of books published not long after celebrating the triumph of capitalism (e.g., Fukuyama 1992). It reminded me, too, of the continual marginalization of Third World politics from the mainstream Western media and consciousness—the fact the 35 million women and men, laborers and peasants, reelected a communist government at the height of the end of the Soviet empire did not rate a column inch in the newspapers of Australia.[7] Finally, it assured me of the complexity of the globalization process, one in which a combination of the significant issues of economic security, social justice, and cultural diversity remain at the forefront of the needs of Third World and other marginalized peoples.

I now turn to briefly examine some of the complexities of the globalization process in the context of some contemporary political and social movements in India. Unlike the work of Robertson, in which a culture-centered mode of globalization is presented, I hope to show that rather than being a culturalist response to a new global order, many of the social and political forces for change (of various political agendas) have their genesis in the preindependent (i.e., pre-1947) Indian social formation. It therefore remains problematic to divorce politicocultural struggles from their economic origins. Be that as it may, it must also be recognized that economically, the modern Indian state is forced to compete globally, which has also raised new political struggles and tensions.

If we consider the political development of the Indian states, we indeed find a degree of opposition to the policies of the central government. For instance, in the state of West Bengal, the left-front government, dominated by the Communist Party of India (Marxist) have (democratically) ruled the state continuously since 1977. The security of their power lies as much in the strength of their cadre system for gaining village-level support as in what some would consider old modernist agendas couched in terms of basic rights, land distribution, equality of access, and so forth (see Kohli 1987). Communist politics have for decades had a strong appeal in West Bengal, and although the demise of the Soviet Union has led to an ideological vacuum for some older party members, at the village level at least, basic land reform, literacy, and women's rights are policies that still appeal to the majority of peasant farmers and village dwellers. Massive industrialization in West Bengal, particularly in the large cities like Calcutta, has always ensured a steady stream of support from the members of various trade unions. Thus, while there is a degree of rethinking strategies on behalf of the CPM policy makers to challenge the policies of liberalization by the central government, there does remain a fairly solid belief that socialist state policies can at least protect the Bengali citizen from the ravages of internationalization (how long this remains a solid conviction remains to be seen).

The CPM in West Bengal has not only been concerned with economic agendas, however. Throughout their time in power, various cultural policies for change have been mooted and put in place. This is particularly true in the area of school education. The policy makers have sought to overturn the inherent biases and inequities of the colonial system of education, which was principally directed to the needs and interests of the middles classes. As such, they have been guided by a belief in the realization of broad based social justice initiatives (mass literacy, political empowerment, the elimination of women's oppression, etc.) as being met through the growth of primary and nonformal education. In a sense, they wished to capture the control of education from the middle classes, a control that has persisted since the British first established formal school education in India two hundred years ago.

As an example of its belief in the justice imperative in schooling, in the early 1980s the government of West Bengal attempted to abolish the teaching of English as a compulsory language at the primary level. This was a direct challenge to the middle classes, who saw the advantages of English proficiency in a nation that was becoming more international and also used the language to preserve their culturally elite status. While citing many international studies to support their argument for the abolition of second-language teaching for young children, the CPM could not harness full public support as the middle classes demanded the right to have English taught in the state schools. Ironically, some left critics admonished the CPM for not going far enough, arguing that if it was really serious about the class biases inherent in English, they should have abolished all English medium schools to ensure that no class has an advantage (Acharya 1982). Despite numerous protests the policy went ahead, although it has only met with minimal success. Indeed, informants during my fieldwork often told me how their children, who went to Bengali state primary schools in Calcutta, were taught English as parents demanded that it be taught. Thus, this political struggle was as much to do with the precolonial and colonial cultural preservation of the elite as it was with (postcolonial) class and economic concerns (for more detailed discussion, see Scrase 1993, 75–77).

This case clearly shows that while a globalizing process has led the Indian middles classes to see a distinct social advantage in maintaining English proficiency (i.e., by increasing their educational, social, and cultural ties between India and the West; the possibilities for immigration; and for doing business with Western transnationals in the increasingly unregulated Indian economy), the genesis of the struggle over its abolition was clearly established during the colonial phase of capital accumulation and modern class formation—in the early stages of the formation of the modern world-system. In other words, the Indian middle classes seek to maintain their cultural hegemony by precisely adopting the cultural logic of globalization to their advantage (i.e., that English is a significant "global" language and must be taught), and so ultimately preserve a hierarchical social order in India (see Scrase 1993, 78). Thus, the logic that globalization can lead to a form of personal liberation, in this particular case is inverted in the sense that the possibility for "justice" (essentially, a bigger slice of the economic cake) is monopolized by the middle classes.

However, can other significant sociopolitical problems in India be read in similar ways? Three major issues that are currently dominating Indian social and political life are the religious conflict between Hindus and Muslims at Ayodhya (the destruction of a mosque and the attempted reconstruction of a Hindu temple); the nationalist and quasi-religious claims for separate statehood in the Punjab (Sikhs versus the "Hindu" state) and Kashmir (Muslims versus the "Hindu" state); and a number of ongoing environmental clashes, including the Chipko ("Hugging the Trees") movement in northern India and the battle over the construction of the Sardar Sarovar dam (in an area largely inhabited by tribals and lower-caste Hindus in the Narmada valley in the state of Gujarat in Western India).

To read these movements only through culturalist accounts (i.e,. the rise of Muslim fundamentalism, Sikh religious identity, and Third World indigenization) denies a number of historical-political and economic factors that have led to their reemergence. For example, the 1960s Green Revolution led to the consolidation of the Punjab as the food bowl of India. Subsequently, many farmers have become extremely wealthy and many more seek potential wealth, and so they viewed the Indian (quasi-socialist) state's policy to purchase their food grains at cheaper than expected rates as an unfair attack on their ability and freedom as capitalist farmers. It becomes politically easy to transfer this economic hostility to one with a religious base: "the Hindu state unfairly treats the hardworking Sikh farmer." Likewise, the Hindu-Muslim conflict is rarely presented in class terms in the Western media, let alone the mainstream Indian media. It remains far too easy for Muslim entrepreneurs and traders in India to blame the Hindu state for their not receiving a fair price for their goods or for Muslim students not getting jobs after graduation than seeing these events in light of the anomalies of contemporary capitalism. For Hindus facing the same plight, the problems lay with the Indian state, whereas for Muslims, the problem lies with the Hindu state.

Finally, with the struggle of indigenous Indians for land, it must be accepted that traditional lands are not only a cultural resource, but equally, land remains an economic resource—for the production of food and providing employment for wages. The Narmada dam project is an example in which the ravages of modernization are thrust upon a marginalized poor despite the numerous local and international voices opposed to the dam construction. The well-known social critic Gail Omvedt wrote recently of the social and ecological devastation of the Narmada dam, including the impoverishment of the rural poor and the rural-to-urban drift that is caused by displacement from one's land (1992, 59):

> Equity cannot be achieved by either a "trickle-down method" or distributing a few "subsidies" from the state to the poor, while the real subsidies continue to be given

to industrial, political, and bureaucratic interests . . .. The Narmada project as currently conceived is a "boondoggle," one that emphasizes green revolution agriculture and so the wasteful use of water joined with high levels of chemical fertilisers and pesticides to win gains in productivity. The result will be not only the submergence of lands and forests and the eviction of tribals and other peasants in the Narmada Valley, but also increased distortions and dependence in the economy as a whole. Such a path of development will mean that the economy will become more and more dependent on petroleum-based imports. It will lead to intensified crises, as society becomes increasingly riven by social conflicts, and as land and other natural resources get destroyed by the ravages of energy-extractive development. In a situation in which the left has discredited itself by its failure to develop an alternative vision to state capitalism, the only beneficiaries will be the fundamentalist, semi-fascist Right (1992, 62–63).

What Omvedt thus called for is an analysis—indeed an awareness—of the interconnectedness of the political economy of development with the larger issues regarding the contradictions of development that beset many Third World societies. Moreover, she pointed to the necessity for those engaged in progressive politics in India to rethink the notion of development, and especially the social, political, and ecological turmoil of its unimpeded progress. The age-old belief of many of the Indians that "development equals prosperity via redistribution" needs serious questioning. This, indeed, becomes an ever more important consideration as India speeds itself along the continuing road of economic restructuring, liberalization, and debt management.

Commenting on the way in which the Chipko movement has been recently interpreted, Vandana Shiva astutely comments:

While the historical evolution of movements involves significant contributions from thousands of participants over extended periods, their climaxes are localised in space and time. This facilitates the appropriation of the movements by an individual or group who then erases the contributions of others. Movements . . . are significant precisely because they involve a multiplicity of people and events which contribute to a reinforcement of social change (1988, 68).

In other words, while environmentalism is seen as a progressive outcome of the globalization process ("that we all share this planet called earth"), Shiva argued precisely the opposite: that these (environmental) struggles for justice and change in peripheral nations like India have had long-term historical roots and, importantly, in the case of Chipko, the movement is an explicitly ecological *and* feminist movement (Shiva 1988, 76). These twin objectives for social justice—women's rights and environmentalism—are thus intimately connected.

CONCLUSION

In concluding this chapter, I wish to stress a point made at the beginning. While globalization describes the process of world social and cultural interconnectedness, and despite the rise of what some observers see as cultural movements emanating from the globalization process, I would argue against positions that seek to celebrate the cultural above the social and the economic in globalization theorizing. Such a move to an ahistorical, antimaterialist position denies the actual social base of many contemporary struggles, reducing them to psychosocial struggles about attaining individual and group solidarity and identity. Moreover, I wish to stress that the politics of resistance in India (as witnessed by the rise of various localized social movements fostering various political agendas) is not new, nor can it be theorized simply as a reaction to, or emergence out of, the latest phase of globalization (see the various articles in *Subaltern Studies I* (1982), edited by Ranajit Guha). What is more significant is to examine the way in which the Indian masses are politically mobilized, involving the playing off of economic gain with various political ideologies and agendas that are currently being defined by the bourgeois central government and various regional, chauvinist governments (such as the Bharatiya Janata party), and to consider these trends in the light of the demise of progressive left-wing politics generally in India.

In regard to the situation in India, therefore, the latest phase of globalization must be analyzed with a degree of caution. While the villager in Central India or the urban squatter in Madras both have (limited) access to the global cultural media (television, videocassette recorders, and satellite television), they do not have such a degree of flexibility when it comes to making a livelihood. In India, driven by the state's preoccupation of maintaining high industrial output and economic growth to pay off the even higher accumulating rates of foreign debt, the once quasi-socialist agendas of Indian central governments have taken a decidedly backward step. In particular, mass social programs are being cut back at the same time that the large and consumption-hungry middle classes have emerged in the major cities. Coupled with the economic crisis, these classes are now demanding, and receiving through voting power, much of the comforts of Western society at the expense of the marginalized poor. Mass production has led, for instance, to the decline of the artisan and craftsperson, new agricultural innovations are made at the expense of the livelihoods of seasonal peasant laborers, and rapid urbanization has led to widespread land speculation and bare existence living for a great number of urban poor in outer urban, poorly resourced slums.

Thus, while the continued globalization of capitalism has seen the arrival of 100 million middle-class people in India, satellite television, the growth of an indigenous computer industry, and the rapid spread of mass communications of various sorts, these changes, as a recent writer has suggested, are the hallmarks of a continuing bourgeois revolution in India (Stern 1993). How long this bourgeois revolution will remain a fait accompli for the middle classes is yet to be seen.

NOTES

1. The literature speaks of numerous terms to describe global social change. To describe these changes in terms of a *process*, apart from globalization, we have the following terms: postmodernization, glocalization, internationalism, shifts toward global interdependence, transnationalization, post-fordism, worldism, and the latest entrant, McDonaldization (Ritzer 1992). Moreover, in terms of changes that constitute a global *structure* of various kinds, we have: the consumer society, the postindustrial society, the risk society, the modern world system, the three worlds, the global ecumene, global unicity, and of course, the global village.

2. Sklair (1991) is one writer in particular who focused his analysis of globalization on the rise of transnational corporations and the global effects of transnational practices, especially through the culture-ideology of consumerism.

3. Although, I might add, Wallerstein (1991) has more recently given attention to the complex way in which culture is formed and mediated within the world system.

4. One only needs to see the writings of, for example, Jeremy Tunstall (1977) or the various contributions to Mattelart and Siegelaub (1983,1989) for trenchant analyses of these processes.

5. As one of the largest nongovernmental organizations, CAA aims to assist Third World and indigenous peoples by giving aid and other forms of developmental assistance. It is similar to OXFAM in England.

6. On this point, Robertson (1992), apparently in a contradiction to his appeals to the autonomy of culture and in one of his more materialistic moods, wrote:

> Global capitalism both promotes and is conditioned by cultural homogeneity *and* cultural heterogeneity. The production and consolidation of difference and variety are an essential ingredient of contemporary capitalism, which is, in any case, increasingly involved with a variety of *micro*-markets (national-cultural, racial and ethnic; genderal; social-stratificational; and so on). At the same time, micro-marketing takes place within the contexts of increasingly universal-global economic practices (1992, 173; original emphasis).

7. Ironically, the fact that India has now adopted the economic liberalization path has led the Australian media to suddenly rediscover India as a likely economic ally in the Indian Ocean region.

REFERENCES

Acharya, Poromesh. 1982. "Abolition of English at the Primary Level in West Bengal." *Economic and Political Weekly* 17, no.4:124–28.

Albrow, Martin, and Elizabeth King, eds. 1990. *Globalization, Knowledge and Society: Readings from International Sociology.* London: Sage.

Amin, Samir. 1990. *Maldevelopment: Anatomy of a Global Failure.* London: Zed.

Arnason, Johann. 1990. "Nationalism, Globalization and Modernity." In Mike Featherstone, ed., *Global Culture: Nationalism, Globalization and Modernity.* London: Sage, 207–36.

Cardoso, Fernando Henrique. 1993. "North-South Relations in the Present Context: A New Dependency?" In M. Carnoy, M. Castells, S. Cohen, and F. H. Cardoso, eds., *The New Global Economy in the Information Age.* University Park: Pennsylvania State University Press, 149–59.

Crook, Stephen, Jan Pakulski, and Malcolm Waters. 1992. *Postmodernization: Change in Advanced Society.* London: Sage.

Featherstone, Mike, ed. 1990. *Global Culture: Nationalism, Globalization and Modernity.* London: Sage.

Fukuyama, Francis. 1992. *The End of History and the Last Man.* New York: Free Press.

Giddens, Anthony. 1990. *The Consequences of Modernity.* Cambridge: Polity.

Guha, Ranajit, ed. 1982. *Subaltern Studies I: Writing on South Asian History and Society.* New Delhi: Oxford.

Harvey, David. 1989. *The Condition of Postmodernity.* Oxford: Basil Blackwell.

King, Anthony D., ed. 1991. *Culture, Globalization and the World-System: Contemporary Conditions for the Representation of Identity.* London: Macmillan.

Kohli, Atul. 1987. *The State and Poverty in India.* London: Cambridge University Press.

Lauderdale, Pat. Forthcoming. "Homogenous Development as Deviance in the Diverse World: Frank Justice Rather than Frankenstein Injustice." In S. Chew and R. Denemark, eds., *The Underdevelopment of Development.*

McGrew, Anthony. 1992. "A Global Society?" In S. Hall, D. Held, and A. McGrew, eds., *Modernity and Its Futures.* Cambridge: Polity.

Mattelart, A., and Siegelaub, S., eds. 1983. *Communication and Class Struggle.* Vol. 2. New York: International General.

———. 1989. *Communication and Class Struggle.* Vol. 3. New York: International General.

Omvedt, Gail. 1992. "Fount of Plenty or Bureaucratic Boondoggle? India's Narmada Project" *Capitalism, Nature, Socialism* 3, no.4:47–64.

Ritzer, George. 1992. *The McDonaldization of Society: An Investigation Into the Changing Character of Contemporary Social Life.* London: Pine Forge Press.

Robertson, Roland. 1992. *Globalization: Social Theory and Global Culture.* London: Sage.

Scrase, Timothy J. 1993. *Image, Ideology and Inequality: Cultural Domination, Hegemony and Schooling in India.* New Delhi: Sage.

Shiva, Vandana. 1988. *Staying Alive: Women, Ecology and Development.* London: Zed Books.

Sklair, Leslie. 1991. *The Sociology of the Global System.* Brighton, UK: Harvester Wheatsheaf.

Stern, Robert W. 1993. *Changing India: Bourgeois Revolution on the Subcontinent.* Cambridge: Cambridge University Press.

Tomlinson, John. 1991. *Cultural Imperialism.* London: Pinter Publishers.

Tunstall, Jeremy. 1977. *The Media Are American.* New York: Colombia University Press.

Wallerstein, Immanuel. 1974. *The Modern World System.* New York: Academic Press.

———. 1980. *The Modern World System II.* New York: Academic Press.

———. 1991. "The National and the Universal: Can There Be Such a Thing as World Culture?" In Anthony D. King, ed., *Culture, Globalization and the World-System: Contemporary Conditions for the Representation of Identity.* London: Macmillan, 91–105.

Wolf, Eric R. 1982. *Europe and the People without History.* Berkeley: University of California Press.

Worsley, Peter. 1984. *The Three Worlds: Culture and Development.* London: Weidenfeld and Nicolson.

Young, Iris Marion. 1990. *Justice and the Politics of Difference.* Princeton, NJ: Princeton University Press.

10

Global Manufacturing, Liberalization, and Indian Leather Workers

Ruchira Ganguly-Scrase

Neoliberal policies are emblematic of the new global order. While it is becoming widely recognized that policies of unregulated international commerce will generate greater income inequality, both within and between nations (Cardoso 1993; MacEwan 1994; Nash 1994, 10–13), the accounts of the lived experience of people in the periphery remain a neglected area of research.[1] In this chapter, I focus on the experience of a group of Indian leather workers (the Rabi Das) undergoing a radical socioeconomic transformation. Based on my study of these workers who reside in Krishnagar, a provincial town near Calcutta, it is argued that they have not benefited from the generation of wealth resulting from the liberalization of foreign investment policy in India.[2] Thus, this chapter adds to the mounting evidence that the dramatic shift in economic policy, in accordance with the structural adjustment requirements of the IMF and rapid opening up to the world market, will polarize Indian society as never before (Singh 1993; Vanaik 1993).

World-systems analysis asserts the primacy of a single global dynamic. Some critics of this approach point to the predictability of outcomes (Trimberger 1979; Roseberry 1989, 12) while others suggest its systemic forces to be unmediated by agency (Ram 1991, 235). It is not my intention to resolve these problems here. Rather, this chapter attempts to integrate the richly textured experiences of people with larger systems (cf. Fischer and Marcus 1986; Nash 1981). Therefore, I make the reasonable assumption that the internal condition of the Rabi Das has been shaped by processes of incorporation into the capitalist world system. In the Indian context, the neomarxist analysis by Caplan (1987) argued that community studies should be deemed incomprehensible if they avoid a consideration of the influences that shape the dynamics of Indian society, namely, the establishment of a colonial presence, the demands of industrialization, the struggle for independence, and the country's absorption into a postcolonial economic system dominated by a capitalist mode of production. My concern as an ethnographer does not lie in the analysis of the macrostructures themselves. Rather, it aims to supplement abstract paradigms of political economy "with more empirical evidence, with . . . ethnographic documentary that would 'fill out' the theoretical scaffolding" (Sullivan 1990, 262). Moreover, the separation of the "micro" and "macro" yields a false dichotomy in ethnographic accounts. Burawoy (1991, 5–6) suggested that the face-to-face, everyday interactions of the micro world often reveal the macro principles of wider forces, such as the economy or even the world-system. Thus, ethnography and theory are inextricably linked. As Geertz (1973, 25) argued, extracting theoretical elements from ethnographic description results in the latter becoming commonplace and vacant. Therefore, implicit in my ethnographic approach is a continual embedding of theory in the ethnographic description.

Recent theorizing on the globalization process has emphasized the significance of the localized analysis of world capitalism (Hall 1991). Needless to say, the linking of the micro world of a neighborhood or "community" to the wider process of global capitalism remains problematic. Most ethnographic studies of the globalization of industrialization focus on the experiences of indigenous people as they confront the *direct* consequences of transnational capitalist production, such as the factory, mine, or plantation (Nash 1979; Taussig 1980; Robinson 1986). By contrast, my account of the artisans involved in shoemaking in India concentrates on the *indirect* effects of international capitalism on their lives. Moreover, while the Rabi Das do not produce for the world market, they are undoubtedly linked to the world economy through their consumption of goods produced nationally and internationally.[3]

In this chapter, I therefore emphasize the subtle, and seemingly inconspicuous, links between the internationalization of the leather industry and the changes in the lives of the Rabi Das. This case study reveals a global logic to the increased economic marginalization and stresses the need to examine the detailed ethnographic and historical aspects at the local level. Following Lakha (1988), I would further contend that historical developments in the Indian setting and its regional variant of class analysis may even become obscured if relations at the level of the world-economy are emphasized at the expense of ignoring politicoideological dimensions. In particular, the way in which the Rabi Das have responded to their increasing displacement from the promised benefits of economic liberalization indicates that the experiences of the poor are not homogenous.

My findings show that only a few Rabi Das gained upward social mobility. In the past, as artisans the leather workers reproduced themselves through their transmission of skills and the ideology of work, but today they face economic redundancy. The vagaries of the international market means that as petty producers, the opportunities for success remain limited despite the degree to which they have striven for self-improvement. Global integration and the rising insecurity of subsistence sectors in the peripheral zones, alluded to elsewhere (Nash 1994), resonates in the experiences of the Rabi Das. However, it is the localized expression of class inequalities that created the subtle shift in the nature of their social and cultural subordination taking them from a caste-based position defined by ritual pollution to a position of cultural subordination, generated by their redefinition as superfluous labor.

Gender relations assumed a new dimension as a result of the changes in women's work. The disappearance of home-based subsistence activities reinforced a repressive domestic ideology, despite the fact that women now routinely enter the labor force. This highlights the major contradictions for women's status in India arising from the pattern of capitalist accumulation (Sharma 1985). Evidently, entry into wage labor does not guarantee an enhancement of women's position in society (Mies 1982). My findings on gender relations confirm that the capitalist restructuring of subsistence economies can successfully accommodate preexisting gender ideologies.

In order to contextualize the Rabi Das experience, I draw attention to the economy and organization of society in Bengal and in Krishnagar. Consideration is given to the particular dynamics of local economic development and its connections to broader processes. I begin with a brief outline of the present condition of the Rabi Das and a look at how they have fared over the last two decades with the capitalist expansion of the Indian economy and its further integration into the global market.

GLOBAL INTEGRATION AND THE PRESENT CONDITION OF THE RABI DAS

Since 1991, India has pursued a policy of economic liberalization, which constituted a reversal of earlier policies of protecting domestic industry. The Indian example is of special interest due to complex geopolitical alliances and the presence of an indigenous bourgeoisie that enabled it in the past to benefit from the political space provided by the superpower rivalry, receiving increasing assistance for its ambitious industrial projects. According to Dutt (1984, 9–36), the Indian capitalist class consists of a genuine national bourgeoisie (rather than a comprador class) which, like any other capitalist class, wants to avoid stagnation. Chronic problems of the Indian economy, embodied in the underutilization of capacity, lack of demand, and lack of investment, necessitate the opening up of new markets. Thus, the desire to open up and institute economic reforms are not merely an outcome of the dictates of the IMF and World Bank ("Uncle Sam the Bully " 1992), but also concur with the interests of the Indian ruling classes.

For the last ten years, the leather industry in India has become export oriented, with foreign exchange earnings exceeding 13 billion rupees.[4] This pushed up the domestic price of leather, with the result that artisans with limited investment are denied access to materials.[5] The growth of the middle class in India also created a heavy domestic demand for high-quality leather products. The increasing effect of the internationalization of capital is also visible in the leather industry. Due to severe environmental pollution (Krishnan 1990, 149) and the rising cost of labor (Gupta 1990, 120), many tanneries from the core have been relocated in the peripheral zones. India is the world's largest single source of raw leather (because of its 15 million-plus cattle population) (India 1985, 190). The recent liberalization of the foreign investment policy led to the formation of many joint ventures. Moreover, the growing potential of the Indian market also led to imported high investment technologies in the leather and the allied chemical industries. Many large transnational companies are now firmly established in India. Bata, which started manufacturing in the 1960s, is the largest organized company and it buys up the bulk of the leather and trade in the local, as well as the international, markets.

Since the 1970s, the introduction of cheap plastics, polythene, and rubber footwear, together with the mechanization of the footwear and leather industries, began displacing the Rabi Das workers. As plastic sandals replaced leather, repair work, which could not be done on plastic sandals, also declined, resulting in diminished incomes. Further, the wearers of plastic sandals, which were cheap, discarded them once they tore. By the late 1970s, while repair work declined, only a few artisans were absorbed into the emerging modern sector of leather production.

Thus, the modernization and internationalization of India's leather industry had serious effects on the Rabi Das. They are unable to compete with the cheap plastic footwear bought by low-income earners, while at the same time, they lost high-income clients who once used custom-made shoes but who now prefer the high-technology fashions. The Rabi Das also lack capital and technology to purchase and process high quality leather to supply the top end of the market. The present state of leather work among the residents of the neighborhood indicates that within the thirty-seven households (with a total population of 225), twenty-six are engaged in leather work. In four households, apart from the head there is one additional member of the family who has a separate enterprise. The majority of the households (50 percent) have taken to repairing bags, suitcases, bicycle tires, and bicycle seats. The two skilled craftsmen who work as wage laborers do so for the successful shop owners.

It would be incorrect to assume, however, that the misfortunes of the Rabi Das are entirely attributed to the operations of the leather industry. Although their livelihoods are tied to the fluctuations in the leather market, they experience commonalities in material inequality with the urban poor in Krishnagar. Nevertheless, there remains the need to contextualize the Rabi Das experiences in view of the particular type of capitalist penetration that has affected the internal development of Krishnagar.

LIMITED DEVELOPMENT IN KRISHNAGAR

The Rabi Das are not unique in experiencing severe social dislocation; they are constitutive of a broader social reality in West Bengal. Krishnagar, like the Nadia district in which it is located, remains largely underdeveloped. Nadia district was first tied to the world market during the colonial period through the commodity production of indigo. Krishnagar, the district headquarters, developed key administration and resource functions to foster colonial capitalism. The major role assigned to Krishnagar was that of coordinating the transportation of raw materials and goods procured from the hinterland to Calcutta. As its main function was to secure the needs of the colonial export trade, developments in the rural areas were neglected. Krishnagar thus became the periphery of Calcutta, which was itself a periphery of the metropolitan center of Britain, the ultimate destination of these goods. Krishnagar's significance could not be compared to the great industrial and port cities such as Calcutta and Bombay, which grew and became important under British rule.

Today, Krishnagar (and the district as a whole) remains agriculturally backward (compared to other districts in West Bengal) and has experienced urbanization without industrialization. The lack of industrialization should be understood with reference to the general decline of industry in West Bengal since Independence. Following Independence in 1947 and the subsequent partition of India, a massive influx of refugees flowed into West Bengal. Krishnagar, which was located in a border district, faced a drastic strain on its already scarce resources. The Bangladesh war in 1971 witnessed a further influx of refugees. The partitioning of Bengal, which resulted in the loss of raw materials, coupled with the political equations of the postindependence period, relegated West Bengal to a much less important position. As the capital shifted to Delhi, Calcutta's loss of its political preeminence contributed to its failure to attract industry to the state. It is also claimed that the central government discriminated by limiting the granting of industrial licences to West Bengal. Despite being the largest urban agglomeration, Calcutta does not receive grants equal to those of Delhi even though it faced a refugee problem after partition and also after the creation of Bangladesh. Calcutta, its hinterland, and the relay towns stand at the very opposite of Delhi, which received appreciably more from the central government, enabling it to place its relay towns and hinterland at the forefront of India's agricultural modernization (Racine 1990, 74–86).

Overt class conflict and the dominance of the communist parties both in and outside parliamentary politics in West Bengal led to a process of the marginalization of the Communist-led Left Front government from the mainstream of national policy formation in India. Kohli's (1987, 95–143) insightful analysis of the role of the (Marxist) (Communist Party of India) (CPM) showed that during the 1960s and 1970s, the party's doctrine of class confrontation eventually led to the demise of the United Front ministry under central government–sponsored repression. The radical demands of the trade unions tended to keep capital away from West Bengal. However, since the return of the Left Front government, dominated by the CPM, in 1977, the party has adopted a reformist and moderate agenda, focusing largely on developmentalist programs in rural areas. Consequently, its power base lies among the agrarian population, while support in the urban areas remain ambiguous. Although the CPM has wrought some remarkable improvements in the agricultural sector in the areas surrounding Krishnagar, it has been unable to stop a decline in the living conditions in urban areas. The Rabi Das perceptions of the CPM are characteristically negative. One of my informants aptly summarized the Rabi Das view:

> After CPM came in we have not gained any opportunities. The common people are completely at a loss. The price of things in the market—what is Jyoti Basu [the Chief Minister of West Bengal] doing [about it]? He has kept the government workers well. What are they doing in the villages? They are giving them loans, and keeping them in line. But as for the small artisan, what are they doing? We can say, even in this day and age Rajiv Gandhi [the former Indian Prime Minister] has given loans to small businesses.

THE RABI DAS

In very general terms, the situation of the Rabi Das may be conceptualized in the following way. They settled in Bengal in the nineteenth century as tanners and shoemakers and were part of a large migration stream from the neighboring state of Bihar to Bengal (*India* 1901, 143). Rural Bihar was badly affected by colonial policies, leading to pauperization and out-migration (Das 1987, 16–20).[6] Since there were no leather workers indigenous to Bengal, there was very little initial competition or threat to their livelihood. However, this was a low-caste occupation and they were literally settled on the margins of Bengali society, confined to the outskirts of town. Their livelihood was dependant on the reciprocal obligations of their patrons, the Bengali landed gentry. All Rabi Das lived in a subsistence economy, giving their requisite services to the landlord. Before 1947, in preindependent and prepartitioned India, ritual taboos prevented the Rabi Das from close social intercourse with the ritually pure higher castes, since tanning and leather work were considered polluting. In the postindependence years, the demise of the land tenure system in Bengal, legal abolition of untouchability, and, more important, the continual mobilization since the 1940s of a local group of Gandhian social reformers who persuaded them to give up the "unclean" practice of tanning, led the Rabi Das to gain a "clean" status. Paradoxically, however, by turning away from the dirty, grinding work, the Rabi Das failed to capitalize on the changes occurring in the burgeoning leather industry in India.

The social reformers introduced changes that enabled the Rabi Das, who were previously considered wretched and degraded, to gain dignity, greater acceptance by the Bengalis, and an entrenchment of the view of themselves as artisans. The social reformers consciously introduced formal education, "respectable" forms of speech, etiquette, measures concerning health and cleanliness, permanent housing, temperance, and ritual changes that raised the status of the Rabi Das and co-opted them into Bengali culture and into the Congress-backed, capitalist, developmental economic ideology. However, this very redefinition of the Rabi Das as artisans seems to have retarded their successful entry into the post-Independence, capitalist, developmental economy.

RABI DAS CLASS IDENTITY: *BHADRALOK/CHOTOLOK* NEXUS

The status that the Rabi Das attained through their interaction with Bengali middle-class social reformers was crucial in terms of gaining respectability in wider society. Ironically, however, this accommodation, coupled with the changing evaluation of social status, played a major role in closing the doors to entrepreneurial success in the leather industry. Thus, an examination of the nature of the local system of class relations helps us to understand the present social dynamic of the Rabi Das. The commonly known class-based patterns of social stratification of advanced capitalist societies cannot explain fully the social condition of the Rabi Das. Most Indian anthropologists emphasize the interlinkage of class with caste, kinship, and family systems, but in Bengal, there is yet another notion that organizes society. This is the great divide between the categories of *bhadralok* ("respectable people") and *chotolok* ("lowly people"), which governs cultural life, social interaction, everyday language, and the like in Bengali society (Sinha and Bhattacharya 1969).

The *bhadralok* are literally called "respectable people," and they emerged as a new social group in the late eighteenth century. The *bhadralok* were distinguished by their refined behavior and cultivated taste, but not necessarily substantial wealth and power. An opposite category was the *abhadralok* (non-*bhadralok*) or, to use a more derogatory term, *chotolok*, meaning "lowly people."

The *bhadralok* were the traditional literati and the first to gain entry into urban professional occupations. They were distinguished by their "social estimation of honor" in the Weberian sense. Although originally linked to upper castes in contemporary Bengali society, they are a distinct status group that is not coterminous with caste or class (Mukherjee 1975).

A major characteristic of the *bhadralok* came to be their aversion to manual labor. In nineteenth-century colonial Bengal, *bhadralok* dominance became evident and *bhadralok* influence in education, social reform and literature was widespread. By the end of British rule in 1947, the *bhadralok* in Bengal had been economically eclipsed (since they had paid little attention to entrepreneurial pursuits) by the traditional castes of Indian merchants and money-lenders from the provinces of Punjab and Rajasthan (Buruma 1986, 70). Changed from their original position for two centuries as a reasonably well-off, educated, and highly cultured status group, the *bhadralok* are now a heterogeneous group and are often poor.

Nowadays, the consumption of material goods has become an increasingly important determinant of status. Conceptually, this reinforces the transition from the emphasis on refined behavior to a focus on material wealth. At the same time, although economically the *bhadralok* have declined, they have maintained their ideological dominance in West Bengal. The overall behavior of the *bhadralok* may be explained in terms of Bourdieu's notion of a "legitimate culture" (Bourdieu 1984), that is, the process by which the dominant classes and class fractions seek to universalize their cultural tastes, language, and bodily representations. The outstanding feature of social interaction in contemporary Bengali society is that people interpret an outwardly poverty stricken appearance with being *chotolok*, indicating the ambiguity and the changing nature of *bhadralok* culture itself. In Krishnagar, the Rabi Das face the contempt and disdain of some *bhadralok* due to their poverty rather than their caste, which a priori defines and demeans them as *chotolok*. Needless to say, the Rabi Das have come to occupy a lowly position which has its origins both in the premodern and the contemporary systems of social stratification.

THE IMPACT OF GANDHIANS

The work of Gandhians among the Rabi Das was governed by a notion of individual mobility through education but also by certain Brahmanical ritual ideas. At times they used existing idioms to rationalize the changes they wanted to bring about. Among other things, the Rabi Das were persuaded to give up their leather-tanning work. The reformers regarded it as a health hazard because of the foul smells and fumes emitted. However, the argument was also put forward by them in terms of such work not being the proper caste occupation for the Rabi Das. They also defined it as an unclean task for those who were really cobblers. Interestingly, the Rabi Das nowadays recall with contempt "the dirty nature of tanning" which, they say, "was not our real work."

As time went on, the Rabi Das men became more pliable as they themselves embarked on the quest for *bhadralok* respectability. They aimed to improve themselves, educate themselves, and raise themselves up to the level of their social superiors. Maintaining cleanliness and *bhadralok* patterns of interpersonal behavior greatly appealed to the youth. They defined an absence of these features among the Rabi Das as stigmatizing. Persistent ridicule by other *bhadralok* of their ways made the Rabi Das continually aware of the difference. The younger people of the day accepted the reformers' version of their own society and the formal education that would free them from economic hardships. The volunteers created a need for respectability and inculcated a belief that it was ,in fact, possible to get out of the inferior social position ascribed by caste. The declining importance of physical untouchability in Bengali society, the legal abolition of untouchability, and some mobility through education helped this belief. Therefore, the conscious adoption of middle-class speech and aspirations, such as the desire for salaried employment, took place. Parents began to encourage their sons to pursue schooling instead of taking up leather work. Thus, it would seem that the rise and fall of Rabi Das artisans is connected as much to the influence of Gandhians as it is to the changing economic circumstances in the post Independence period.

HISTORICAL PHASES AND RABI DAS FORTUNES

The work of the Rabi Das males can be classified into three historical periods. These coincide with the general patterns in the world economy and are broadly reflected in the Rabi Das experience, namely, (1) the integration of India in the colonial phase and the relative stability of accumulation in the postwar years, (2) the fiscal crisis precipitated by the rising oil prices in the 1970s and (3) the current triumph of neoliberalism on a world scale.

The first phase started in the nineteenth century with their settlement in Krishnagar, when they worked as tanners and shoemakers, and ended when the social reformers brought tanning to a halt in the late 1940s. It seems that the rewards of their work in the initial period of settlement were adequate but, by the time the social reformers appeared in their midst, they had declined precipitously.

In the next phase, the Rabi Das, equipped with literacy, sought employment other than their hereditary caste occupation. In the third and the current phase, the decline in the availability of leather work, together with other forms of employment, has left them in a quandary.

It should be obvious that in the first phase, when the Rabi Das worked at tanning and shoemaking, they were pursuing an occupation that was protected by caste mores. Being in possession of a very low-status occupation, they had no competitors or threats from outside.

The social reformers provided them with a new life-style, good housing, sobriety, literacy, schooling for children, refined speech, and etiquette. They also helped them discover a dignity in their craft and a taste for *bhadralok* status. Fortunately, this came about at a time when they could also build themselves an economic niche as craftsmen. Hard work and entrepreneurialism did not make them rich. However, it did enable them to have faith in the volunteers, their Congress, and the postindependence government. It was as if the Protestant ethic had delivered its promise of success. Some of the questions that need to be raised are these: was the transformation inculcated into the Rabi Das a necessary, or even sufficient, condition for the economic success in the second phase? Is it not possible that they would have succeeded in the economic arena, simply because there was a demand for their work and product? Can we argue that by inculcating middle-class (*bhadralok*) values, the volunteers weakened, if not destroyed, their potential for turning into ruthless entrepreneurs? I envisage at least a theoretical possibility that some persons among the Rabi Das would have succeeded as entrepreneurs had they used kinship and communal (that is, premodern) ties to turn the other Rabi Das into a pliant, exploitable workforce. If this is so, it can be argued with some validity that the Gandhians' gifts of *bhadralok* aspirations and dignity in work in fact retarded this process.

The question is, why do the Rabi Das, old and young, hold no blame against the reformers for the current malaise? It was the reformers who taught that artisanship was the way, not so much to riches, but to an honest and clean livelihood that was worthy of respect. The reformers gave the Rabi Das a work ethic and an implicit promise of unending artisanal work life. In doing so, the reformers were true to the Gandhian ideology but at odds with the economic reality of capitalist industrial development. Of course, the reformers themselves were not prescient, and even after they became aware that artisanal activity by itself was not viable, they did little to change their belief or to take action to safeguard the future of their wards, such as establishing an artisan cooperative.

The answer to the question lies in the fact that the reformers gave the Rabi Das that which they value the most, even now. To the old men, who remember the past, it is the dignity of work, the education with which to see the world in new ways, and the "clean life" that are important, while to the young it is the *bhadralok* "diacritical marks" (such as dress habits and speech etiquette) that are significant.

GENDER HIERARCHIES

It is in the arena of emerging gender relations that the effects of the new economic policies of restructuring assume critical significance. The devaluation of the rupee, an outcome of structural adjustment, drastically affected the household survival of the Rabi Das. Growing inflation and declining living standards meant that to ensure survival, increasing numbers of women entered into wage labor. Paradoxically, however, the increasing entry of women (specifically, unmarried girls) into wage labor is accompanied by the universal reluctance of the young men to take up shoemaking, which once was the sole income for the household.

Changes in the leather industry largely prompted the decline of male child labor. The need for male child labor diminished as boys are no longer required in the work now performed by the Rabi Das. While parents recognize that for their sons, leather work is not a viable occupation, they like them to find other sorts of work. Under the circumstances, it is the girls who are sent out to work as domestic servants while the sons are allowed the luxury of waiting until a suitable job is found.

Structural adjustment policies have heightened the sexual division of labor. The outside work that women are now forced to do because of economic necessity has not resulted in the loosening of patriarchal control. On the contrary, strict control is maintained over women's mobility. It is sanctioned by preexisting ideologies associated with notions of what are "appropriate" gender roles. The proper conduct for a woman is continually emphasized. A commonly expressed sentiment is, "A woman is the keeper of the family's honor, and once a certain level of well-being is reached, she will cease wage labor and be kept in the home." Highly routinized statements like this are used about the propriety of a woman's behavior so that she does not risk becoming sexually or morally "loose." The family impresses on a young working woman that her current lot is only temporary and will cease one day, when things become better. Ideologically, such statements serve to keep women in a constantly dependent position even as they continue to work indefinitely.

The ideologies of kinship and gender intersect with the current economic transformations in complex and contradictory ways. The tendency to define women as the signifiers of family honor and community are congruent with the emergence of neofamilial and communal ideologies in India. As structural adjustment policies fail to provide the basic needs of people, alternative ideologies based on Hindu and Muslim fundamentalism gain currency.[7] Both the state and fundamentalist movements play a key role in representing women as the repositories of communal and national identity. More significantly, the weakening of patriarchal control over women in the family, stemming from capitalist development, is militated by the renewed control over women by the state. The state plays a major role in indirectly sponsoring the rise of fundamentalist organizations, promoting many conservative ideologies through the media and so forth (Chhachhi 1989). In this context, Rabi Das women are under constant pressure to conform to a model of femininity based on their familial identity. The ideal role for a woman is to occupy herself in domestic work.

Existing hierarchical relationships based on gender and age are accommodated to the changing economic circumstances. Although for many Rabi Das women, laboring outside their homes is a necessity, they are still considered supplementary earners. For example, I found that in households where women's income underpinned the survival of the household, they always said that their wages were *upri* ("on-top," or supplementary). In fact, women worked because they accept the premise of "the domestic economy" ideologically, whereby men were considered the ultimate providers while women were responsible for domestic work. Although occasionally women protested, mostly they hoped to go back to housework through the economic success of their sons, if not their husband. Women did not necessarily feel exploited by their husbands because they were committed to the well-being of their family and felt greater exploitation from working in *bhadralok* households as domestic servants than they did at home. Despite the relative affluence of the urban middle classes in Krishnagar, Rabi Das women who worked for them as domestic servants could not expect high wages.

Women's experiences reflect their multiple burdens and are indicative of the deep class divisions that exist in Krishnagar. Men are simultaneously limited by job opportunities, which confine them largely to the hereditary caste occupation, and are further constrained by the operations of the leather industry. Their success remains limited in this expanding industry since the capital required to establish themselves as competitors is beyond their reach. An inability to capitalize businesses in this otherwise lucrative industry generates an overwhelming sense of frustration.

While the Rabi Das do not characterize the past as idyllic, what frustrates them is that the potential for expansion and affluence was foreclosed by the sudden changes in the leather industry. They are quite aware that there is money to be made from a developed leather industry but do not have the necessary capital to start up and compete with large firms. They feel completely powerless as the comments of a Rabi Das man conveys:

Our sons are not turning to this craft. It is almost ruined due to polythene. Bata
has displaced us . . .. The way the jute mills are closing, the way they are being
ruined because of synthetics, our trade is also being destroyed because of
polythene. Our government is exporting leather overseas and our countrymen are
wearing cheap plastics. The export market buys a lot. The government earns
crores (millions). We could say that the government should reduce the price [of
leather], but how can a government run without revenue? That is justified. What
can we do? We are in hard times.

Ironically, such views exemplify the legitimation of the state's ideology of its fair
and just mediating role. Despite the limited concrete assistance and improvements
effected in India, "both the state and the ruling classes . . . promulgat[e] a view that
they are concerned with the welfare of the masses" (Caplan 1987, 186–87). Studies
of the Indian Five Year Plan (Chatterjee and Sen 1988) have demonstrated that
policies have little significance in terms of economic indicators of production or
distribution and function mainly as political-ideological instruments of manufacturing consent. For the Rabi Das there is a continual tension between acceptance and
rejection of the discourses of welfare. They are in the double bind of preferring the
government as a neutral arbitrator (as opposed to kin), while rejecting its rationalist
mode of operation. Thus, the government's failures are shifted onto themselves as
the inevitable imperfections of a generally responsible regime.

DESPAIR, NOT CLASS STRUGGLE

The specific situation of India in the new global political economy can be seen
on two levels, one on affluent internationalized sector and the other inconsequential
to the global economy of which the Rabi Das are a part. However, the response of
the Rabi Das to this process have *not* been radical class struggle spearheaded by the
Communist party. Indeed, there is an atmosphere of overwhelming sense of
frustration and despair. The unemployed, disenchanted, and disenfranchised youth
have become supporters of the Conservative and Pro-Hindu parties. On the whole,
the Rabi Das constitute a conservative political force. The historical association
with the Gandhians and their efforts at individual self-improvement have partly
paved way for a conservative ideology. While there are pockets of resistance
emerging across India, my findings suggest that the responses of the poor cannot be
homogenized. Scrase noted (in Chapter 9 of this volume) that forces of resistance
are not merely a response to the recent globalization process but a continuing
struggle by people to defend their rights to earn a livelihood. His account is a
significant reminder of the anti-systemic struggles taking place in the periphery, an
issue often glossed over in the contemporary literature celebrating globalization.
While it is important to counter the bias, it would be equally dangerous to valorize
resistance. The case of the Rabi Das is an exemplar of accommodation. In
Krishnagar, most of the urban poor are supporters of the CPM and have been
vehemently opposed to the imposition of the IMF and the Dunkel Draft, and they

wish for an alternative social system. By contrast, the Rabi Das want a stake in the system rather than to see it dismantled.

Historically, the Rabi Das gave their support to the Congress party, mainly due to the Gandhian reformers' loose associations with Congress in the 1950s through their active campaign to bring the Rabi Das housing subsidies, water, electricity, and schooling. The volunteers brought important Congress personnel, such as the state governor and well-known Congress members of parliament (MPs) to visit the neighborhood. The Rabi Das gained a measure of prestige through their association with famous dignitaries and the elders still speak with pride about these famous visitors. Although the old nationalist volunteers at present do not in any way encourage the Rabi Das to vote for the Congress due to high levels of corruption in the party, local Congress politicians at the municipal, state ,and national levels continue to capitalize on the Gandhian legacy.

One possible route for the Rabi Das out of their economic malaise, and the only avenue to seizing the opportunities in the expanding leather industry which is open to them, is the formation of some type of joint enterprise or cooperatives. However, the Rabi Das also reject this strategy. Underlying the reluctance to form co-operatives is the absence of a community organization. Ironically, it was the Gandhians who were partially responsible for destroying the indigenous Rabi Das community council (the caste *panchayat*) in their efforts to stop alcohol consumption. The council was the venue for resolving communal and intrafamilial disputes, but it was also a venue for convivial drinking. The social reformers were able to convince the Rabi Das that when the council met to deliberate on complaints, the fines it imposed on the offending party were simply a way of raising money for alcohol consumption. With the passing of drinking, the *panchayat* died. Today there is no community decision-making body that can serve as a basis for cooperatives.

CONCLUSION

On a concluding note, I would argue that the case study of the Rabi Das reveals that, not only is there a global logic to their increased economic marginalization, it also demonstrates the fact that success and failure are tied to highly localized processes. Rabi Das subordination in the New World Order must be understood as an outcome both of their structural location and their ideological and political circumstances, which have prevented them from taking advantages of the changing economic conditions.

A frequent criticism directed at dependency and world-system analyses has been the relegation of communities, classes, and groups to a secondary status in developing an overall picture of world capitalist development. Although over a quarter of a century, these approaches have become sophisticated in analyzing the Indian situation in the 1990s, the challenge is to interweave the workings of the global and the local factors. By this, I do not imply that local outcomes are derivative of the global economy. I noted at the outset that the Rabi Das conditions are shaped by the transnationalization of the leather industry. However, I have also shown throughout this chapter that there is a major element of the localized history that gives particularity to the Rabi Das experience, namely, the ideological influence of the Gandhians, that is *independent* of the global processes. Therefore, it is important to recognize the complex and contradictory ways in which ideologies cross-cut economic transformations.

In this chapter, I have outlined the human costs of the Indian economy's further integration into the world market and presented accounts of the lived experience of a community of artisans. I have argued that the internationalization of the leather industry and the general underdevelopment of Krishnagar have indeed contributed to the economic marginalization of the Rabi Das. However, the way in which the Rabi Das has responded to their condition have been unique. Unlike their class counterparts, they have not mobilized against capital. Instead, they want to reap the benefits of the liberalization of the Indian economy. This is, in part, due to the influence of Gandhian social reformers, who were successful in inculcating *bhadralok* middle-class values among the Rabi Das.

For this reason, I would stress the significance of looking at the local system of class relations and its effect on people. Although the Rabi Das did not benefit economically from their adoption of middle-class mores, it is important to recognize the extent of social respectability that they gained. As India becomes more integrated into a global culture, in the future the value of *bhadralok* respectability may become meaningless as the possession of material wealth alone becomes the definer of middle class status. Until this happens, the Rabi Das will continue to feel disenchanted.

Finally, the local system of class also impacts the way in which gender relations are formulated. Growing impoverishment requires women to work outside their homes in wage work. Laboring outside the home is contrary to the ideal of a woman's role, yet even though women are now expected to earn a wage and move beyond the boundaries of the family and community, strict controls are imposed on their mobility. Thus, repressive domestic ideologies are reinforced at the same time that women are expected to work for a wage.

NOTES

1. The recognition of the intra- and international effects is exemplified by the current debates in a number of critical journals such as *Monthly Review: Capitalism, Nature, Socialism; Economic and Political Weekly;* and *Development and Change*.

2. The research for this chapter is based on fieldwork carried out between December 1988 and April 1990 in Krishnagar, a small, and not yet industrialized, town in West Bengal. For further details, see Ganguly-Scrase (1993).

3. The links between the local and global economies are demonstrated in the everyday survival of people in Krishnagar, who rely on goods of diverse types which are produced internationally and then marketed in their town. Agencies for some of the large business houses of India as well as some transnational corporations such as Pepsi have their offices and outlets in the town. There are also fertilizer and agrotechnical shops (which largely sell farming equipment and chemicals marketed by transnational companies).

4. Opening Address by R. K. Srivastava, Conference of All India Leather Industries Association, Calcutta, February 1990.

5. Based on author's interviews with (a) the participants of Lexpo 1989, which included members of both small co-operatives and large exporting enterprises; (b) members of two voluntary agencies; and (c) three independent exporters.

6. Oral histories of the Rabi Das also reveal a belief that their ancestors migrated to Bengal because of its egalitarian tradition, which permitted them to overcome the social discrimination and deprivation suffered in Bihar rather than merely in search for economic rewards.

7. The failure of neoliberal policies has created a crisis of legitimation for the postcolonial Indian state, which in turn has asserted its legitimacy by emphasizing a homogenous national identity. A consequence of this process has been the increasing identification of women in terms of their family and community. For details, see "Review of Women's Studies in India" (1993) and Hassan (1994). Moreover, recent work on the role of the state in constructing gender identities in India shows that the growing demands by the women's movement to protect women against violence have paradoxically relegated women to the familial sphere. For details, see Mukhopadhyay (1994).

REFERENCES

Bourdieu, P. 1984. *Distinction: A Social Critique of the Judgement of Taste.* Cambridge, MA: Harvard University Press.

Burawoy, M., ed. 1991. *Ethnography Unbound: Power and Resistance in the Modern Metropolis.* Berkeley: University of California Press.

Buruma, I. 1986. "A Tale of Two Bengals." In *Far Eastern and Economic Review*, 3 April.

Caplan, L. 1987. *Class and Culture in Urban India: Fundamentalism in a Christian Community.* New York: Clarendon Press.

Cardoso, H. 1993. "North-South Relations in the Present Context: A New Dependency?" In Carnoy, M. Castells, S. Cohen and F. H. Cardoso, eds., *The New Global Economy in the Information Age.* Pennsylvania State University Press, 149–59.

Chatterjee, P., and Sen, A. 1988. "Planning and the Political Process in India: Duality and Differentiation." In A. Bagchi, eds., *The Political Economy of Indian Planning.* Calcutta: Oxford University Press.

Chhachhi, A. 1989. "The State, Religious Fundamentalism and Women: Trends in South Asia." *Economic and Political* Weekly 24, no.11.

Das, A. 1987. "Changel: Three Centuries of an Indian Village." In *Journal of Peasant Studies* 15, no.1.

Dutt, S. 1984. *India and the Third World: Altruism or Hegemony?* London: Zed Press.

Fischer, M. J. and Marcus, G. E. 1986. *Anthropology as Cultural Critique. An Experimental Moment in the Human Sciences.* Chicago: University of Chicago Press.

Ganguly-Scrase, R. 1993. "Labor Class and Community: An Ethnography of the Rabi Das of Krishnagar, India. Unpublished Ph.D. thesis, University of Melbourne.

Geertz, C. 1973. *The Interpretation of Cultures.* London: Hutchinson.

Ghosh, S. K. 1983. "The Indian Bourgeoisie and Imperialism." *Bulletin of Concerned Asian Scholars* 15, no. 3, 2–17.

Gupta, S. 1990. "Training Needs for the Leather Products Sector." *Indian Leather: Digest of Leather News* 23, no. 11, 113–23.

Hall, S. 1991. "Old and New Identities: Old and New Ethnicities." In A. D. King, ed., *Culture, Globalization and the World System: Contemporary Conditions for the Representation of Identity.* Macmillan, 19–39.

Hassan, Z., ed. 1994. *Forging Identities: Gender Communities and the State.* New Delhi: Kali for Women.

India. 1901. *The Census of Bengal.*

———. 1985. *The Seventh Five Year Plan 1985–90.* Vol. 2. New Delhi: Government of India, Planning Commission.

Kohli, A. 1987. *The State and Poverty in India: The Politics of Reform.* Cambridge: Cambridge University Press.

Krishnan, T. 1990. "Relocation of Tanneries—New Concept for Treatment of Pollution of Tanning Industries." *Indian Leather: Digest of Leather News* 23, no. 11, 145–54.

Lakha, S. 1988. *Capitalism and Class in Colonial India : A Case of Ahmedabad.* Delhi: Sterling Publishers.

MacEwan, A. 1994. "Globalization and Stagnation." *Monthly Review* 45, no. 11, 1–16.

Mies, M. 1982. *The Lace Makers of Narsapur: Indian Housewives Produce for the World Market.* London: Zed Press.

Mukherjee, S. N. 1975. "Bhadralok in Bengali Language and Literature: An Essay on the Language of Class and Status." *Bengal Past and Present* 95, no. 2, 225–37.

Mukhopadhyay, M. 1994. "Construction of Gender Identity: Women, State and Personal Laws in India." Unpublished Ph.D. thesis, University of Sussex.

Nash, J. 1979. *We Eat the Mines and the Mines Eat Us: Dependency and Exploitation in Bolivian Mines.* New York: Columbia University Press.

————. 1981. "Ethnographic Aspects of the World System." *Annual Review of Anthropology* 10, 393–423.

————. 1994. "Global Integration and Subsistence Insecurity." *American Anthropologist* 96, no.1, 7–30.

Racine, J. 1990. "Calcutta and Her Hinterland: A Regional and National Perspective." In J. Racine, eds., *Calcutta 1981: The City, Its Crisis and the Debate on Urban Planning and Development.* New Delhi: Concept Publishers, 51–88.

Ram, K. 1991. *Mukkuvar Women: Gender Hegemony and Capitalist Transformation in a South Indian Fishing Community.* Sydney, Australia: Allen and Unwin.

"Review of Women's Studies in India." 1993. *Economic and Political Weekly,* no. 17, 2–44.

Robinson, K. 1986. *Step Children of Progress: The Political Economy of an Indonesian Mining Town.* Albany: State University of New York Press.

Roseberry, W. 1989. *Anthropologies and Histories: Essays in Culture, History and Political Economy.* New Brunswick, NJ: Rutgers University Press.

Sharma, M. 1985. "Caste, Class and Gender: Production and Reproduction in North India." *Journal of Peasant Studies* 12, no. 4, 56–88.

Singh, A. K. 1993. "Social Consequences of New Economic Policies." *Economic and Political Weekly* 28, no. 7, 279–85.

Sinha, S., and Bhattacharya, R. 1969. "Bhadralok and Chotolok in a Rural Area of West Bengal." *Sociological Bulletin* 18, 50–66.

Sullivan, R. 1990. "Marxism and the 'Subject' of Anthropology." In M. Manganaro, ed., *Modernist Anthropology: From Fieldwork to Text.* Princeton, NJ: Princeton University Press, 243–65.

Taussig, M. 1980. *The Devil and Commodity Fetishism.* Chapell Hill: University of North Carolina Press.

Trimberger, K. 1979. "World-Systems Analysis: The Problem of Unequal Development." *Theory and Society* 8, no. 1.

"Uncle Sam the Bully" (editorial). 1992. *India Today,* 31 May, 11.

Vanaik, A. 1993. "Imperialism, Soviet Collapse and Implications for the Post Colonial World." *Economic and Political Weekly* 38, no. 5, 37–46.

11

Globalization, Hegemony, and Political Conflict: The Case of Local Politics in Zurich, Switzerland

Stefan Kipfer

For a number of years now, the "global economy" has entered the realm of daily political discourse through images constructed and diffused by editorialists, advertisers, and newscasters. In these representations of the global economy, which constitute the core of the "rhetoric of globalization" (Robertson 1991), it appears most often as an established entity acting as an external force of constraint on the specific, institutionally bounded spheres of "politics." In this reifying account, neoliberal proponents of the globalization thesis draw heavily on postulates of neoclassical economics, according to which the economy is seen as a mechanical, Newtonian system driven by the time- and space-less laws of atomistic behavior (Altvater 1993). Following this logic which, unfortunately, some Marxists are prone to reproduce (Block 1986), globalization can be seen as the transposition of economic necessity to an abstract level beyond jurisdictional boundaries.

As Karl Polanyi (1957) pointed out long ago, the bourgeois belief in the self-realization of capital is utopian. Although capitalist strive toward the elimination of spatial and temporal boundaries during periods of economic crisis, the reproduction of capital ultimately depends on its access to the conditions of production (labor-power, ecology, and urban space), which cannot be produced by capital itself but must be mobilized politically in particular times and spaces (O'Connor 1988). As recent clashes in Chiapas, Los Angeles, and the French countryside have indicated, the mobilization of noncommodities for the purpose of global accumulation is a fundamentally conflictive process. "Globalization' can thus be seen as a process of restructuring which is concretized by multiple 'projects-in-the-making' to change the ways in which spaces are controlled and re-inserted into the world economy (Swyngedouw 1992).

In this chapter, I attempt to demonstrate the relatively contingent nature of globalization in an unlikely setting: the city of Zurich, Switzerland. An empirical case study of global city formation, local politics, and social movements in the city of Zurich will indicate that even in a country where the hegemony of capital has historically been deeply entrenched in the fabric of society, the process of urban transnationalization is far from "natural" (*naturwüchsig*, as Marx would say) because local social movements and reformist forces have contested the hegemonic capacity of dominant sociopolitical forces to control and transform urban space.[1] Before telling the story of Zurich politics, it will be necessary to discuss nonreductionist ways of conceptualizing political conflict in structural change, for recognizing the relevance of local politics in the process of transnationalization is not just a question of empirical research but also a function of one's theoretical orientation.

WORLD-SYSTEM THEORY, STRUCTURAL CHANGE, AND POLITICAL CONFLICT

A critique of neoliberal ideologies of globalization must depart from an awareness of the historical and geographical specificities of capital and the role of political agency in structural change (Keil and Kipfer 1994). Due to its connections to the rich geographical materialism of the Annales School, world-system theory (Wallerstein 1974) seems, in principle, well suited to analyzing the concrete temporal and geographical dimensions of "globalization." However, world-system theorists have been accused of operating with rather rigid categories of time and space rooted in the "long sixteenth century" (Freidmann 1990) and, therefore, interpreting the current transnational restructuring of capital as a gradual movement (a set of cyclical fluctuations and secular tendencies) within an existing world-system (Ross and Trachte 1990, 55–60). While world-system theory is helpful in relativizing the magnitude of globalization, the very long-term perspective adopted by world-system theorists resists efforts to understand transnationalization as a qualitative transformation of capitalist development.

A second limitation of world-system theory is related to its problematic, exchange-oriented conceptualization of capitalism (Brenner 1970) and its ontological privileging of world-systematic explanations of historical change (Skocpol 1977). If one accepts that ultimately, the world-system is the decisive level of analysis and that "it is not the primacy of economic motives in historical explanation that constitutes the decisive difference between Marxism and bourgeois thought, but the point of view of totality" (Wallerstein 1974, 387), then one is likely to overemphasize the weight of worldwide forces in shaping subglobal spaces. Although world-system analysts have refuted simplistically determinist arguments about the totalizing nature of the world system (Timberlake 1985, 3; Sokolowsky 1985), the role of sociopolitical forces and mediating instances and agents of structural change (rather than contingent factors constrained by the exposition of a particular social space within a long-standing structure of worldwide exchange relations) remains undertheorized within the world-system paradigm (Cox 1987, 357–58).

In contrast, the metatheoretical perspective of historicist, neo-Gramscian political economy (Demirovic 1992; Cox 1987) accepts the historical and geographical contingencies of capitalist development as the starting point for analysis. Central to a historicist approach is the assertion that (always incomplete) stabilization of *metropolitan* capitalism is predicated on two forms of hegemony: the integration of sociopolitical forces (Gramsci 1971, 180–82) as well as the norms and practices of everyday life that regulate the historically and geographically specific social forms of capital accumulation. Capitalism is interpreted not from above, as a long-standing world economy, but from below, as a complex of collective practices which bind structures of accumulation and organize the access of capital to the conditions of production, including the structured coherence of urban space (Goodwin, Duncan, and Halford 1993). Globalization—the (unstable) transnational integration of production, finance, and class relations—can thus be understood as a crisis of restructuring of the hegemonic practices and regulatory forms that had underpinned postwar capitalism at multiple (international, national, local, etc.) scales of social interaction.

If the reference to "eternally necessary economic laws must be understood as an attempt to stabilize the will of struggling groups" (Demirovic 1989, 74), then it becomes immediately obvious that political conflict is a central factor in the transformation of historically specific forms of accumulation. While historical structures represent condensations of social conflict themselves, sociopolitical forces play an important role in the process of structural change by intensifying contradictions of historical structures and providing alternative ideas for the future. New social movements, for example, helped undermine the "normalities" of Fordism, which had temporarily stabilized the operation of power relations and prevented the social costs of production from being imposed on capital (Roth and Mayer, n.d.; O'Connor 1988). Globalization, which thrives on the contradictions of postwar capitalism, is thus best understood as a process mediated by hegemonic politics among contending sociopolitical forces, which articulate different spaces of accumulation.

GLOBAL CITY FORMATION AND RESTRUCTURING: THE CASE OF ZURICH

While it is important to emphasize that processes of global city formation build, in part, on the residues of previous world economic structures (King 1990), contemporary global cities exemplify primarily the qualitative politicoeconomic transformations after Fordism. As headquarter cities and basing points for global financial markets, global cities are good examples of the spatial reorganization of the world economy: they articulate the spatial contingency of transnationalization as well as the destabilization of national political economies (Sassen 1991). Internally, global city formation builds on a finance-led service economy, the flexibilization of Fordist production structures, and a displacement of subordinate social spaces by dominant land uses, such as office space, gentrified residences, high-tech infrastructure, and spaces of cultural representation. Restructuring and sociospatial displacement tend to politicize the urban process and further undermine the structured coherence (Harvey 1989) and the urban growth machines (Logan and Molotch 1987) of postwar cities, which had already been weakened by the urban rebellions after the late 1960s (Keil 1993; Lefebvre 1968).

The current status of Zurich as a second-tier global city (Friedmann 1986, 72; Thrift 1987, 209) with important financial markets, headquarter functions, and high-technology networks is a result of the restructuring of Swiss Fordism since the mid-1970s (Hitz, Schmid, and Wolff 1994). Swiss Fordism can best be described as a set of highly integrated, liberal, corporatist (Katzenstein 1984) social forms, which sustained a secondary imperialist economy centered on the internationally oriented financial, machinery, and chemicals industries (Ziegler 1976). This liberal-corporatist mode of regulation was overdetermined by isolationist, localist, antiurban, and xenophobic traces of national culture and comprised (1) a corporatist state form centered on large-scale capital and stabilized by an encompassing system of rationalizing political discourse (semidirect democracy and 'consensual' government); (2) bipartite arrangements of "labor peace" between organized labor and capital supported by a discriminatory labor-market policy based on immigrant workers; and (3) a mode of spatial organization based on decentralized industrial structures, a balanced city-system, and localized, patriarchal forms of social control.

Partly due to the effectiveness of the immigration system in exporting unemployment, the institutional arrangements of Swiss Fordism have remained relatively stable compared to those in Anglo-Saxon countries with their "divided cities" (Fainstein, Gordon, and Harlow 1992). Nonetheless, tensions have developed within Swiss Fordism as multinationals have restructured and integrated their operations transnationally. The growing concentration of control functions, financial transactions, producer service networks, and high-tech infrastructures in the Zurich region (Hitz, Schmid, and Wolff 1994; Lehrer 1994) has meant that peripheral regions and mid-sized industrial corporations have become increasingly subordinated to decisions made in Zurich boardrooms (Katzenstein 1984). The disproportionate growth and partial autonomization of the Zurich region from the national economy caused tensions between different capital fractions and were criticized as "un-Swiss" phenomena: violations of the decentralist, localist, and isolationist traits of national identity.

In Zurich itself, global city formation was connected to three major forms of sociospatial restructuring, all of which can be said to have magnified the social costs of capitalist urbanization. First, expansion of the Central Business District (CBD), or city expansion, involving an inflation of land rents and the expansion of dominant spaces of the global city (office space, financial data banks, stockmarkets, luxury stores, upscale apartments, etc.), displaced subordinate land uses and led to a decrease, recomposition, and segmentation of the inner-city population in the city of Zurich (Scherr 1992; Dürrenberger, et al. 1990). Second, city expansion was closely related to the formation of a disaggregated, multinodal urban region of about 1.5 million inhabitants, which comprises sprawling residential areas and ex-urban business districts interlinked by rapidly growing commuting flows (Hitz, Schmid, and Wolff 1994). Finally, land rent inflation, European integration and the recent crisis in the machinery industry have induced large industrial corporations (e.g., Sulzer, ABB, and Örlikon-Bührle) to automate, rationalize, or relocate their operations and convert industrial areas into more profitable commercial space.

GLOBAL CITY FORMATION AND LOCAL POLITICS IN ZURICH

In principle, spatial restructuring could simply be interpreted as an expression of a crisis-induced switching of surplus capital from productive sectors into the speculatory circuits of finance and real estate (Harvey 1993) within the high-interest-rate regime of the late 1970s and 1980s (Altvater 1989). The global demand for financial services was certainly a force behind the inflation of land and rent prices as well as the localizing strategies of expansion by financial capital and the move of Zurich industrial firms into real estate speculation (Dürrenberger et al. 1990:12, 25; *Hochparterre* [various issues]). However, in Zurich, abstract laws of motion were made visible by local reform coalitions and the youth and squatter movements, which questioned the unconditional mobilization of urban space, for transnational accumulation. Forces of restructuring were thus mediated by local political struggles for cultural hegemony and the control of urban space which destabilized the structured coherence of the Zurich urban region and the integrative capacity of local growth machines.

From "Manhattanization" to "Stabilization," or, Reorganizing the Zurich Growth Machine

During the last twenty years, the transnationalization of the Zurich region has run parallel to a growing fragmentation of sociopolitical forces in that city. Already by the mid-1970s, it had become evident that an openly expansionist, cosmopolitan strategy of global city formation could not be pursued without sacrificing the "consensual" technocratic arrangements of postwar urbanization. The reorganization of the local growth machine—a result of popular mobilization and a shift in the political atmosphere after 1968—blocked large-scale urban expansion strategies and renewed a moderate tradition of urban reform, thus accelerating the tendency of large-scale capital to regionalize operations and leading to growing tensions, not only between state and capital but also within business organizations. Based on this recomposition of social-political forces and reinforced by the real estate inflation of the 1980s, the relationships between local state and capitalist interests took on more ad hoc forms while the cohesion among dominant forces was considerably reduced.

In the mid-1960s, urban-based capitalists in Zurich regrouped in a "peak organization" (*City Vereinigung*) designed to integrate the divergent economic-corporate interests of different business groups (inner-city merchants, big retail chains, financial institutions) and establish long-term, informal, and natural connections with the local state (Blanc and Ganz 1986). In 1969, the leadership of the City Vereinigung proposed a vision of urban growth intended to promote Zurich as a European metropolis (Allemann 1969). Modeled on American urban renewal programs and shared by influential city planners (Sidler 1971), this vision was put forward as a "cosmopolitan" alternative to the perceived "provincialism" of Zurich politics, which was a source of persistent skepticism about slash-and-burn modes of redevelopment. According to this strategy, the inner city was to become an exclusive center of business and commerce and be easily accessible by means of a network of urban expressways and subways, while formerly working class areas west of the CBD were to make room for a row of office towers to meet the needs of a metropolitan service economy (Blanc 1993, 127–32).

This strategy of urban internationalization failed in the aftermath of 1968. In a series of popular referenda between 1969 and the mid-1970s, the Zurich electorate rejected a bid for the Olympic Games and proposals for subway and high-speed train systems as well as other building blocks of urban expansion, such as road projects and parking garages. As a result, the completion of inner-city expressways and office tower complexes was either delayed or canceled altogether. Popular mobilization against urban expansionism signaled the end of the postwar growth consensus, under which most political forces in the city, by and large, accepted the necessity to subordinate the city to the technocratically managed imperatives of economic expansion and automobile traffic. As neighborhood groups and various political forces (young Social Democrats, Communists, unionists, reformist urban intellectuals, centrist politicians, and individual capitalists) combined in a loose antigrowth coalition during referendum campaigns, the segregation of urban functions, traffic emissions, and the subordination of the "city of living" to the "city of work" were no longer accepted as inevitable consequences of natural urban growth (Blanc 1993, 163–69, 185–86, 202–5).

Popular vetoes and political confrontation resulted in a political stalemate and renewed the tradition of reform of the "red" Zurich of the 1930s. Informed by the loose concept of urban stabilization (coined by consulting reports written for the city of Zurich) and more wide-ranging notions of urban livability and neighborhood planning borrowed from communist Bologna, Italy (Kommission des Gemeinderates 1975), a heterogenous grouping of reformist forces (statist Social Democrats, libertarian labor activists, socially conservative centrists, and, later, Greens), led by the Social Democratic party, managed to institute concrete reform measures. These reform steps included residential quotas in official zones, a six-story height restriction for new building projects, and measures of traffic management (parking restrictions, speed limits, street furniture, and automated traffic guidance systems) to protect residential neighborhoods and public transportation routes from car traffic. When additional reform-minded Social Democrats were voted into the multiparty local executive in 1986 and a loose red-green-middle coalition won the majority in both the council and executive in 1990, building permit policies were restricted further and a new official plan was adopted in 1992. If implemented, this plan would exclude ecologically sensitive areas from building zones and abstain from preemptively rezoning urban space, thus blocking the unconditional conversion of existing land uses (including industrial land) into commercial office space.

Planning reforms in the city of Zurich had unintended consequences that impacted on the direction of spatial expansion. On the one hand, popular mobilization against city expansion and restrictions on the operation of land markets effectively blocked the whole-scale redevelopment of the area west of the Sihl, the former working-class district peripheral to the city which, in the late 1960s, was designated as the main expansion area for the CBD (Allemann 1969, 7). On the other hand, the gradual "infiltration" of the local state (notably, the planning department) by reformist elements during the late 1970s and early 1980s destabilized the natural connections between the local state and organized business that had been institutionalized in the Urban Planning Commission between 1960 and 1986. Restrictions on urban expansion and a deteriorating business climate reinforced the tendency of banks, insurance corporations, and headquarter firms to relocate selected control functions and back offices (administration, data processing, training, telecommunications) to peripheral and ex-urban towns with fewer development guidelines, lower tax rates, and more spatial reserves (Jeker 1988; 12 Dec. 1993).

Indirectly, the recomposition of sociopolitical forces at the local level led to a greater differentiation among capitalist interests themselves, as the locational perspective of transnationally connected financial interests (banks and insurance corporations) and large retailers became increasingly regional in scope, while the economic-corporate interests of inner-city merchants and small retailers remained tied to the inner city and opposed to the establishment of regional shopping malls and the forces of CBD expansion (Lüchinger 1982). During the 1980s, tensions within the urban growth machine centered on the City Vereinigung intensified when big landowners, developers, and financial institutions (including pension funds) pursued short-term, purely return-oriented strategies of rent maximization at the expense of local retail capital and mid-sized industrial corporations. In 1986, these tensions led to a change of leadership within the City Vereinigung in favor of a representative close to dominant financial interests. Two years earlier, the largest business interests in the Zurich region (banks, insurance corporations, large retailers, developers, and some industrial groups) had formed a new organization, Interessengemeinschaft Zürcher Unternehmen (IZU), which adopted an aggressively neoliberal and explicitly regional agenda (Interessengemeinschaft 1988, 1993).

In the meantime, the relationships between the local state and capitalist interests have become more ad hoc. In the city of Zurich, natural, long-term, and informal links between urban elites and the local authorities have been replaced in part by project-based bargaining processes between large investors, landowners, and the planning department (Cattacin and Kühne 1991, 112). Pioneered by large-scale projects to develop areas surrounding the main railway station (HB-Südwest) and convert large, partly vacant industrial zones into office space, these ad hoc planning forms can be interpreted as piecemeal modes of world-market integration that actually reinforce tensions between small retailers, mid-sized industrial firms, and big investors. For reformist exponents of the planning department and the red-green-middle coalition that was in office between 1990 and 1994, project planning is considered a means to attach conditions to development projects and promote "urban quality" (residential stability, environmental protection, and urban design) as a central component of the international competitiveness of the Zurich economy (Stadtrat von Zürich 1990; Aeschbacher 1994).

Urban reform measures were generally modest and sometimes proved—as in the case of residential stabilization—class-biased and difficult to implement. These measures were also limited because they remained isolated within the jurisdictionally fragmented Zurich urban region. Although the regionalization of CBD expansion provoked resistance elsewhere (Willi 1992), reform measures in the city of Zurich faced multiple obstacles from the cantonal state and wealthy suburbs. Finally, local reform politics in Zurich rode on conservative political undercurrents, for the continuity of reform politics (spearheaded by Social Democrats) made it imperative to include socially conservative representatives from centrist (Christian Democratic and Protestant) parties, for whom stabilization meant the conservation of the localist and conformist elements of Swiss society at the exclusion of social experiments proposed by social movements (Aeschbacher 1994). This much said, reformist forces managed to veto slash-and-burn urban renewal, a "negative" achievement which, itself, had an effect on the course of global city formation and the homogeneity of the local growth machine (Scherr 1993).

Youth Protest and the Squatter Movement: Loosening the Grip of Cultural Hegemony

The new social movements in Switzerland can be considered agents of structural change insofar as they challenged the bureaucratizing commodifying and collectively individualizing tendencies of the postwar order and destabilized particularities of Swiss Fordism, such as a "consensual" (effectively conservative) political rationality (Church 1989), as well as the imperatives of order, cleanliness, and hard work, which cemented the comparative advantage of Swiss capital. Due to the degree of political activity and the severity of social conflict, Zurich was the most important center for movement politics in Switzerland (Kriesi 1984, 183). At the core of Zurich movement politics during the last two decades, youth and squatter movements were forces of disruption in the process of urban transnationalization. While reformist forces were instrumental in eroding alliances among institutionally oriented sociopolitical forces, social movements further politicized the urban process and questioned deeper, cultural dimensions of hegemony.

In the years after 1968, the central themes of the Zurich youth and squatter politics of the late 1970s and 1980s—antiauthoritarian protest, calls for autonomous self-determination, and innovative political practices—had already been established. In 1968 and 1970, antiauthoritarian protesters (radical students, anarchist "spontaneists" (Spontis), and disgruntled working-class youth) experienced the repressive powers of the state when police brutalized rock music fans and youth protesters calling for an "autonomous youth center" (AJZ) and when the local authorities closed a supervised youth center only a few months after its opening. With their actions, youth protesters and support organizations contributed strongly to the change in political atmosphere that put a brake on strategies of unhampered urban expansion (Arbeitsgemeinschaft 1968). Some young activists became new left forces of change within the Social Democratic party and the Stalinist Communist party, joined renters' and neighborhood protests, and complemented referendum campaigns with roadblocks and the first housing occupation in 1971 (Verein 1982, 55; Kriesi 1984, 194–5; Geiger 1994).

By the mid-1970s, the first movement wave of 1968 had ended in the cul-de-sac of sectarian communism, the mainstreaming of some activists, and the establishment of a counter-culture based on alternative institutions like communes, cafés, day care centers, and printing shops. Small numbers of these "older" movement segments—notably, the spontaneists—merged with a new movement scene ("Szene"), a loose network of communes and personal contacts heavily infused with anarchist (*Autonomen*) and subcultural tendencies, which was to sustain the youth protest of the early 1980s (Fischer 1994). The immediate causes of the youth riots of 1980 were related to the pressures exercised on the Szene—located in the western vicinity of the financial district—by the forces of city expansion and cultural repression. These pressures triggered protests against repeated closures of youth centers and rock music venues and led to housing occupations, roadblocks, and eviction boycotts of tenants and activists against growing traffic volume and the displacement of low-cost housing by petty speculation (Schmid 1993; Kriesi 1984, 189–95, 199–204).

In May 1980, built-up tensions erupted in massive riots when a demonstration against the renovation of the Zurich opera house—a project that brought the marginalized status of the alternative culture into sharp relief—spilled over into violent clashes between protesters and the police. The opera house riots were the starting point of almost two years of struggle for an autonomous youth center. Between 1980 and 1982, about 500 activists and 4,000 movement 'participants,' most of whom were under the age of twenty-five and shared a working-class background, made up the core of a highly fluid and spontaneous movement that had the capacity to mobilize about 10,000 demonstrators and was loosely coordinated by base-democratic plenary sessions and informal information channels. After numerous bloody (and, in a few cases, fatal) clashes with the police, secret negotiations between youth and local authorities, and repeated attempts to run the autonomous youth center (AJZ) against all odds (notably, the obstruction of the local state and the encroaching drug trade), these struggles ended in a growing rift between youth activists and sympathizers and the final closure of the AJZ in early 1982 (Kriesi 1984, 214–16).[2]

The youth movement of 1980 signaled a shift in movement politics. The new movement activists took up antiauthoritarian practices and programmatic demands from previous generations, but their call for autonomous, self-determined, and antiauthoritarian spaces, despite the antiimperialist discourse of radical anarchist groups (Autonomen), had become more individualist, more antitheoretical, and less inclined toward strategies of general social transformation (Fischer 1994). In the eyes of observers from the generation of 1968 (Lüscher 1984; Kriesi 1984), the youth movement appeared a senseless celebration of spontaneity, intensity, and disorder. As a force of discontinuity in a city where alternative cultural forms were systematically repressed as provocations of consensual politics, a strict work ethic, and the functional administration of urban space, the movement self-consciously defied the instrumental rationalities implied in the rituals of "sensible" politics adhered to, not only by dominant forces but also by the organized left, older, "institutionalized" movement segments and small, sectarian cadre parties (Funk 1986; Lüscher 1984; Kriesi 1984, 232).

Although the failure to wrest an AJZ from the global city of Zurich inevitably had demobilizing, and even self-destructive, effects on those movement activists with uncompromising perspectives (Fischer 1994), the events of 1980 profoundly influenced the squatter politics of the 1980s. Housing occupations and demonstrations against the destruction of affordable residential space were an integral, if secondary, part of the movement of 1980 but, as in other cities (Hamburg, Amsterdam, Berlin, and Frankfurt), squatting became the main focus of radical movement politics after 1982. On the one hand, the demands for autonomous spaces and participatory, spontaneous, and passionate forms of mobilization, as well as the skepticism against state-centered and theoretical politics, were taken up by squatters and articulated by new generations of activists. On the other hand, however, spiraling land rent inflation and progressing CBD expansion led to a resurgence of radical protest at the end of the 1980s (Guigni and Kriesi 1990) and made economic necessity a motivating force for some squatters (Hofer 1993) for whom squatting had previously been a matter of anarchist principle or a way to protect niches of alternative living (Lehrer 1993; Fischer 1994).

During the last twenty years, an estimated 100 to 200 housing occupations occurred in Zurich. Although houses were occupied in many Zurich neighborhoods—there were even occupations in bourgeois residential districts—the most important occupations (at the Stauffacher [1980–1990] and the Wohlgroth [1989, 1991–1993]) were undertaken in the originally working-class and heavily immigrant neighborhoods to the west of the city and the central railway station. The strategic location of many squatter activities was partly a result of the necessity of defending the social networks and alternative institutions in those areas against urban development pressures and partly of the conscious desire to establish alternative social relations as a strategy of mobilization against the expanding tentacles of the imperialist CBD. Not surprisingly, therefore, squatters who occupied houses destined for renovation or demolition were evicted within a very short period of time up until 1989, when the growing breadth of housing protests pressured local authorities to relax eviction policies (WOZ, 22 Dec. 1989).

During the 1980s, squatter politics articulated a variety of social movements such as the radical women's movement, the Third World Solidarity movement, and the left alternative movement (Lehrer 1993). In this way, the general desire for autonomous spaces and alternative modes of life were concretized and enriched by particular tendencies and practices such as radical feminism—there was even a women-only occupation, solidarity actions with would-be Kurdish refugees, and left-alternative currents of individuals hoping to construct ecological utopias in the belly of the imperialist beast ("p.m." 1990; *Karthago* 1989). This heterogeneity of the squatter movement (which was partly compensated by extensive interpersonal contacts, movement institutions, and common points of mobilization) revealed a growing internal differentiation of social movements during the 1980s. While certain squatters started to pursue (mostly unsuccessful) strategies of legalization and negotiation (Karthago 1989), dwindling numbers of radical anarchists stuck to their confrontational stance in a surge of radical protest, and others faced the threat of marginality (homelessness and drug addiction) in their relentless search for cultural niches (Fischer 1994; Schmid 1993; Hofer 1993; Sutter 1994; Guigni and Kriesi 1990).

Overall, the isolation of squatters and youth protesters from reformist forces was a major limitation for movement politics in Zurich. In 1982, links between youth protesters and sympathizers broke down. During the 1980s, the nature of support for youth protesters and squatting activities by institutionally oriented forces remained ad hoc and limited to a few cases, such as the parliamentary support of small movement parties (Progressive Organisationen 1981) and the Stauffacher occupations, in which squatters and a support organization of neighborhood groups, Social Democrats, and Greens blocked redevelopment for years (Karthago 1989). Cooperating with movement activists was unthinkable for most exponents of the institutional left because of the autonomist tendencies of movement politics and the generational rift between culturally marginalized youth protesters, organized labor, and "suburban" segments of the remaining Swiss working class (Kammerer 1993; Scherr 1993; Kivrak 1994).[3] As a result, Zurich (unlike Geneva) witnessed no virtuous circle of radical squatter mobilization and strategies of housing reform by Communists and Social Democrats (SAU 1989).

If the isolation of social movements from the institutional left can be excused by pointing to the conservative connotations of labor politics in Switzerland, the gap between movement activists and the bulk of the immigrant population touches on a problematic aspect of the squatter movement itself. Immigrant workers are indispensable for the service and manufacturing sectors of the global city of Zurich and tend to be particularly affected by discrimination in the housing market, yet they played only a marginal role in youth and housing protests (Kivrak 1994).[4]

Radical squatters engaged in solidarity actions with refugees, but many squatters did not adequately problematize the seclusion of immigrants from Swiss political life (Schmid 1993). In an early rationalization of their territorial politics, for example, activists failed to clarify the role of disenfranchised immigrant workers in struggles aimed at protecting vernacular (and heavily immigrant) neighborhoods against the expansion of the central business district.

Despite the limitations and the unconventional, antiinstitutional, and antitheoretical leanings of squatters and youth activists (which do not fit the label of *revolutionary* in the traditional Marxist sense) movement politics had an effect on structural change in general and global city formation, in particular. Besides concrete achievements, which included changes in housing policy (relaxed eviction procedures and more proactive, affordable housing policies), the legalization of a squatter settlements, and the creation of semiinstitutionalized, alternative cultural venues and supervised youth centers, years of struggle made what used to be marginalized subcultural practices (such as rock music and unconventional behavior) more acceptable and contributed to a partial democratization of everyday life (Schmid 1993; Geiger 1994; Fischer 1994). Most important, squatters and youth protesters challenged the process of global city formation in three ways.

First, social movements reinforced the growing differentiation of sociopolitical forces. In the early 1970s, radical student and youth politics were instrumental in breaking up the cohesive growth coalition underpinning the technocratic urban growth patterns of the postwar system. In turn, the youth riots in 1980 reinforced tensions within the reformist camp and almost caused a split within the Social Democratic party when conservative labor unionists adamantly opposed concessions to the youth movement (Kammerer 1993; Jacobi 1994). Finally, the (unsuccessful) referendum campaign for the legalization of a marginally alternative housing project in 1994 revealed tensions between reactionary neopopulists and liberal elements within the local elite.

Second, squatters contested the capitalist urban process in Zurich. Occupying houses adjacent to, or on, major redevelopment zones, squatters obstructed the expansion of the CBD into vernacular neighborhoods. In strategic areas of the city of Zurich, squatters blocked major redevelopment schemes, temporarily insulated houses or housing blocks from petty speculation, and resisted attempts of dominant actors such as banks, developers, and pension funds to revalorize urban space by converting existing residential and small commercial uses into office space and luxury apartments (Scherr 1986; Spielhofer 1994). In this way, housing occupations and the antiimperialist discourses and symbolic protests of anarchist and left-alternative squatters against the Zurich financial center ("p.m." 1990; Fischer 1994; Lehrer 1993) articulated the social costs of city expansion and made visible the concrete economic-corporate interests that inscribe supposedly abstract, transnational economic forces into local space.

Third, despite (or maybe because of) their niche orientation, squatters and youth activists destabilized the cultural dimensions of hegemony in Zurich and marked an oppositional presence in a city known for its clean and orderly functioning. The uncompromising defiance of the imperatives of social stability and cultural quietism, as exemplified by the 1980 riots and repeated housing occupations, politicized the "hidden" but repressive character of normal life, which remained unquestioned by the institutional left. In turn, the illiberal orientation of the local elite (Loacker 1994)—indeed the very visibility of crude coercion against what were clearly not insurrectionary forms of mobilization—was an indication of the latent instability of the dominant order. The imaginative, passionate, and base-democratic practices of movement activists thus opened up cracks in the cultural foundations of Zurich's attractiveness as a financial center and headquarter city (Scherr 1993). In the process, movement politics revealed glimpses of a utopian (nonhierarchical, self-determined, sustainable, and nonimperial) future that was different from a view involving "qualitative" strategies of intercity competition and the alienating facets of the capitalist city.[5]

The 1990s: Reorganizing Consent?

After two decades of structural change and political conflict, the Zurich urban region appears more fragmented than ever. While creeping European integration and the most severe recession since the 1930s forced large numbers of Swiss workers to face the prospect of unemployment for the first time, neoliberal strategies of deregulation are the order of the day. In the Zurich region, the machinery industry and what remains of the textile and chemicals industry faced serious crises of restructuring, while cantonal and local states adopted cutback measures to respond to growing budget deficits. Public and private sector unions have come under the most severe pressure in decades (Wohnlich 1994; Jacobi 1994), while activists fight against the demobilizing, fragmenting, and marginalizing effects of economic crisis on their dwindling movement bases (Kivrak 1994).

Large-scale capital, represented in the IZU has seized the opportunity of the moment to propose a neoliberal strategy to flexibilize urban planning and foster interterritorial competition within a self-defined urban region of 2 to 3 million people to promote the Zurich economy as a "bridgehead" to the European Union (Interessengemeinschaft Zürcher 1993). While this vision is unlikely to re-establish the hegemonic cohesion of the Zurich region, a more effective, openly authoritarian hegemonic strategy is promoted by the Swiss Peoples party (SVP) as well as conservative neighborhood groups and small business interests in city. These neopopulist forces have singled out drug addicts and nonestablished foreigners (mostly would-be refugees) for police repression to reverse the achievements of social movements and ghettoize marginal groups in the inner city. In this context, the future of progressive politics in Zurich will depend on the possibility of combining the struggles of antiracist activists (Kivrak 1994), green-alternative forces (*Kraftwerk* 1993), pressured unionists, disillusioned reformists, and movement party members to bridge the divides among subordinate social groups and establish germs of an alternative to the neoliberal mode of world market insertion with its fascistic undertones.

CONCLUSION

In this chapter, I proposed that instead of positing a unidirectional and linear link between the global economy and subglobal change, one needs to account for constellations of sociopolitical forces and the norms and practices circumscribing the latter's interaction as the mediating factors through which particular spaces are inserted into the world-economy. In the case of Zurich, urban transnationalization was a moment in the reorganization of the world economy and the restructuring of the Swiss political economy. However, without mentioning the role of reformist forces and social movements, which challenged the cohesion of the local growth machine and disrupted the normalcy of everyday life, it would be impossible to understand the process through which global city formation was transformed from a hegemonic project (Jessop 1990:209-10) twenty years ago into a fragmented process composed of visibly contested economic-corporate strategies of globalization.

If a nonreductionist analysis of globalization is necessary so as not to theoretically close windows of political opportunity, such an analysis can still be no more than a starting point for political strategizing. Political responses to globalizing capital can combine with social instability in many ways. In the Zurich case, oppositional forces were certainly constitutive elements in structural change but remained too fragmented and isolated themselves to preclude the possibility of a contradictory articulation of neoliberal globalization with fascistic neo-populism. It would be wrong, therefore, to mystify social movements in metropolitan cities as privileged agents of political transformation. For those who have to make political choices in the capitalist core, however, the political challenge lies in pursuing two-pronged strategies of transnationalization to, first, bridge the differences among subaltern social groups in an already highly internationalized social context, and, second, connect oppositional forces in the core with anticapitalist struggles in peripheral spaces in order to resist the transnational forces of capital.

NOTES

I would like to thank the editors, Kamal Kipfer, Ute Lehrer, Roger Keil, Claudio Iacoe, and Rob Martin, for their helpful comments and criticisms on earlier drafts of this chapter.

1. The empirical part of this chapter is based on primary documents, secondary sources, and interviews with (partly anonymous) movement activists, union organizers, representatives of business organizations, members of the local executive, municipal councilors, and urban planners that I conducted in June 1993

and June 1994. Field research in Zurich was generously funded by the Faculty of Environmental Studies, York University, Toronto.

2. According to estimates, there were about 20,000 sympathizers of the youth movement in Zurich in 1980, most of whom were activists from previous movement generations (Kriesi 1984, 195).

3. In Swiss political culture, the terms *work* and *labor* (*"schaffe"*) represent a discourse of order and discipline.

4. Only about 6 percent of the youth movement of 1980 were immigrants, compared to an immigrant share of 20 percent of the population of the city of Zurich (Kriesi 1984, 216).

5. Concerning such a utopian future, an "anticipatory imagination" (Ernst Bloch) is necessary for this argument (Evers 1985, 52–54).

REFERENCES

Aeschbacher, Rudolf (Evangelische Volkspartei Zürich). 1994. Interview by author. Zurich, 14 June.

Allemann, Richard. 1969. "Provinzstadt oder Europäische Metropole?" Zurich: City Vereinigung.

Altvater, Elmar. 1989. "Fordist and Post-Fordist International Division of Labor and Monetary Regimes." In Michael Storper and Allen Scott, eds., *Pathways to Industrialization and Regional Development.* London: Routledge, 21–43.

———. 1993. *The Future of the Market.* Trans. Patrick Camiller. London: Verso.

Arbeitsgemeinschaft 'Zürcher Manifest.' 1968. *Wandzeitungen und Plakate die während der Veranstaltungen "6-Tage Zürcher Manifest" entstanden sind.* Zurich (photocopy).

Blanc, Jean Daniel. 1993. *Die Stadt—Ein Verkehrshindernis? Leitbilder städtischer Verkehrsplanung in Zürich: 1945–75.* Zurich: Chronos.

Blanc, Jean Daniel, and Martin Ganz. 1986. "Die City-Macher." In Theo Ginsburg, Hansruedi Hitz, Christian Schmid, and Richard Wolff, *Zürich ohne Grenzen.* Zurich: Pendo.

Block, Fred. 1986. "Political Choice and the Multiple "Logics" of Capital." *Theory and Society* 15, nos.1–2:175–90.

Brenner, Robert. 1970. "The Origins of Capitalist Development: A Critique of Neo-Smithian Marxism." *New Left Review,* 104:25-92.

Cannellotto, Bruno, Daniel Rice, and Robert Riemer (Gewerkschaft Bau/Industrie Zürich). 1994. Interviews by author. 7 June.

Cattacin, Sandro, and Armin Kühne. 1990. "Stadt und Staat." *Jahrbuch Schweizerische Vereinigung für Politische Wissenschaften* 30:101–20.

Church, Clive. 1989. "Behind the Consociational Screen: Politics in Contemporary Switzerland." *West European Politics* 12, no.2:12–34.

Cox, Robert. 1987. *Production, Power, and World Order: Social Forces in the Making of History.* New York: Columbia University Press.

Demirovic, Alex. 1989. "Die Hegemoniale Strategie der Wahrheit: Zur Historizität des Marxismus bei Gramsci." *Argument Sonderband* 159:69–89.

———. 1992. "Regulation und Hegemonie: Intellektuelle, Wissenspraktiken und Akkumulation." In Alex Demirovic, Hans-Peter Krebs, and Thomas Sablowski, eds, *Hegemonie und Staat: Kapitalistische Regulation als Projekt und Prozess.* Münster: Westfälisches Dampfboot, 128–57.

Dürrenberger, G., H. Ernste, F. Furger, C. Jaeger, D. Steiner, and Z. Truffer. 1990. *Das Dilemma der Modernen Stadt.* Berlin: Springer.

Evers, Tilman. 1985. "Identity: The Hidden Reverse Side of New Social Movements in Latin America." In David Slater, ed., *New Social Movements and the State in Latin America* (Amsterdam: Commission on Economic Development in Latin America CEDLA):43–71.

Fainstein, Susan S., Ian Gordon, and Michael Harloe. 1992. *Divided Cities: New York and London in the Contemporary World.* London: Basil Blackwell.

Fischer, Stefan (Paranoia City). 1994. Interview by author. Zurich, 25 June.

Friedmann, Harriet. 1990. "Rethinking Capitalism and Hierarchy." *Review* 8, no. 2:255–64.

Friedmann, John. 1986. "The World-City Hypothesis." *Development and Change* 17, no. 1:69–84.

Funk, Beat. 1986. "Als die Wünsche erstarrt . . . Zur Geschichtswerdung der 'Bewegig' aus dem Geiste der Angst." *Lücken im Panorama: Einblicke in den Nachlass Zürichs* (Geschichtsladen Zürich):101–41.

Geiger, Thomas (Paranoia City). 1994. Interview by author. 7 June.

Ginsburg, Theo, Hansruedi Hitz, Christian Schmid, and Richard Wolff, eds. 1986. *Zürich ohne Grenzen.* Zurich: Pendo.

Giugni, Marco, and Hanspeter Kriesi. 1990. "Nouveaux Mouvements Sociaux dans les Années 80." *Jahrbuch Schweizerische Vereinigung für Politische Wissenschaften*, 30:97–99.

Goodwin, M., S. Duncan, and S. Halford. 1993. "Regulation Theory, the Local State, and the Transition of Urban Politics." *Society and Space* 11, no. 1:67–88.

Gramsci, Antonio. 1971. *Selections from the Prison Notebooks.* Ed. and Trans. Quintin Hoare and Geoffrey Smith. New York: International Publishers.

Harvey, David. 1989. *The Urban Experience.* Oxford: Basil Blackwell.

Hitz, H., Christian Schmid, and Richard Wolff. 1994. "Urbanization in Zurich: Headquarter Economy and City-Belt." *Environment and Planning D: Society and Space* 12:167–85.

Hochparterre. Various issues.

Hofer, Andreas. 1993. Interview by author. Zurich, 11 June (photocopy).

Infoladen Für Häuserkampf. 1988. *Zonen.* Zurich.

Interessengemeinschaft Zürcher Unternehmen (IZU). 1988. *Überlegungen der Zürcher Wirtschaft zur Entwicklung der Stadt Zürich.* Zurich: IZU.

————. 1993. *Impulse für die Entwicklung des Raumes Zürich.* Zurich: IZU.

Jacobi, Heinz (Schweizerischer Verband des Personals öffentlicher Dienste [VPOD] Zürich). 1994. Interview by author. Zurich, 13 June.

Jeker, R. A. 1988. *Der Dienstleistungsplatz Zürich.* Zurich: Credit Suisse.

Jessop, Bob. 1990. *State Theory: Putting Capitalist States in their Place.* University Park: Pennsylvania State University Press.

Kammerer, Bruno (Sozialdemokratische Partei, Zürich). 1993. Interview by author. Zurich, 12 June.

Karthago am Stauffacher. 1989. Zurich: Paranoia City.

Katzenstein, Peter J. 1984. *Austria, Switzerland, and the Politics of Industry.* Ithaca, NY: Cornell University Press.

Keil, Roger. 1993. *Weltstadt, Stadt der Welt: Internationalisierung und lokale Politik in Los Angeles.* Münster: Westfälisches Dampfboot.

Keil, Roger, and Stefan Kipfer. 1994. "Weltwirtschaft/Wirtschaftswelten: Globale Transformationen im Lokalen Raum." In Peter Noller, Walter Prigge, and Klaus Ronneberger, eds., *Stadt-Welt.* Frankfurt: Campus, 83–93.

King, Anthony. 1990. *Global Cities: Post-Imperialism and the Internationalization of London.* London: Routledge.

Kivrak, Mehmet. 1994. Interview by author. Zurich, 27 June.

Kommission des Gemeinderates zur Vorberatung des Geschäftes. 1975. "Entwicklungsprogramm der Stadt Zürich bis 1985. *Bericht III: Die Arbeit der Kommission und Anträge.* Zurich: City of Zurich.

Kraftwerk 1: Projekt für das Sulzer-Escher Wyss Areal. 1993. Zurich.

Kriesi, Hanspeter. 1984. *Die Zürcher Bewegung: Bilder, Interaktionen, Zusammenhänge.* Frankfurt: Campus.

Lefebvre, Henri. 1968. *Le Droit à la Ville.* Paris: Anthropos.

Lehrer, Ute. 1993. Interview by author. 22 July.

————. 1994. "Images of the Periphery: The Architecture of FlexSpace in Switzerland." *Environment and Planning D: Society and Space,* 12:187–205.

Loacker, Norbert. 1994. "Der Geometrische Staat." *Politikinitiativen* 6:6–31.

Logan, John, and Harvey Molotch. 1987. *Urban Fortunes: The Political Economy of Place.* Berkeley: University of California Press.

Lüchinger, Hans Georg. 1982. *Eine Standortbestimmung der City Vereinigung Zürich.* Zurich: City Vereinigung.

Lüscher, Rudolf. 1984. *Einbruch in den Gewöhnlichen Ablauf der Ereignisse.* Zürich: Limmat.

Mayer, Margit. 1992. "The Shifting Local Political System in European Cities." In Mick Dunford and Grigoris Kafkalas, eds., *Cities and Regions in the New Europe: the Global-Local Interplay and Spatial Development Strategies.* London: Belhaven, 253–274.

O'Connor, James. 1988. "Capitalism, Nature, Socialism: A Theoretical Introduction." *Capitalism, Nature, Socialism* 1, no. 1:11–45.

"p.m." 1986. "Zürich—Abschied von einer Stadt des Imperiums." In Theo Ginsburg, Hansruedi Hitz, Christian Schmid, and Richard Wolff, eds., *Zürich ohne Grenzen*. Zurich: Pendo, 228–35.

———. 1990. "bolo'bolo." *Nizza*, 10–11 April.

Polanyi, Karl. 1957. *The Great Transformation*. Boston: Beacon Press.

Progressive Organisationen der Schweiz (POCH). 1981. *Bewegig is Parlamänt und id' Partei*. Zurich.

Robertson, Roland. 1991. "Social Theory, Cultural Relativity and the Problem of Globality." In Anthony King, ed., *Culture, Globalization and the World-System: Contemporary Conditions for the Representation of Identity*. Binghamton: State University of New York Press, 69–89.

Ross, Robert, and Kent Trachte. 1990. *Global Capitalism: The New Leviathan*. Albany: State University of New York Press.

Roth, Roland, and Margit Mayer. n.d. [1992]. "New Social Movements and Transformation to Post-Fordist Society." Unpublished manuscript.

Sassen, Saskia. 1991. *The Global City: New York, London, Tokyo*. Princeton, NJ: Princeton University Press.

SAU (Center for Applied Urbanism). 1986. "Aussersihl—Zwischen Schlachtfeld und Spielwiese." In Theo Ginsburg, Hansruedi Hitz, Christian Schmid, and Richard Wolff, eds., *Zürich ohne Grenzen*. Zurich: Pendo, 100–111.

———. 1989. "Zürcher Falken und Genfer Tauben." *Wochenzeitung*, 22 Dec.

Scherr, Niklaus (Zurich's renters' association). 1986. "Hütet Euch am Stauffacher." In Theo Ginsburg, et al., eds., *Zürich ohne Grenzen*. Zurich: Pendo.

———. 1992. "Nur noch für die Miete arbeiten?" *Widerspruch* 23:91-96.

———. 1993. Interview by author. Zurich, 11 June.

Schmid, Christian. 1993. Interview by author. Zurich, 5 June.

Schweizerische Handelszeitung (SHZ). Various issues.

Sidler, Gerhard. 1971. "Die Entwicklung der Stadtzentren in den USA—Folgerungen für Zürich." Zurich: City Vereinigung (speech transcript).

Skocpol, Theda. 1977. "Wallerstein's World Capitalist System: A Theoretical and Historical Critique." *American Journal of Sociology* 82, no. 5:1075–89.

Sokolovsky, Joan. 1985. "Logic, Space and Time: The Boundaries of the Capitalist World Economy." In Michael Timberlake, ed., *Urbanization in the World Economy*. Orlando, FL: Academic Press, 41–54.

Spielhofer, Guido. 1994. "Kein Gott, Kein Staat, Kein Mietvertrag." *Die Beute* 1:67–71.

Stadtrat von Zürich. 1990. *Ziele und Politische Schwerpunkte (Amtsdauer 1990–1994)*. Zurich: City of Zurich.

Sutter, Monique. 1994. Interview by author. Zurich, 18 June.

Swyngedouw, Erik. 1992. "The Mammon Quest: 'Glocalisation,' Interspatial Competition and the Monetary Order: the Construction of New Scales." In Mick Dunford and Grigoris Kafkaalas, eds., *Cities and Regions in the New Europe*. London: Belhaven.

Thrift, Nigel. 1987. "The Fixers: The Urban Geography of International Commercial Capital." In Manuel Castells and Jeffrey Henderson, eds., *Global Restructuring and Territorial Development.* London: Sage, 203–33.

Timberlake, Michael. 1985. "The World-System Perspective and Urbanization." In Michael Timberlake, ed., *Urbanization in the World Economy.* Orlando, FL: Academic Press, 3–22.

Verein Unabhängiges Aussersihl. 1982. *Aussersihl War und ist Ausser Sich.* Zurich: Verein Unabhängiges Aussersihl.

Wallerstein, Immanuel. 1974. "The Rise and Future Demise of the World Capitalist System: Concepts for Comparative Analysis." *Comparative Studies in Society and History* 16:387–415.

Willi, Erich. 1992. *Zürich-Nord: Lebensraum/Wirtschaftsraum.* Zurich: Überparteiliche Arbeitsgruppe Zürich-Nord.

Wohnlich, Kaspar (SMUV Region Zürich). 1994. Interview by author. Dietikon, 27 June.

WOZ. *(Wochenzeitung).* Various issues.

Ziegler, Jean. 1976. *Eine Schweiz—Über Jeden Verdacht Erhaben.* Trans. Klara Obermüller. Darmstadt: Luchterhand.

12

Environmental Transformations: Accumulation, Ecological Crisis, and Social Movements

Sing C. Chew

In world-system analysis, the process of capital accumulation is considered the motor force of world history. According to Frank and Gills (1992a, 1992b), this process has played a central role in world system history for at least several millennia. However, for Wallerstein (1974, 1992), its ceaseless nature emerged with the modern world-system in the sixteenth century. Regardless of whether this process has been the underlying feature over the last several millennia or only the last four hundred years, one of the manifestations of the ultimately self-defeating process of world accumulation is the appearance of environmental degradation and crisis. The exploitation of nature as a process parallels the exploitation of human labor. In world-system studies, however, much less attention is paid to the former process of exploitation over the long term in comparison to the latter.[1] This neglect leaves a gap in our understanding of the dynamic interrelationship between the natural environment and the economic, political, and social processes of the world system.

If we examine world history, the exploitation of nature as a consequence of the accumulation process has occurred for at least 5,000 years (Ponting 1991). Over the entire period, environmental degradation and depletion have led to the relocation of commodity production processes and, as well, the decline of civilizations and centers of accumulation. This shows that in addition to the social and economic barriers to the process of accumulation, nature also defines the parameters of world-system expansion and the conditions of production and accumulation in world history.[2] Besides the limits established by nature for the accumulation process, social struggles and resistance in response to the exploitative use of nature arose throughout the course of world history. Frank and Fuentes (1989, 1990) Frank argued that these purportedly new social movements (such as the women's, peace, and ecological movements) have existed throughout the ages, while others, such as Touraine (1981), Melucci (1989) and Gorz (1982), have identified these new social movements as outcomes of cultural and materialistic innovations that are consequences of a particular stage of societal evolution: postindustrial society. Sharing this postindustrial theme, Habermas (1989) treated the new social movements as defensive resistance to the processes of colonization of the *lebenswelt* (life-world). Habermas's work facilitates our understanding of the motivation and mobilization of social movements in their struggle with the state or capital, especially in the arena of the environment. Eder (1990, 1993), building on Habermas's work, suggested that the terrain of social resistance for the core zone, in the late twentieth century and into the future, has shifted to the struggle over the environment. Despite these differences in terms of the historical time line of resistance to the accumulation process, it is clear that the move away from the working class as the agent of change to an analysis of social movements suggests that the transformation of society as a one-class project, especially for the North, is a thing of the past. Eder (1993) argued that such changes widen the scope for critical politics and that class conflicts can now be centered on the problem of the exploitation of nature. Such a shift in the field of struggle adds further to the various points of crisis and transformation in the late twentieth century world-system.

If the environment becomes a contested terrain, the social movements oriented to ecology become a key factor in the process of global transformation, especially for the late twentieth century. However, how anti-systemic are these ecological movements? For Wallerstein (1990), these movements are part of the family of anti-systemic movements that play a part in transforming the world-system. Frank and Fuentes (1989), however, we are not convinced that these movements are anti-systemic if this term means to destroy the system and replace it with another. However, if anti-systemic implies the modification of the system by changing its systemic linkages, then these movements do show a transformative potential.

How have these themes played out in world-system history, and especially in the late twentieth century? What follows is a brief attempt to examine the assault on the forests and the consequent social resistance to the process of accumulation, which utilizes some concepts from world-system analysis.

ACCUMULATION, ECOLOGICAL CRISIS, AND SOCIAL MOVEMENTS

If one examines world history over the long term, one can see that it has involved the extraction of natural resources such as wood to meet the reproductive and expansionary dynamics of societies and civilizations. Wood, therefore, is an important commodity which facilitated directly, or indirectly, the process of accumulation in world history. The long history of forest utilization, from the ancient civilizations of Mesopotamia and China to the present, is an exploitative one. It is often undertaken within and between the trade and territorial (and including extraterritorial) linkages of societies, civilizations, and empires (Attenborough 1987; Marsh 1864; Perlin 1989; Butzer 1971; Thirgood, 1981). Trees fueled the socio-economic transformation of every society and, in some cases, provided the means for societies to become the core accumulation centers of the world-system. One may see a continuity in this pattern of accumulation not only in recent history but even as far back as early China, third millennium b.c. Mesopotamia, Bronze Age Crete, Mycenaean Greece, Greece of the Classical period, second century b.c. Rome, and India as early as 2000 b.c. The extraction of wood resources most often led to ecological degradation, and in some cases, to the collapse of empires and civilizations (Perlin 1989; Ponting 1991). It also resulted in expeditions and conquests to seek other areas for wood (Perlin 1989; Thirgood 1981; Attenborough 1987). Thus, for ancient empires and hegemonic powers, the deforestation occurred not only within the proximity of the developed centers, but also in the outer domains of these empires or in their external arenas. The cases of Rome, Mycenae, and China are examples from the ancient period, while from more recent times (i.e., from the fifteenth century onward) we have Portugal, Spain, Holland, England, France, the United States, and Japan. The ceaseless assault on forests as fuel for the accumulation process has hitherto known no bounds and continually shifts to other areas that are more fertile and less inhibitive (in the sense of social resistance) areas for continued accumulation after the nearby forest resources have been exhausted (Chew 1992, 1994). Therefore, nature has been sacrificed at the expense of human exuberance and greed.

Over world history, those states or kingdoms that are located hierarchically in more advantageous positions in the total accumulation process extracted wood products to meet their social-economic transformative needs through tributes, conquests, or trading relations. This social-economic linkage engenders center-periphery relations and, over time, structures the dynamics of the trading patterns, as well as the political economy of the region in question.[3] If we review this patterning, we find that as early as 2100 b.c., the Ammanus region to the northwest was supplying the wood requirements of southern Mesopotamia. In fifth century b.c., Athens exploited Amphipolis for its wood through conquests and settlement. During Roman times, Liguria, Umbria, and Etruria were conquered to provide wood for Rome prior to the Christian period, and after the first century a.d., it was western Europe (including England) and North Africa. Similarly, Asia beginning from the second century a.d. experienced the provision of wood as tribute and as trade exchange between China and the states located in southern India and Southeast Asia. The height of such center-periphery relations was during the period of the Tang and Sung dynasties, in which city-states located in the Malay archipelago (Annam, Java, and Sumatra) provided wood products as part of their tribute missions to China.

Post-1450 a.d., center-periphery relations shifted toward the states of western Europe, beginning with Portugal, Spain, and Holland, and extracted the forest resources of the Mediterranean and England. They then expanded to Asian countries such as India, Java, Sumatra, and the Philippines. England and France pursued a more Continental extractive geopolitical strategy, focusing on eastern Europe, Russia, and the Baltic countries and later directing their efforts at North

America from the seventeenth or eighteenth centuries onward. England was to penetrate the forests of Southeast Asia in the nineteenth century.

In the late twentieth century, the United States and Japan replaced England and France as the two main centers of wood consumption and consequently, accumulation. At this stage, the dynamics of wood exploitation are occurring in the parts of the world-system that are the most amenable to the accumulation of capital.[4] Consequently, we find extensive wood operations by American and Japanese multinationals in North America, Latin America, Asia, Siberia, and West Africa. For Japan, whose wood resources were severely exploited in the past, global efforts are made now by its *sogo shoshas* to maintain a constant supply from foreign sources.[5] Japanese dependency on imported wood has risen from 5.5 percent in 1955 to 55 percent in 1970 and 66.5 percent in 1986 (Nectoux and Kuroda 1990, 27). With a more bountiful indigenous wood supply, the United States has been more fortunate than Japan. However, this has not stopped the multinational operations of U.S. based corporations from exploiting the temperate and tropical forests in the periphery of the world system.

Core-periphery relations have resulted in differential accumulation rates and fostered the ascendance of core states in the world system. In the late twentieth century, besides the United States, we find Japan exhibiting a global accumulation strategy in the timber and lumber sectors of the world economy. For nearly two decades, Japan has been the world's major importer of tropical timber hardwood. The total volume of tropical wood imports into Japan amounted to 29 percent of the world trade in tropical hardwoods in 1986 (Nectoux and Kuroda 1990, 5). The high levels of consumption reflect an age of exuberance similar to what the United States experienced in the postwar era (Devall 1993).[6] In the paper products area, over the last thirty years Japan has emerged as the world's largest importer of forest products, second largest producer of paper and paperboard, third largest producer of pulp, and second largest consumer of paper in the world, after the United States (Penna 1992, 1). Its total consumption of paper and paperboard has increased over 548 percent during the last thirty years (Penna 1992, 3). Furthermore, Japan, because of its proximity to Southeast Asia, has treated the region as its own woodyard, just as England did with British North America in the eighteenth to nineteenth centuries. Over the last decade, it has been importing unfinished logs from countries in Southeast Asia (such as from Malaysia, Indonesia, and Papua New Guinea) on a yearly average of 11 million cubic meters, or about 38 percent of its total volume of log imports (Kato 1992:95; Mori No Koe, Apr./June 1993, 8). By the end of the 1980s, this slowed, not because of a drop in consumption, but because of a diminishing resource and bans enforced by the states in Malaysia, Indonesia and the Philippines on the export of raw logs.[7]

The activities of Japan's *sogo shoshas* and *keiretsus* reflect the intensiveness and breadth of the capital accumulation process.[8] Overall, investments in the pulp and paper industry in Japan grew steadily, from 1.8 billion yen in 1980 to 4.7 billion yen in 1989 (Graham 1993, 39). This also includes direct investments in other parts of the world-economy such as in the United States, Canada, Chile,

Indonesia, Thailand, Malaysia, Portugal, New Zealand, Australia, and Papua New Guinea (Penna 1992, 29–30). The concentration in the industry increased dramatically over the last thirty years (Penna,1982, 18). In 1960, the top ten Japanese pulp and paper corporations produced 61 percent of the pulp, 64 percent of the paper and 42 percent of the paperboard in Japan. By 1990, however, the top ten corporations accounted for the manufacture of 83 percent of the pulp, 74 percent of the paper, and 57 percent of the paperboard. The concentration of capital naturally has led to an immense power on the part of Japan's pulp and paper industry over its peripheral producers in the world, such as in Southeast Asia. Tadem (1990, 23) indicated that Japan has been labeled an economic imperialist by some of the Southeast Asian wood producers, for it levies a 20 percent import tax on finished wood products and nothing on unprocessed logs. This measure is designed to protect Japan's labor intensive wood manufacturing industry (Tadem 1990, 24). Attempts by peripheral producers to control supply are met with price slashing in order "to break up any wood and forest product cartel in the region" (Tadem 1990, 25).

Exploitative accumulation processes that lead to environmental degradation and crises also promote the emergence of social movements with different, or revised, worldviews. These perspectives question the existing materialistic relationships between society and nature and, in the twentieth century, insist on the political rights and intrinsic value of other living beings.[9] However, social resistance to environmental degradation is not just a feature of the late twentieth-century world-system. This resistance, including the development of an environmental worldview, occurred repeatedly through world history. The information on groups that participated in alternative life styles and with different value orientations towards nature prior to the Christian period is limited. We have some indication that the practice of vegetarianism by Pythagorean groups in Classical Greece was a rejection of the dominant culture with its bloody sacrificial rites (Eder 1990). During the Roman expansionary period, there was recorded resistance by countermovements to Roman imperial ecological dispositions, especially by peasant farmers in the outlying areas of the empire (Grove 1990). Of course, there was also the emergence of intellectuals whose works covered ecological conservation issues, which can be linked to periods of environmental crisis in terms of wood supplies. In the Christian era, and especially with European colonialism after the seventeenth century, there was an increasing awareness of the relationship between colonial rule and environmental destruction, leading to various types of legislation to protect the environment of the colonies. Starting in 1677 with the deforestation of the Mauritius, there was the stark realization that the chopping of the ebony forests would have an ecological impact and, coupled with more general social unrest, there was emerging resistance by intellectuals of the day (Grove 1990, 1991, 1992). French scientists (such as Philibert Commerson, Pierre Poivre, and Jean Jacques Henri Bernardin de St. Pierre) undertook initiatives to protect the environment. For them, responsible stewardship was "an aesthetic and moral priority as well as a matter of economic necessity" (Grove 1992, 43). Laws were passed for the

Mauritius covering forest protection and water pollution from the indigo and sugar mills. French conservationists were also followed by their British counterparts in Tobago and India. In addition, there are indications throughout the history of the post-seventeenth century world-system of social unrest and resistance to imperial ecological edicts and interventions from the farmers and peasants of Africa and Asia (Grove 1990).

In the late twentieth century, this resistance occurs in areas where the exploitation of the forests impacts on the reproductive capacities of local communities and where severe environmental degradation occurs—both consequences of systematic capital penetration. During this period, these social movements (such as the environmental groups) in certain locations and cases have replaced labor as the primary resistance to capital. Across the zones of the world-system, capital (multinationals, ranchers, and large-scale capitalist farmers) and labor (in certain cases) are on one side of the "fence," and environmental movements, peasants, and native aboriginal peoples are on the other. For example, in Brazil resistance to the rainforest assault in the 1970s to the 1980s was led by Chico Mendez (Mendez 1990). The social struggle is also being repeated in India, with the Chipko environmental movement trying to save the forests of India and the Himalayas (Guha 1989; Sethi 1993). In Southeast Asia, the native aboriginal peoples of Malaysia resisted the incursions of local and foreign timber capital into their place of abode, and in the core zone of the U.S. Pacific Northwest, the struggle is to save the ancient forests from further destruction.

In core societies like the United States, the emergence of radical environmentalism in the 1970s—with its critique of the mainstream environmental movement as being "less responsive to grassroots demands for more rapid change in public policy, too bureaucratized and centralized, and too 'shallow' in ideology" (Devall 1992, 51–52)—changed the landscape of resistance to one of capital penetration and accumulation. "Direct action" taken in the form of ecotage, guerrilla theater, demonstrations, and "bearing witness"by radical environmentalists and ecowarriors are some outcomes of this resistance (Manes 1990; List 1993; Devall 1991, 1992; Foreman 1991).[10] Ecological activism takes the theme, "resist much, obey little" (Devall 1991, 138). This radical wing of the U.S. environmental movement, with its specific ecosophy, does exhibit the anti-systemic nature of the movement.[11] The "deep ecological" stance is uncompromising, with a critique focused on the excessive system of production and reproduction to satisfy exchange values, not use values, and a demand that the existing system must not only change its basic ways of organizing and reproducing itself, but recognize the intrinsic values of other living beings. The agreement to change the intensive and expansive exploitative practices to meet ecocentric demands, such as "let nature rest," would ultimately mean a qualitative transformation of the nature of current social organization and production systems that are based on the incessant process of capital accumulation and profit maximization.

One of the current terrains of conflict between environmental movements and capital in the core zone of the world-system concerns the clear-cutting of ancient forests (centuries-old trees) in the Pacific Northwest and the threat to biodiversity in that region. Here, the battle is to save the last stands of the ancient forest, with its multilayered canopy, from further deforestation. In terms of cutting the ancient forest, the record for the Pacific Northwest is worse than the deforestation of the Amazon forests of Latin America, according to the U.S. National Aeronautics and Space Administration (NASA) (*New York Times* 11 June 1992). It is estimated that during this century, almost 88 percent of these centuries-old trees have been cut, leaving only 12 percent or 2.4 million acres remaining. Such a scenario led environmental groups to file injunctions for the protection of certain species (the spotted owl and marbled murrelet, for example) that are threatened, to have initiatives on state ballots to protect the ancient forests, and to demonstrate by blockading logging roads with their bodies, tree sitting, and blocking entrances to mills and docks where logs are loaded.[12] The latter tactic resulted in a concerted demonstration, called "Redwood Summer," over the summer of 1990 to blockade logging roads and mill entrances in northern California. Environmentalists from all over the United States arrived in northern California to denounce the corporate plunder of old-growth forests (Pickett 1993, 207–12; Devall 1992, 60). The outcomes of such "timber wars" are unclear. The number of injunctions filed over timber harvest plans have slowed the pace of cutting, and the level of tension has increased in northern Californian communities, where the struggles between the environmental movement and the timber companies and the various levels of state agencies are being played out. Devall (1992, 60) revealed counter-movement tactics by logging industry interests to expose environmentalism. State agencies have undertaken investigations and surveillances of radical environmentalists as a consequence of their radical action (Foreman 1991; Manes 1990). These struggles underline the continued challenges to capital and the state by the environmental movement.[13] For the former, a barrier, though not an insurmountable one, has been erected—a consequence of a revised *lebenswelt* of our relationship with the environment.

In Southeast Asia, environmental movements, along with the native aboriginal peoples, have attempted to disrupt the process of accumulation. In East Malaysia, the struggle is over the destruction of traditional life styles and the degradation of the environment by local and foreign capital. East Malaysia is the world's largest exporter of tropical hardwood logs, where in Sarawak (East Malaysia), over half the forests (4.9 million hectares) have been awarded as forest concessions without any competitive bidding. Logging licenses are granted to timber companies without any regard or notice to the native aboriginal peoples. According to Gedicks, it is not "unusual for the native people to wake up in the morning and see bulldozers and chainsaws leveling their farms, desecrating sacred ancestral burial grounds, and opening roads through their property" (1993, 28). Such dislocations have transformed these people from an independent, self-sustaining life style to one dependent on government assistance or low-wage work in the timber industry (Hurst 1990).

It is clear that the Malaysian state, either in its pursuit of developmental policies or in enhancing the interests of some elected politicians, is responsible for the trend and intensity of the exploitation of its tropical rainforests. Having been advised and encouraged by multilateral agencies such as the World Bank and the Asian Development Bank during the postindependence era to target timber as a major export for developing the country, the state in Malaysia proceeded, in concert with local economic elites (and, in some cases, foreign corporations), to exploit this natural resource without much restraint, ignoring even the plight of its native aboriginal peoples (Hurst 1990).[14] The total annual timber cut in 1989 for Malaysia was about 800,000 hectares per year (Utusan Konsumer 1989). In East Malaysia, in the 1960s the forests of Sarawak covered about 76.5 percent (9.4 million hectares) of the land area. The rate of deforestation for Sarawak is quite extensive: 2.82 million hectares were cut between 1962 and 1985. Thus, in twenty-two years, 30 percent of Sarawak's forests were cut. It is expected that if the current pace continues, by 1995, more than 60 percent of the forests of Sarawak will be lost (Gedicks 1993, 28).

The assaults on the forests led to radical protests by some of the aboriginal groups, supported by environmentalists in the region. Environmental movements such as the Consumers Association of Penang, the Sahabat Alam Malaysia, and many others in Southeast Asia, as well as Rainforest Action Network, Mori No Koe, and Rainforest Information Center (based respectively in America, Japan, and Australia), managed over the last decade to mobilize public (national and global) attention concerning the destructive effects of the type of development that the timber companies and states are pursuing in Southeast Asia, and especially in East Malaysia.[15]

The Penan protest in Sarawak, East Malaysia, is one of the most publicized events in the region. The rainforests of Sarawak are home to about 220,000 native aboriginal peoples known as Dayaks, including the Penan people.[16] The conflict between the Dayaks, including the Penan living in the Baram and Limbang districts of Sarawak, came to the forefront of environmental politics in March 1987, when barricades were set up to block logging roads. Assisting these native aboriginal peoples in their struggle with the timber concessionaires and the state was an environmental group, Sahabat Alam Malaysia (Friends of the Earth). Government action followed with arrests (up to 103 citizens) and fines of up to $6,000 Malaysian dollars, the banning of public rallies, and the closing of three newspapers. Despite these actions and the concomitant heightened pace of harvesting practices, the protesters blockaded logging roads, which led to further arrests (a total of 500 since 1987). The Sahabat Alam Malaysia responded with an international campaign to draw world attention to the trial of the native protesters (Rush 1991). In 1989, it organized a World Rainforest Movement Meeting in Penang, Malaysia, with the participation of environmental groups from Indonesia, the Philippines, Thailand, India, Japan, Australia, Canada, Great Britain, and the

United States. The declaration called for action "for the forests, their people, and life on earth" (Gedicks 1993, 31). Included in this declaration was a call to ban all tropical wood imports to the core zone. In North America, the Rainforest Action Network participated with an educational campaign. Environmental groups in Europe lobbied the European Parliament, leading that institution to appeal to Malaysia to cease persecuting the native aboriginal protesters. In Japan, a Sarawak Campaign Committee (Mori No Koe) was formed to lobby against the destruction of the tropical rainforests of Sarawak and to undertake educational efforts to reduce the consumption of tropical hardwoods in Japan.

The Malaysian government responded to counteract this negative publicity by allocating $4 million U.S. for activities to counter the antitropical timber campaign by the environmentalists in the industrialized countries (Mori No Koe, July 1992). To date, the environmental movement's response has been the organization of an International Alliance of the Indigenous Tribal Peoples of the Tropical Rainforests in Malaysia in 1992, with the adoption of a "Charter of the Indigenous Tribal Peoples of the Tropical Rainforests" (Gedicks 1993, 32). Meanwhile, the blockade of logging roads continued over the summer of 1993; more than a thousand native aboriginal peoples participated in a blockade that lasted for seven months at Ulu Sungai Sebatu in the Baram district of Sarawak (Mori No Koe, Dec. 1993, 9).[17]

The outcome of such ongoing environmental struggles is unclear. What is certain is that across the zones of the world-system, resistance to capital and authoritarian states in the late twentieth century will not only come from "classical" social movements, such as labor unions, but increasingly from the "new" social movements, such as the ecological groups which are beginning to organize transnationally in their struggles. The exploitation of the environment as an issue is one that traverses and transcends nation-states of the world-system. It impacts everyone, and the potential for a truly transnational "people-to-people" resistance to capital and state systems can thus be realized. The transnational linkages and collaborations between some ecological movements, albeit with different social-political agendas and located in different zones of the late twentieth century world-system, show signs of changing the systemic linkages of a global system differentiated by nation-states. Therefore, ecological movements have the potential to be transnational within the world-system and, furthermore, to be transformative. Even if the movement's objectives are not achieved, it is possible that these protests across the zones of the world-system will limit (and perhaps stall) the options available to capital and the state and help draw attention to the plight of the ancient forests of the Pacific Northwest, the rainforests of Southeast Asia, and the native aboriginal peoples. In the process, this movement will assist in the transformation of social relations and our conceptions of nature.

CONCLUSION

Our brief look at world history suggests that, along with world-systemic social-structural factors, nature defines and limits the parameters of expansion and the conditions of production and accumulation in world system history. Environmental degradation and crisis have recurred for at least the last 5,000 years. This suggests that as the accumulation process intensifies, environmental degradation increases concomitantly and environmental crisis–like conditions emerge sparking societal ecological consciousness and conservation practices. Therefore, viewed through this long-term perspective, the current concern and debate over environmental crises reflect similar practices of prior historical periods of the world-system.

The question, however, remains as to whether current world accumulation processes will lead to qualitative and quantitative transformations of the global environment that have not yet been witnessed in world-system history. Such an answer cannot be easily provided due to the limited materials and information available for assessing the consequences of world accumulation processes over the long period of world-system history. Computer-simulated models have shown that we have overshot the natural limits of sustainability as a result of our excessive consumptive patterns, which are typical of life-styles (though differing levels across societies and zones) in the world-system (Meadows, Meadows, and Rander 1992). In words of Meadows and colleagues the sinks of the planet are beginning to fill and natural resources are being used up in an exponential fashion. It appears that whereas in the past, environmental crisis tended to be more localized and limited in nature, in the late twentieth century, we may be seeing, as a consequence of a ceaseless "cumulation of accumulation," an environmental crisis that poses a global threat to the reproduction of the world-system.

Whether this question can be answered satisfactorily for the long run should not be our only concern, for the current global transformation of the environment through the process of capital accumulation must also be addressed—and challenged. Such challenges have already been started in concert by the environmental movements across the zones of the world-system. The global nature of the problem cannot be addressed on a nation-by-nation basis, for inhibiting capital flows in one part of the world-system may merely shift the environmental degradation to another part of the system via capital's mobility and the receptiveness of states to promote the accumulation process under the umbrella of development and jobs. The outcome of such struggles is uncertain. At the very least, they will limit or impact the choices available to capital and the state, while at the very most, they will engender the emergence of an "ecosophically" sensitive, culturally diverse, and socially nonhierarchical world system.

NOTES

Thanks to Bob Denemark, Bill Devall, Gunder Frank, Dave Smith, and Jan Tye-Chew for their comments on an earlier draft of this chapter.

1. There are some exceptions. See, for example, Braudel (1975) and Frank and Gills (1992a, 1992b).

2. See O'Connor's (1991) recent work, which deals with the second contradiction and introduces the crisis aspects of the cost side of the accumulation of capital.

3. Analyses of center-periphery relations of world history prior to 1450 have been undertaken to explore this concept. See, for example, Algaze (1993), Chase-Dunn and Hall (1991), Kohl (1987), and Ekholm and Friedman (1982).

4. Presently, besides capital from the core zone establishing timber operations in the periphery, Colchester (1994, 45) reported that Asian timber companies, in concert with local capital, are undertaking logging operations in Guyana.

5. The *sogo shosha* is a trading house that has financial and trading functions. It provides financing for timber operations and credit for processing and sales. There are approximately 8,500 of these trading houses in Japan; however, the 15 largest handle the majority of timber imports into Japan (Nectoux and Kuroda 1990; Penna 1992).

6. It should be noted that due to mounting pressure by environmental groups in North America, a more consistent supply of wood resources is now being sought in Siberia (Goto 1993, 6). Since the 1960s, Japan has imported wood from the former Soviet Union, although formerly, Soviet wood could not compete against wood from North America in terms of quality and an antiquated production process marred by outdated machinery. With the constriction of wood supply, however, Siberia is now seen as a potential resource base. Mitsubishi and Sumitomo, in conjunction with Svetlaya, are participating in a joint venture deal with Hyundai Corporation of Korea to exploit the Siberian taiga (Goto 1993, 6).

7. Indonesia started to restrict the export of logs in 1979, while Malaysia took nearly a decade longer to ban the temporary export of logs (in January 1993) and to lift the ban with quota level exports (in May 1993) (Mori No Koe, Apr./June 1993, 6).

8. *Keiretsu* are Japan's industrial conglomerates. They might have, within their holdings, *sogo shoshas* (Penna 1992). Examples of *keiretsus* are Mitsubishi and Sumitomo.

9. For the twentieth century, see the work of Naess (1973), Devall (1991, 1993), and Devall and Sessions (1987).

10. "Bearing witness" means to stand forth or to be an example for others. According to Devall (1992, 59), it involves "the exploration of their own spiritual awakening in an age of environmental crisis, this means bearing witness for the mute forests that are being burned and chainsawed in the name of progress, greed, or ignorance."

11. For an overview of the ecosophy that has guided this radical wing of the movement, see Devall (1992).

12. For a concise account of the controversy surrounding endangered species, see Grumbine (1992).

13. Ecosocialists such as Foster (1993:12) have argued that such actions by environmentalists will contribute little to the overall green goal of forming a sustainable relationship between human beings and nature. His solution is to foster class alliances between environmentalists, loggers, and lumber workers.

14. The state in Malaysia is by no means unique in its treatment of native aboriginal peoples. For example, during the nineteenth century, the U.S. state, in a series of strategies to develop its western frontier, also ignored the plight of its native people, the Native Americans.

15. For a brief overview of environmental action in Southeast Asia, see Rush (1991, 55–96).

16. The Penan tribe numbers 9,500 persons, who depend totally on the rainforest for their food (Mori No Koe, Dec. 1993, 4).

17. This blockade took the lives of nine persons, including six children who died of malnutrition and other infections (Mori No Koe, Dec. 1993 9).

REFERENCES

Algaze, G. 1993. "Expansionary Dynamics of Some Early Pristine States." *American Anthropologist* 95, no. 2:304–33.

Attenborough, David. 1987. *The First Eden: The Mediterranean World and Man.* Boston: Little Brown.

Braudel, Fernand. 1975. *The Mediterranean and the Mediterranean World in the Age of Philip II, Vol 1.* London: Fontana.

Butzer, Karl W. 1971. *Environment and Archaeology from an Ecological Perspective.* Chicago: Aldine-Atherton.

Chase-Dunn, T., and T. Hall, eds. 1991. *Core-Periphery Relations in the Pre-Capitalist World.* Boulder, CO: Westview Press.

Chew, Sing C. 1992. *Logs for Capital The Timber Industry and Capitalist Enterprise in the 19th Century.* Westport, CT: Greenwood Press.

———. 1994. "Environmental Imperatives and Development Strategies: Challenges for S.E. Asia." In J. Lele, ed., *Asia Enters the 21st Century: Meeting and Making a New World.* Kingston, Canada: Queen's University Press.

Colchester, Marcus. 1994. "The New Sultans." *Ecologist* 24, no. 2 (March/April): 45–52.

Devall, Bill. 1991. "Political Activism in Time of War." *Revision* 13, no. 3: 135–41.

————. 1992. "Deep Ecology and Radical Environmentalism." In R. Dunlap and A. Mertig, eds., *American Environmentalism*. Philadelphia: Taylor and Francis, 51–62.

————. 1993. *Living Richly in an Age of Limits*. Salt Lake City, UT: Peregrine Smith.

Devall, Bill, and G. Sessions. 1987. *Deep Ecology*. Salt Lake City, UT: Peregrine Smith.

Eder, Klaus. 1990. "The Cultural Code of Modernity and the Problem of Nature: A Critique of the Naturalistic Notion of Progress." In J. Alexander and P. Sztompka, eds., *Rethinking Progress: Movements, Forces, and Ideas at the end of the 20th Century*. New York: Unwin and Hyman, 67–86.

————. 1993. *The New Politics of Class*. Newbury Park, CA: Sage.

Ekholm, K., and J. Friedman. 1982. "'Capital' Imperialism and Exploitation in Ancient World-Systems." *Review* 4, no. 1:87–109.

Foreman, D. 1991. *Confessions of an Eco-Warrior*. New York: Harmony Books.

Foster, John. 1993. "The Limits of Environmentalism without Class: Lessons from the Ancient Forest Struggle of the Pacific Northwest." *Capitalism, Nature, Socialism* 4, no. 1:11–42.

Frank, André Gunder. 1990. "Civil Democracy: Social Movements in Recent World History." In S. Amin, G. Arrighi, A. Frank, and I. Wallerstein, eds., *Transforming the Revolution*. New York: Monthly Review Press, 139–80.

Frank, André Gunder, and Marta Fuentes. 1989. "Ten Theses on Social Movements." *World Development* 17, no. 2:179–91.

Frank, André Gunder and Barry Gills. 1992(a). "The Five Thousand Year Old System: An Interdisciplinary Introduction." *Humboldt Journal of Social Relations* 18, no. 1:1–80.

————. 1992b. "World System Cycles, Crises, and Hegemonical Shifts." *Review* 15, no. 4:621–88.

Gedicks, Al. 1993. *The New Resource Wars*. Boston: Southend Press.

Gorz, Andre. 1982. *Farewell to the Working Class*. London: Pluto.

Goto, Daisuke. 1993. "Logging in Siberia: Japan's Involvement." *Japan Environmental Exchange Newsletter* (Tokyo), July.

Graham, Alistair. 1993. "Wood Flows around the Pacific Rim (a Corporate Picture)." Paper presented at the First International Temperate Forest Conference. Tasmania, Australia.

Grove, Richard. 1990. "Colonial Conservation, Ecological Hegemony, and Popular Resistance: Towards a Global Synthesis." In John Mackenzie, ed., *Imperialism and the Natural World*. Manchester, UK: University of Manchester Press, 15–50.

————. 1991. "Threatened Islands, Threatened Earth; Early Professional Science and the Historical Origins of Global Environmental Concerns." In D. J. R. Angell, J. Comer, and M. Wilkinson, eds., *Sustaining Earth: Response to the Environmental Threat*. New York: St Martin's Press, 15–29.

————. 1992. "Origins of Western Environmentalism." *Scientific American*, July, 268:42–47.

Grumbine, Edward. 1992. *Ghost Bears*. Covelo, CA: Island Press.

Guha, R. 1989. *The Unquiet Woods*. Berkeley: University of California Press.

Habermas, Jurgen. 1989. *The Theory of Communicative Action*. Vol. 2. Boston: Beacon Press.

Hurst, Philip. 1990. *Rainforest Politics*. London: Zed Press.

Kato, T. 1992. "Structural Changes in Japanese Forest Products Import During the 1980s." In *The Current State of Japanese Forestry*. Tokyo: Japanese Forest Economic Society, 87–101.

Kohl, Phil. 1987. "The Ancient Economy, Transferable Technologies, and the Bronze Age World System." In M. Rowlands, M. Larsen, and K. Kristiansen, eds., *Centre and Periphery in the Ancient World*. Cambridge: Cambridge University Press, 13–24.

List, Peter, ed.. 1993. *Radical Environmentalism*. Belmont, CA: Wadsworth.

Manes, Chris. 1990. *Green Rage*. Boston: Little Brown.

Marsh, George. 1864. *Man and Nature, Or Physical Geography as Modified by Human Action*. New York: Charles Scribner.

Meadows, Donella, Dennis Meadows, and Jorgen Rander. 1992. *Beyond the Limits*. Post Mills, VT: Chelsea Green.

Melucci, Alberto. 1989. *Nomads of the Present*. Philadelphia: Temple University Press.

Mendez, Chico. 1990. *Fight for the Forest*. London: Latin American Bureau.

Mori No Koe. 1993. *Japan and the World's Forests* (periodical). Tokyo: Sarawak Campaign Committee.

Naess, Arne. 1973. "The Shallow and the Deep: Long Range Ecology Movement: A Summary." *Inquiry* 16:95–100.

Nectoux, Francis, and Yoichi Kuroda. 1990. *Timber from the South Seas*. Geneva: World Wildlife Fund.

O'Connor, James. 1991. "The Second Contradiction of Capitalism: Causes and Consequences." *Capitalism, Nature, Socialism (CNS)* Pamphlet 1. Santa Cruz, CA: Center for Political Ecology.

Penna, Ian. 1992. *Japan's Paper Industry*. Tokyo: Chikyu no Tomo.

Perlin, John. 1989. *A Forest Journey*. Cambridge, MA: Harvard University Press.

Pickett, Karen. 1993. "Redwood Summer Retrospective." In P. List, ed., *Radical Environmentalism*. Belmont, CA: Wadsworth, 107–12.

Ponting, Clive. 1991. *A Green History of the World*. London: Penguin.

Rush, James. 1991. *The Last Tree: Reclaiming the Environment in Tropical Asia*. Boulder, CO: Westview.

Sethi, Harsh. 1993. "Survival and Democracy: Ecological Struggles in India." In P. Wignaraja, ed., *New Social Movements in the South*. London: Zed Books, 122–45.

Tadem, E. 1990. "Conflict over Land Based Natural Resources in the ASEAN Countries." In T. G. Lim, and M. Valencia, eds., *Conflict over Natural*

Resources in Southeast Asia and the Pacific. Singapore: Oxford University Press, 13–50.

Thirgood, J. V. 1981. *Man and the Mediterranean Forest: A History of Resource Depletion.* London: Academic Press.

Touraine, Alain. 1981. *The Voice and the Eye.* New York: Cambridge University Press.

Utusan Konsumer. 1989. *Newsletter.* Penang, Malaysia: Consumers Association of Penang.

Wallerstein, Immanuel. 1974. *The Modern World-System.* Vol. 1. San Diego, CA: Academic Press.

———. 1990. "Anti-systemic Movements: History and Dilemmas." In S. Amin, S., Arrighi, G., Frank, I. Wallerstein, eds.. *Transforming the Revolution.* New York: Monthly Review Press, 13–53.

———. 1992. "The West, Capitalism, and the Modern World-System." *Review* 15, no. 4:561–620.

13

Left Internationalism and the Politics of Resistance in the New World Order

André C. Drainville

In the last twenty years or so, the global crisis of accumulation has presented itself as a collection of particular events: currency devaluations, debt, and budgetary and monetary crises. These episodes are ruptures in the structures that previously generated growth and disciplined accumulation in social formations at the center of the world economy: the Bretton Woods monetary regime, embedded liberalism, Fordism, and Keynesianism.

The crises within the crisis have spawned a succession of calls to order. As early as 1976, for example, finding themselves faced with runaway inflation, shrinking productive investments, and rising strike rates, the heads of states of the G7 industrialized countries came together in the hope of nurturing a sense of "common purpose and vision." At the end of their Bonn summit in 1978, the G7 proposed to meet falling growth with "a comprehensive strategy covering growth, employment and inflation, international monetary policy, energy, trade and other issues . . . [which] is a coherent whole whose parts are interdependent.[1] From the IMF's "system of guidance" came grand designs of SDR (Special Drawing Rights)-based monetary orders, amid declarations about the necessity to anchor state policies on transnational targets of monetary growth and public expenditure reductions.[2] The Organization for Economic Cooperation and Development (OECD) called for "rotating Keynesianism," and spoke of the "collegial management of the developed world's interests."[3] More recently, the Bank for International Settlements (BIS), while recognizing that "the best supervision ultimately begins at home," has insisted on international regulatory coherence in financial supervision. The World Bank has called for the ordered restructuring of world debt, and the United Nations has put forward plans for a "development security council" that would be responsible for the overall coordination of economic policy in the world-economy.[4]

These *mots d'ordre* (calls to order) are not merely appeals to interstate solidarity in moments of crisis. They also announce a new world order in the making. The process by which this order is constructed in the world-economy has been documented and theorized by a growing body of literature, which updates and politicizes the work of world-system analysts. This literature is variously labeled, "transnational historical materialism," "Gramscian international political economy," or, more matter-of-factly, the "new IPE."[5] I have elsewhere referred to this literature as "Open Marxism" to underline its desire to capture power relationships in the world-economy as a historically and spatially contingent reality.[6]

Open Marxism has made a remarkable contribution to the analysis of the dialectics of order in the world-economy. However, it has had much less to say about the dialectics of change. Because it has explored the construction of the new world order in the world-economy through the historical experience of what Fernand Braudel used to call the "minority phenomenon at the center of capitalism," the realm of elites where capitalists—and with them, capitalism—live and die, Open Marxism has constructed global accumulation as a self-sufficient transnational machine that is impenetrable to the dialectics of change.[7]

As a result of its preoccupation with the particular experience of *bourgeois conquérants* (triumphant bourgeoisie) in the world-economy, Open Marxism has generated little in terms of strategic thought and instead has been content with issuing general invitations to "organizations and movements that might form part of a counter-hegemonic bloc includ[ing] Amnesty International, green parties and ecological groups, socialist think-tanks like the Transnational Institute, peace groups such as OXFAM, and religious organizations such as the World Council of Churches."[8]

This chapter is an effort to reflect on this invitation and to begin thinking more historically about the dialectics of change in the world-economy. In the first part of the chapter, I will try to draw strategic lessons from the historical experience of left internationalism. In the second part of the chapter, the partial insights offered by the history of left internationalism are used to refocus the analysis of the new world order on the dialectics of change. Particular attention will be paid here to what Peter Waterman has called the "new" internationalism of social movements, which has opposed a punctual, varied, and multiform resistance to the new world order.

LEFT INTERNATIONALISM AND THE DIALECTICS OF CHANGE IN THE WORLD ECONOMY

In terms of strategic and tactical approaches to change in the world economy, the history of left internationalism since the "short" nineteenth century can be told in three episodes. First, in the period between 1840 and 1914, competing ideologies of left internationalism began to present (frequently conflicting) programs that attempted to make sense of, and structure, the spontaneous, isolated, punctual, bounded, ever-changing, and occasionally contradictory resistance of workers, farmers, and city dwellers, men and women—all those shaken by the restructuring of the space of the European world-economy.

In the fifty years or so between the end of World War I and the beginning of détente, competing programs of left internationalism became institutionalized in rival internationals offering distinct blueprints for the reinvention of social relations. In this period, ongoing resistance internationalism became, in and of itself, an object of interprogrammatic struggle, which the Third and Fourth internationals, as well as various social democratic internationals, divided and locked up in competing mastodonic projects. Also in this period, which ranges from the anti-Russian war of 1918–1920 through the Cold War, internationalism from below was structured from above by the dynamics of interstate relations.

The third period, which Peter Waterman has called the "new grass-roots internationalism of social movements,"is not new at all in the sense of the questions that it raises or the social forces it mobilizes.[9] This "new" internationalism is but a chapter of the ongoing history of internationalism from below: the spontaneous and somewhat prepolitical internationalism of those shaken by the constant restructuring of production in the world-economy. What is new, though, is the context within which this internationalism now exists. In the last twenty years, the (interstate, interparty, inter-Internationals) structures that had shaped from above this *courte durée* internationalism have lost their overdetermining importance, and a more multiform internationalism has become apparent. This is an internationalism not shaped by shared allegiances to political blueprints or imprisoned by the discipline and *esprit de corps* of interstate relations, but rather dictated by the specificity of lived situations inside the general framework of the world-economy.

The Short Nineteenth Century

The years between 1840 and World War I were a classical age of sorts for left internationalism.[10] In this period, the First and Second internationals met and were dissolved, and as social movements began to locate organizational questions directly in the world-economy, a wide variety of internationals were convened: the Democratic Friends of All Nations (1844), the Fraternal Democrats (1845), the International Committee (1855), the International Council for Women (1888), the Congrès International de la Condition et des Droits des Femmes (1900), the International Woman Suffrage Alliance (1904), the Postal, Telegraph and Telephone International (1911), l'Union des Femmes du Monde Entier pour la Paix (1915), and so on.

With regard to socialism *as a strategy for the world-economy*, socialist a priorism, which installed the proletariat as a universal subject and socialism as an undifferentiated, cosmopolitan, global project, attempted in this period to fashion a revolutionary combination out of a more fragmented resistance internationalism, defining socialism in the world-economy as an immediate, and somewhat bounded, intervention in everyday life that is always reshaped by the conditions of the moment.

The different ideological programs that together make up the programmatic history of left internationalism in the nineteenth century shared, to an extent, the cosmopolitanism ambitions of bourgeois internationalism that attempted to construct undifferentiated universal order on the basis of moral values and political forms transcending national specificities. Enlightenment cosmopolitanism yielded, for example, the Abbé de Saint-Pierre's Projet de Paix Perpétuelle (1729), a republican edifice held together by universal adherence to the general principle of non-interference, and Immanuel Kant's *Project for Perpetual Peace* (1795), which sought to construct a universal and everlasting federal order out of small republics.[11] Redefined by David Hume and Adam Smith in a period when the bourgeoisie was giving a cosmopolitan character to production and consumption in every country, liberal cosmopolitanism emphasized the civilizing and homogenizing effect of the international division of labor and market liberalization on all countries of the world.

Similarly, socialists, Marxists, anarchists, collectivists, and mutualists in the nineteenth century attempted to design alternative cosmopolitanisms based on universalizing the experience of waged workers. What had been solid would melt into air, what had been holy would become profane—and left internationalism could install immovable core values and universal actors at the center of a cosmopolitan project for global order. Workers of all countries could be imagined as uniting and joining in with the shedding of identical chains.

Thus, the history of left internationalism in the period prior to World War I can be told as a programmatic history, a parade of conflicting programs covering a wide variety of subjects. In the First International, this history recalls debates over the organization and financing of the International Working Men's Association (IWMA), the role of Russia in Europe, the responsibilities of trade unions in working-class struggle, the political organization of workers into a class unto itself, the relationship with the League of Peace and Freedom, and above all, the nationalization of the means of production: the how, why, and when of collectiviz-ing ownership of land, farms, and mines. In the period of the Second International, programmatic conflicts took a more tactical turn: they featured debates over revisionism, Alexandre Millerand's participation in a bourgeois coalition government, the place of anarchists in the International, the signification of May Day protests, the possibilities for general social strikes, colonial policy and its role in the development of production forces, and, of course, the best strategy to mobilize the working class against the war and the meaning of this mobilization for the building of socialism. Through these questions took shape the debates that defined the Second International. These debates went on between revolutionaries and reformists, with Marxists giving priority to organized struggle for state power and anarchists, trade unionists, and syndicalists giving priority to mobilization in the economic realm, along with realists, and pacifists.

Thus told, the history of the short nineteenth century misses an important dimension of left internationalism *as a political movement of the world-economy*: in a sense, it is a history that is written above the level at which it was being made and that does not properly acknowledge the importance for the politics of change in the world-economy of the rise, from the 1840s on, of a left internationalism from below. This resistance was formed in the *courte durée* of events such as the growth of a European division of labor in agriculture as well as the overall increase in the mobility of production factors and the transformation of work structures, and it made all social forces more vulnerable to the vagaries of internationalized capital and deeply upset the whole dynamics of social relations.[12]

The Period between the End of World War I and Détente

In the fifty years or so between the end of World War I and détente, the relationship between internationalist programs from above and *courte durée* internationalism was, in a manner of speaking, clarified and regulated. In this period, internationalism from above organized and structured *courte durée* internationalism and inserted it, sometimes forcefully, into cosmopolitan programs.

Several factors contributed to this dominion of internationalist programs and ideologies over internationalism from below. First, the division of left internationalism between social-democrat and communist wings, which was already evident at Zimmerwald in 1915 and confirmed by the creation of the Third International, transformed various moments of internationalist solidarity into various terrains of programmatic struggle and left little room for an internationalist movement not defined in terms of party or state allegiances. The history of antifascist brigades during the Spanish Civil War illustrates well this transformation of internationalism from below. Started as somewhat fragmented, "primitive unprepared and leaderless" units of anarcho-syndicalist, communist, and Trotskyist workers at the onset of the war, the brigades themselves became important stakes in fractional struggles within the left. The Comintern, moved by Stalin's diplomatic strategy toward France and Great Britain, called for the liquidation of all Trotskysts in Spain and presented the victory against Trotskyism as a more important goal than even a victory against fascists.[13]

The ascendancy of internationalism from above in this period was also nurtured by the preponderance of interstate conflicts in the left agenda. The Russian civil war, World War II, the Cold War, and related peripheral conflicts (in Korea, Indochina, Egypt, Yemen, etc.), as well as the debates over a New International Economic Order (NIEO) and the debt crisis, all contributed to turning internationalism into an interstate affair, in which international solidarity was measured by statebound allegiances.

In the postwar period, Fordist regulation in the West also contributed to the structuring of left internationalism. More specifically, Fordism transformed trade unions into collaborators of states in the management of the workforce within a national framework and encouraged a corporatist approach to economic foreign policy, which turned left internationalism into little more than a foreign policy venture by American unions intent on pursuing their anti-communist campaigns abroad and widening their corporatist alliance with the state. This was particularly evident, for example, in the comanagement by unions and states of the Marshall Plan and the North Atlantic Alliance, and also in the shared strategic position toward communist-affiliated unions.[14]

In this context, *courte durée* internationalist resistance was, with few exceptions (the international mobilization that took place during the Sacco and Vanzetti trial comes to mind), considerably transformed by cosmopolitan programs.[15]

The "New" Internationalism

In the twenty years since détente, the political structures that had set the stage for the enclosing of *courte durée* internationalism have changed profoundly. In the age of the new world order, resistance has become the dominant form of expression of left internationalism.

First, the political dynamic of interstates relations has lost, in the last twenty years or so, both the cadre that had disciplined it since the end of World War II, and its capacity to overdetermine the left agenda. The predominance of the East-West axis as an organizing principle of international relations, which had begun to be put into question as early as the Bandung Conference of 1955 and the rise of the nonaligned movement in the mid-1950s, and been further shaken by the United Nations–centered debate on a new international economic order, the debt crisis, and Eurocommunism, has now definitively been brought to an end by the disappearance of actually existing socialism. For left internationalism in the post–Cold War world, this disappearance means that internationalist movements of solidarity have, to a certain extent, begun escaping the process of being automatically rerouted through interstate relations. Simply put, they do not have to explain themselves in terms of East-West relations. More generally, the end of the Cold War also means that the sense of immediacy of *courte durée* internationalism—its punctuality as well as its globalism—has begun structuring left internationalism as a transnational movement of resistance.

The crisis of Fordism in the West and the growing transnational segmentation of production have also contributed to this reinvention of left internationalism as a movement of resistance. While Fordist regulation provided a national framework for the regulation of accumulation and the management of social relations, left internationalism was, in effect, an international movement of social actors either in the business of petitioning the Keynesian state or working to reform it. For example, labor internationalism was largely the result of national labor federations meeting (at the International Confederation of Free Trade Unions, for example), feminist internationalism was a gathering of national associations of women (the

National Organization for Women in the United States, the National Action Committee in Canada, the National Abortion Campaign in Great Britain, etc.), and socialist internationalism was assembled as a meeting of parliamentary representatives. The crisis of Fordism, which is both a crisis of transnationally coordinated, but nationally regulated, accumulation and a crisis of relevance for the Keynesian state, has put into question the construction of left internationalism as an international movement.

Furthermore, the accelerating segmentation of production in a context of capitalist restructuring since the beginning of the crisis has turned all social actors into reluctant citizens of the world-economy and widened the material basis of a left internationalist resistance. When wage workers were the most vulnerable to the ebbs and flows of global accumulation in advanced capitalist countries, left internationalism universalized their experience and constructed an internationalist political project defined primarily in terms of their interests. In the post-Fordist period, however, social relations in general have become a category of global accumulation and thus serve as a multifaceted starting point for a broader, more varied internationalism ("based on recognition of the interconnections between capitalism, racism, sexism, and statism").[16]

As well, the transnational restructuring of capital has put into question assumptions that the capitalist conquest of the world would lead to a global homogenization of social relations. Rather than ushering in the global equalization in conditions of exploitation and social relations that Marx, Lenin, Rosa Luxemburg, and others had foreseen, the spreading of capitalist production relations throughout the world has gone hand in hand with an increasing differentiation in the ways in which capitalist social relations are organized within specific sites of the world-economy. Thus, if capitalist production increasingly provides the framework on which hangs the organization of social relations everywhere, accumulation increasingly exists differently in different social milieus. In this context, contemporary left internationalism has been at once more *global* (in the sense that it brings together a wider variety of social movements touched directly by the ongoing restructuring of the world-economy in ever more sites of production) and more *ruptured* (inasmuch as it involves increasingly specific struggles over the local ways of life of global capitalism).

For unionized wage workers, who have traditionally been the privileged subject of left internationalism, resistance internationalism has meant, above all, that centralized agencies created to marshal efforts at building international networks of solidarity have been transformed to accommodate a growing emphasis on member-led solidarity efforts and local fights for jobs and better working conditions. Union locals themselves have become increasingly involved in international campaigns, and a greater emphasis has been put on setting up resistance and organizing direct actions in locations where production itself takes place.[17]

In the spirit of the new labor internationalism, the Congress of South African Trade Unions decided in 1989 to disaffiliate itself from the World Federation of Trade Unions as well as the World Congress of Labor and declared its intention to build effective worker-to-worker solidarity with progressive trade union centers in other countries. Similarly, the Canadian Union of Public Employees has emphasized, in a recent member's guide to global solidarity, the importance of "direct contacts" and "worker-to-worker alliances" in the internationalization of labor.[18] Recognizing that "workers are [all] up against the same corporate agenda" and that organizational support given to foreign workers helps prevent job losses at home, the Communication, Energy and Paperworkers Union of Canada created a Humanity Fund for International Solidarity in the late 1980s that is directly targeted at foreign trade unionists.[19] In the same spirit, the International Commission for the Coordination of Solidarity among Sugar Workers (ICCSASW) began in the early 1980s to organize a membership-level solidarity campaign among sugar workers of the world.[20] The Centrale des Métallurgistes de Belgique, recognizing that recovery in domestic steel production went hand in hand with the growth of Third World production, moved to increased collaboration between peripheral steel workers and Belgian union militants and called for the cancellation of Third World debt.[21] In the 1980s, Latin American Trade unions also intensified their efforts to confront the international organization of multinational corporations with a grass-roots mobilization of its membership.[22] In the spirit of resistance internationalism, the International Metal Workers Federation led an international campaign for the released of Moses Mayekiso, the general secretary of the National Union of Metal Workers of South Africa, while the U.S./Guatemala Labor Education Project coordinated an international campaign on behalf of Lunafil textile workers in Guatemala that succeeded in securing safer working conditions.[23]

The newest wave of internationalism has also brought groups such as the Southerners for Economic Justice, a worker-based coalition for the defense of the unorganized working poor of the American South, to work toward a "Worker's Bill of Rights" that would serve as an international point of departure for struggles over work safety, pay equity, and fair trade.[24]

In the same spirit, the process of regional integration in the Americas has prompted unions in the United States to organize coalitions with Mexican workers and progressive religious organizations, such as the Methodist Federation for Social Action (MFSA), which have also become increasingly involved in struggles of labor rights. The MFSA, for example, participates actively in the Coalition for Justice in the Maquiladoras, which has been fighting to impose standards of conduct on (mostly American) multinationals and been involved in struggles against union busting.[25]

For the women's movement as well, internationalism has increasingly meant a descent toward the concrete and a greater plurality of organizational forms. In the nineteenth century, the international women's movement was principally concerned with putting forth an alternative cosmopolitanism based on the universalization of innately female values. For example, the International Council for Women (1889) was founded on the basis that "the cause of women is the cause of religion and morality all the world over," and proposed to represent, as founding member Lady Aberdeen put it, the "mothers of the world" to install the higher moral values of women as guiding principles for world order.[26] In the same period, the International Women Suffrage Alliance (1904) fought for equal citizenship rights for women on the bases both of the need for equity and the moral contribution of women to the cause of justice around the world. More immediate concerns were, of course, also part of the early phase of women's internationalism. The international women's meeting held at the Paris World's Fair, for example, demanded that women's domestic work be regulated and that a fair wage for it be paid by the state.[27] Women also fought for international conventions on the regulation of night work and childbirth (adopted in 1906 in Bern and in 1919 at the first session of the Conférence Internationale du Travail[28]). In both cases, however, these timely struggles were seen as mere parts of a larger universalist agenda (concerned, for example, with the protection of women's motherly duties and the preservation of women's reproductive labor).

In the last twenty years, the international women's movement has been shaped increasingly by what Gita Sen and Caren Grown have called an "ethic [of struggle] drawn from women's daily lives."[29] Socialist-feminists in particular have emphasized that the development of capitalist production on a world scale has depended on the super-exploitation of women, the maintenance of putting-out production in the center as well as the periphery, and gender-based, primitive accumulation. Accordingly, feminist internationalism has been defined, of late, not merely by symbolic events such as International Women's Day, but (mostly) by struggles over basic needs, sexual tourism, abortion rights, household consumption, wages for housework, the putting-out system, world market factories, gendered work in "free production zones," and workplace safety.[30]

The new internationalism of the social movements, is also made up of a wide variety of resistance movements involved in challenging the capitalist organization of social production in the world-economy. Antiracist struggles and struggles over the construction of a *citoyenneté mondiale* (global citizenship) have put into question the manner in which global capitalism particularizes individuals and finds spatial fixes for the organization of global capital. Indeed, local and regional campaigns over the dumping of toxic waste in peripheral zones, the European social charter, the systematic use of contractual labor, work condition in the maquiladoras, the GATT's "zero option" on the deregulation of food and medicine prices, the environmental consequences of the North American Free Trade Agreement (NAFTA), and the liberalization of international trade, and intellectual property rights (especially in Third World countries) have all put into question the prerogative of transnational capitalists to manage social production in the world-economy as their private endeavor.

Thus, in the last twenty years, the crisis of the manifold structures that had hitherto disciplined accumulation and interstate relations in the postwar period (Fordism, Keynesianism, the international division of labor, the Cold War, Pax Americana, etc.) has transformed the framework within which left internationalism had invented itself as a largely interstate, cosmopolitan movement. In this context, left internationalism has been increasingly a movement of resistance, and it is as a movement of resistance that the left has confronted the discipline of the new world order.

Left Resistance and the New World Order

Starting in the late 1960s, "new social movements" proclaimed socialism dead, its historic subject extinct, and its holism dangerous. André Gorz bid farewell to the working class, while Ernesto Laclau and Chantal Mouffe announced that there was no more totality and that bourgeois "society was not a valid object of discourse."[31] This signaled what Martin Jay called the "disintegration of the hopeful notions of socialist holism" and the "abandonment of the yearning for an alternative totality.[32]

In the same spirit, the new left internationalism appears to mark, if not the wholesale defeat of socialist internationalism and the appearance of piecemeal reformism, at least its weakening in a series of particularized struggles having little to do with socialism, or with any political project at all. On the face of it, the new internationalism of social movements appears as a collection of reflex responses of social movements to the pressures generated by the transnational restructuring of production. It concerns defending established spaces, boundaries, social practices, and modes of life endangered by transnational restructuring. It is a prepolitical gesture, a mob action, or a collection of urban riots (against the IMF, for example, as in Caracas, Buenos Aires, Abidjan, and Libreville) owing more to what Gramsci would have called a type of economicocorporatist consciousness than to anything resembling a critical understanding of the workings of the world-economy.[33]

The new internationalism is concerned with protecting jobs threatened by global restructuring, defending the right to organize unions without threats from hired guns, and access to reasonably priced medication in the face of GATT's efforts to defend the intellectual property rights of pharmaceutical producers the world over. It involves, as with the Zapatista National Liberation Army in Chiapas, protecting the peasants' title to their land as well as access to electricity and drinkable water, both of which are threatened by the North American Free Trade Agreement.[34]

As a political movement, the instant political communities formed to protect jobs, union rights, cheap medication, land reform, or abortion rights are little more than sacked potatoes that scatter as soon as the immediate menaces holding them together momentarily recede. Befitting a movement with a fragmented and fluctuating constituency, the new internationalism has little in terms of programs or blueprints. It speaks not of universal subjects, but of *difference*; not of ideologies, but of values. It seems to involve little beyond a vague humanism, a concern for the victims of the world economy. Alain Lipietz, writing about the *internationalisme modeste* (modest internationalism) of ecologists, referred, for example, to internationalism as the solidarity of the oppressed while, citing Václav Havel, Peter Waterman wrote of an "international community of the shaken."[35] In this sense, the new internationalism is on a par with left internationalism of an earlier period, when the London Working Men's Association spoke of humanity facing the bourgeois oppressors and the Fraternal Democrats spoke of the solidarity of people "who grow corn and eat potatoes, who make clothes and wear rags, who build houses and live in wretched hovels."[36]

Some elements of programmatic unity, of course, can be found in the new left internationalism to satisfy those who, like Giovanni Arrighi, Terence Hopkins, and Immanuel Wallerstein, are looking for an ideology to unite what they call "the family of world anti-systemic movements."[37] Those elements have come, in particular, from critical political ecologists and feminist theoreticians who have written about the unity of all social forces and who wish to further social control over the "constructed environment" and personal as well as social spaces (whether defined as ecosystems, women's bodies, cities, national economies, or workplaces) in a way that attempts to give a sense of coherence to the disparate struggles over environmental degradation, the gendering of work, consumerism, racism (including "environmental racism"), and refugee migrations. In this sense, internationalism of necessity radically puts into question both the spatial and the temporal foundations of the world-economy. As a movement concerning space, the new internationalism confronts the national, racial, ethnic, gender, and regional particularizations and compartmentalizations that form anchoring points for the free circulation of capital in the world economy. Furthermore, the new internationalism, because it involves immediate and contingent issues, also puts into question the time-delayed promises offered by the capitalist world-economy. To the liberal discourse on the universal benefits of comparative advantages, it asks: "What about jobs now?" Similarly, in regard to World Bank agroexport experts, it asks about feeding the periphery, while it asks the IMF about day care, health and safety programs, and social welfare.

However appealing may be these efforts to give a sense of priority and historic aims to the struggle against the new world order of capital, these broad-based programs are located so high above the struggles of which they wish to make sense, and are so completely divorced from lived internationalism, that they appear to be of limited usefulness in understanding what is new and important about left resistance to the new world order.

It is not as a program or an ideology that the radical, transformative nature of the new internationalism can be seized, but as a political movement. The new internationalism of social movement is a collection of particular demands, timely and necessary acts of solidarity that have become internationalized by the globalization of everyday life. It is, in fact, an *internationalism of necessity*, not brought about by shared allegiances to political programs and ideologies or by a particularly developed humanist consciousness but by the shared social and historical experience of life in the world economy. It is a class movement in the broadest sense of the term, as Gramsci understood it: a movement of marginalized people sharing a structurally precarious position.[38] In this sense, the new internationalism is the political movement of a class created in the world-economy itself by a transnationalization of production that has broadened the circle of everyone's humanity.

Herein lies the radical possibilities of the new internationalism of social movements. Unlike the internationalism assembled in the Internationals or at the International Confederation of Free Trade Unions (ICFTU), the World Federation of Free Trade Unions (WFTU), or the UN conferences on the new international order (in communication, on the land, in the seas, etc.), this is not an internationalism guided from above but one deeply grounded in the immediate necessities of the material world. The evanescent, fragmented, limited, timely, specific, and short-sighted expressions of internationalist solidarity that together make up the new left internationalism of social movement are radically important because they express a material cohesiveness that is increasingly part of daily life in the world economy. In this context, the frailty of the instantaneous political communities assembled to protect jobs, attack racism, defend abortion rights, and secure control over natural and constructed environments matters less than the structural experience of a shared life in the world-economy.

Thus, the new internationalism is not radical because it represents a leap of consciousness, proclaims ex cathedra its anticapitalism, or invents new and broader solidarities, but rather because it is an increasingly ordinary, everyday expression of the deep fellowship of the moved and the shaken of the world-economy. It is radical because it expresses a shared marginalization that is more deeply rooted materially than that projected by cosmopolitan projects of the nineteenth century or desired by the Internationals. This is not the crystalline internationalism of those who share a similar position on the mathematical equations explaining the capitalist accumulation process, but the cloudy internationalism of those who live in a capitalist world-economy and resist global capitalism as a historically specific and contingent mode of social organization.

The new internationalism has radical implications because it reveals the fragility of the social foundations of the new world order. This is of considerable importance in understanding the limits and possibilities of the present moment. Open Marxism has pictured global accumulation as a coherent machine and concluded that political actions in the world-economy had to be inserted within counter-hegemonical strategies; that they had to be parts of the offering of an alternative order in the world. For Open Marxism, the task at hand is to patiently build new, national, historic blocs "capable of sustaining a long war of position until [they are] strong enough to become an alternative basis of polity."[39] In the context of this war of position, incrementalism is to be resisted and timely and bounded struggles conducted for specific gains by actors peripheral to the emerging counter-hegemonical bloc should be avoided.[40]

If, however, we take seriously the rise of a new internationalism, we begin to recognize that the power of transnational capital is far from sufficient to attain the consensual and socially grounded order assumed by Open Marxism. From the point of view of the new internationalism, the new world order takes on the appearance of a bourgeois *bonne entente* (machination, cabal) imposed on the world; its coercive nature becomes more evident and its social moorings seem to disappear.

There are, of course, some elements of social consensus in the construction of bourgeois rule in the world economy, but this consensus has been, *and remains*, a wholly bourgeois affair. It involves only the transnational class in formation that Open Marxism has been documenting. Furthermore, it is in national social formations, and not in the world-economy itself, that are to be found the superstructures of civil society about which Antonio Gramsci wrote of as the social underpinning of hegemony, and there are negotiated the conditions of transnational bourgeois rule. The social foundations of hegemony remain national constructions (or, perhaps, regional ones, as Jacques de la Rosière recognized in his contribution to the Delors Report).[41] There is no social consensus in the world-economy itself. As a reality of the world-economy, the new world order is a coercive one. What is negotiated socially is negotiated outside the realm of the world economy.

The coercive, nonembedded nature of bourgeois power *in the world-economy itself* is manifested in its reliance both on fixed and rigidly defined objectives as a mean to order and on a set of institutions (central banks, fluid international policy bodies, etc.) That are becoming increasingly insulated from civil society.[42] Though the organs of regulation of the world economy, from the OECD, the BIS, and the IMF to the Trilateral Commission and the Bilderberg meetings, operate a kind of Poulantzascian reading of the conditions of accumulation in the world-economy that defines the exigencies of global accumulation and establishes boundaries to states' management of their national economies, the actual governance of the world economy is anything but a consensual affair. Rather, the global reading has relied for its enforcement on cosmopolitan artifices that attempt to override the local specificities of global accumulation. In different periods, this global order has been prompted by the gold standard or the Bretton Woods rules on monetary relations, most favored nation clauses, monetarist appeals to rigid conditions for monetary growth, calls for fixed GNP/debt ratios and targets in public spending reductions, and so forth.

The coerciveness of bourgeois power in the world-economy has been particularly evident of late, when global organs of management of the world-economy have begun to talk triumphally about the global "restoration of capitalism" and the liberal unity of the whole of the world-economy. "In our time," said David Beckman of the World Bank, "the whole world lives one history."[43] Increasingly, this shared history is forged out of a common experience of the brutality of monetarism, structural adjustment programs, and targets for the reduction of public spending engendered by the organs of management of the world-economy. The new world order represents, not only a revival of nineteenth-century ideas about the white man's burden and an effort to recenter the United Nations on the Security Council, it is also a neopolitical program from above that says, "market, yes, state, no," and leaves no alternatives to the marketization of social relations.[44]

In this context, in which bourgeois power in the world-economy relies increasingly on coercion and has failed to establish footholds of its own in civil society, patient counter-hegemonical strategies of wars of position appear wanting. More should be possible sooner, and the partial and limited sorties that new left internationalism organizes against capital are appropriate to the form of transnational power in the time of the new world order.

While left political practice within national social formations takes shape in a milieu that is forever in the process of construction and in which states give coherent and manageable—if changing—forms to social relations that are framed by a power structure embedded in civil society, left internationalism is faced with a less consensual order. Though historical hegemonies, underwritten by the capitalist integration of the world economy, can be said to have organized global accumulation, and though global regimes of sorts (from the monetary regime of the gold standard system to the postwar regime of embedded liberalism) have disciplined global accumulation, social relations in the world-economy have remained diffused, ever-changing, and continually confronted by an organized, and coercive, transnational bourgeoisie. Accordingly, where left politics within national social formations can be constructed as a reformulation of the whole—an alternative order defined in reference to a totality—left internationalism has to take on more timely forms.

Where the left within national social formations has to be mindful of the social infrastructure of bourgeois power and weary of adventurism, left internationalists are confronted by a nonembedded order that is little more than a collection of edicts and *mots d'ordre* pronounced on behalf of an emerging transnational bourgeoisie by internationalizing elements of the state apparatus. In this context, the task of the left is not so much to construct an alternative order underneath or beside the existing one, or even to assemble a counter-hegemonic bloc. Rather, it is to intervene in the exercise of bourgeois power, to facilitate the building of social coalitions (what Marx called the creation of "fraternal concurrences") and the making of an internationalist subject.[45]

Thus, the new internationalism of social movements is of radical importance in understanding the politics of change in the contemporary world economy, both because it reveals the increasing social fragility of the new world order and because it indicates that a historic bloc of sorts is already being assembled to topple it. This bloc, of course, is not the relatively enduring Gramscian grand alliance of social forces guided by a hegemonical fraction and sharing a common allegiance to a program for the reinvention of social relation. Rather, it is a mutable and ever-changing collection of narrowly focused social movements that are continually reminded of their transitory nature by the unrelenting restructuring of production in the world-economy.

CONCLUSION

To speak of left internationalism in general is to make odd bedfellows of Parisian communards (where, according to the *Paris-Journal* of 1871, "the plebe of the whole world could be seen rising"); anarcho-syndicalists, antifascist brigades of the Spanish Civil War, Kim Il Sung, "alternative" transnational consumer networks, the Zapatista National Liberation Army, the Comintern, coffee brigades in Nicaragua, world peace brigades, and the surrealist socialism of the Situationist International.[46] Political trials such as those of Antonio Gramsci or Sacco and Vanzetti, having activated internationalist resistance, are also part of the fractured history of left internationalism, as are, in the eyes of André Gunder Frank and Maria Fuentes, luddites and Quakers, feminists, chartists, the Sierra Club, Bob Geldof (of Live Aid fame), peasant movements at the periphery of the world economy, the Boxers Rebellion in China, the Boer's War, Mao's long walk, Diên Biên Phu, the Paris Commune, and the Bandung conference.[47] Internationalism has remained a largely untheorized practice, being dismissed, even in the age of the new world order and triumphant global liberalism, as "mere romanticism."[48] Nonetheless, discussions of left internationalism have never been more essential. The global restructuring of accumulation, which has been ongoing since capitalists first ventured into the world-economy but has become particularly manifest in the last two decades, when transnational neoliberal discipline and internationalizing state apparatuses have imposed a global strategy out of the crisis, make it essential to think about the possibilities and the difficulties of political organization in the world-economy.

Resistance in the world-economy, where bourgeois power is not embedded and which does not come equipped with social infrastructures, does not simply lead to reforming organized capitalism, nor does it represent an adventurist dash against the establish power of capital. Rather, it is an attempt to gain social control over production in the particular setting of the world-economy, where it is most fragile, and to give space to the construction of a socialist framework for local, national, and regional attempts to build counter-hegemonies. This is the radical meaning of the new internationalism of social movement in the context of the new world order.

NOTES

A first draft of this article was partially written during a research trip at the International Institute of Social History in Amsterdam which was made possible by the Social Science and Humanities Research Council of Canada and Laval University. I am grateful to Robert Cox, Stephen Gill, Carol Levasseur, Lorraine O'Donnell and Leo Panitch for their generous comments and friendly advice.
   1. See Hajnal (1989), 21–22, 47–57.
   2. On IMF guidance, see Fleming, (1975).

3. Organization for Economic Cooperation and Development, *Facing the Future: Mastering the Probable and Managing the Unpredictable* (Paris: OECD, 1979), 78. On rotating Keynesianism, see Lipietz, (1985), 121.

4. Bank for International Settlements (BIS), *62nd Annual Report* (Basle, Switzerland: BIS, June 1992), 212. The United Nations Development Program was released on April 24, 1992. It proposed to bring the World Bank and the IMF "under a newly constituted United Nations Development Security Council responsible for the coordination of global economic policy" *Guardian* 24 April, 1992, 11.

5. Murphy and Tooze (1991). See also Stephen Gill, ed., *Gramsci, Historical Materialism and International Relations* (Cambridge: Cambridge University Press, 1993).

6. Drainville (1994).

7. Braudel (1985), 93–94.

8. Stephen Gill and David Law, "Global Hegemony and the Structural Power of Capital" in Stephen Gill, ed., *Gramsci, Historical Materialism and International Relations* (Cambridge: Cambridge University Press, 1993), 122.

9. Waterman (1988). In the same spirit, Pierre Milza noted that the number of grass-roots, political, public, and nongovernmental organizations active in the world-economy has grown by 2,500 percent since the beginning of the twentieth century. See Pierre Milza, "Introduction," in *Les internationales et le problème de la guerre au XXe siècle.* (Rome: University of Milan, 1987), 3.

10. F. van Hoolthon and Marcel van der Linden, "Introduction," in *Internationalism in the Labor Movement 1830-1940*, 2 vol. (Leiden, Holland: E. J. Brill, 1988), vii. On the beginning of "anti-systemic social movements" in this period, see also Immanuel Wallerstein, "Anti-systemic Movements: History and Dilemmas," in Amin, Arrighi, Frank and Wallerstein (1990), 130–53.

11. Gregory Claeys, "Reciprocal Dependence, Virtue and Progress: Some Sources of Early Socialist Cosmopolitanism and Internationalism, 1750–1850" in F. Van Hoolthon and Marcel van der Linden, eds., *Internationalism in the Labor Movement 1830-1940*, 2 vol. (Leiden, Holland: E. J. Brill, 1988), 235–58.

12. On the relationship between the dynamics of global accumulation and European social movements, see Mark Traugott, "Interdependencies in Global Crisis: France and England in the Mid-Nineteenth Century," pp. 13–24 and Robert Bezucha, "The French Revolution of 1848 and the Social History of Work," pp. 24–39 both in Burke (1988). On the social impact of the increased mobility of all factors of production in the nineteenth century, see "International Factor Mobility, 1875–1914," ch. 5 in Foreman-Pack (1983), 127–58.

13. Julius Braunthal *History of the International*, Vol. 2:1914–1943, trans. Henry Collins and Kenneth Mitchell (New York: Frederick A. Praeger, 1967), 457.

14. Harvey A. Levenstein, *Communism, Anticommunism and the CIO*. (Westport, CT: Greenwood Press, 1981), 190–224.

15. On internationalist support in the Sacco and Vanzetti case, see Louis Stark, "The Facts in the Sacco and Vanzetti Case," *New York Times*, 17 April, 1927; Art Shields, "The Sacco-Vanzetti Case and the Grim Forces behind It," in Sacco-Vanzetti Defense Committee, *Are They Doomed?* (pamphlet), kept in the Emma Goldman archives, International Institute for Social History (IISH), Amsterdam, folio 22, 16611–787.

16. Waterman (1988), 297.

17. See Michael Allen, "Wordly Wisdom," *New Statesman and Society* (21 May 1993) xii-xiii. See also Jeroen Peijnenberg "Workers in Transnational Corporations: Meeting the Corporate Challenge" and Werner Olle and Wolfgang Schoeller, "World Market Competition and Restrictions upon International Trade Union Policies" (reprinted from *Capital and Class*, no. 2, 1977, 56–75), both in Waterman, (1984), 108–20, 39–58.

18. Canadian Union of Public Employees (1992). (Pamphlet).

19. CWC Humanity Fund, "International Solidarity: Why Should We Care?" (Introductory course) (1991).

20. In 1993, for example, the ICCSASW campaigned on behalf of Nicaraguan sugar workers against the privatization of sugar refineries and defended the rights of Dominican and Haitians cane cutters to organize unions. See *Sugar World: A Newsletter on Issues of Concern to Sugar Workers* 16, nos. 2, 3 (March and May 1993).

21. Centrale des Métallurgistes de Belgique (CMB), *Les défis à la solidarité: Le fil rouge* (Bruxelles: CMB/FGTB [Federation generale des travarilleurs Belges], April-May 1990); Jo Cottenier and Kris Hertogen, *Le temps travaille pour nous: Militant syndical dans les années 1990* (Bruxelles: Editions EPO, 1991), 167–68.

22. Joseph Giguère and Demis Sulmont, "Outline for a Strategy of International Trade-Union Solidarity in Latin America" in Waterman (1992), 44–49.

23. "Solidarity Success Stories," *Horizon* (Nanaimo: Global Village), 8, no. 7, (1992):5.

24. Southerners for Economic Justice, Inc., *1992 Program Review*, (Durham, NC: Southerners for Economic Justice, Inc., 1992).

25. Methodist Federation for Social Action (MFSA), *Social Questions Bulletin* 82, no. 6, (Nov./Dec. 1992).

26. Cited from a letter by Isabella M. S. Todd to Susan B. Anthony (an [ICW] founding member), 17 Feb., 1884, in Deutsch (1992), 21, also see Eeghen (1938), 4.

27. France, Ministère du Commerce, de l'Industrie des Postes et des Télégraphes, *Congrès international de la condition et des droits des femmes tenu à Paris du 5 au 8 Septembre 1900* (Paris: Imprimerie Nationale, 1901).

28. Bureau International du Travail, *La règlementation du travail féminin* (Série "Études et Documents," no. 2) (Geneva: Bureau International du Travail, 1931).

29. Sen and Grown, (1987), 79.

30. See Temma Kaplan, "On the Socialist Origins of International Women's Day," in F. van Hoolthon and Marcel van der Linden, eds., *Internationalism in the Labor Movement 1830–1940* (Leiden, Holland: E. J. Brill, 1988) 1:188–94; Mies, (1986); Mies, Bennholdt-Thomsen, and von Werlhof (1988); *Abortion Rights—A Socialist Perspective* (pamphlet, International Informie [IIAV] collection, 1977). On the relationship between the international division of labor and the growth of the putting-out system, see Luijken and Mitter (1987). See also Maureen Mackintosh, "The Sexual Division of Labor and the Subordination of Women," and Diane Elson and Ruth Pearson, "The Subordination of Women and the Internationalization of Factory Production," both in Young, Wolkowitz and McCullagh (1981).

31. Gorz (1994); and Mouffe (1985).

32. Jay (1988).

33. Concerning these riots, see Didier Bigo, "Contestation populaires et émeutes urbaines: Les jeux du politique et de la transnationalité," *Cultures et Conflits* (1992):3–22.

34. Bertrand de la Grange, "Mexique: La révolte dérangeante des Indiens du Chiapas," *Le Monde* 3 Feb. 1994), 2.

35. See Alain Lipietz, "Pour un internationalisme modeste," ch. 7 in *Vert espérance: L'avenir de l'écologie politique* (Paris: La Découverte, 1993), 72–83, and Václav Havel, "Anti-Political Politics," cited by Waterman (1990), 36. On antipolitical politics as the power of the powerless and the awakening of the oppressed, see also "Le pouvoir des sans-pouvoirs," in Václav Havel, *Essais Politiques* (Paris: Calmann-Lévy, 1989), 67–157.

36. Quoted in Julius Braunthal, *History of the International*, Vol. 1:1864–1914, (trans. Henry Collins and Kenneth Mitchell), (New York: Praeger, 1967), 63.

37. Giovanni Arrighi, Terence K. Hopkins and Immanuel Wallerstein, *Anti-systemic Movements* (London: Verso: 1989), 51. On the need to unite and combine anti-systemic movements, see also Immanuel Wallerstein, "1968: Révolution dans le système mondial," *Les temps modernes*, nos. 514–15 (May-June 1989), 154–76.

38. Dante Germino, *Antonio Gramsci: Architect of a New Politics*, (Baton Rouge: Louisiana State University Press, 1990), 56.

39. Cox (1991), 349.

40. Cox (1993), 53.

41. J. de Larosière, "First Stages towards the Creation of a European Reserve Bank: The Creation of the European Reserve Fund," in Committee for the Study of Economic and Monetary Union, ed., *Report on Economic and Monetary Union in the European Community*, (Luxembourg: Office for Official Publications of the European Communities, 1989), 177–84.

42. Stephen Gill called this the New Constitutionalism "the move towards construction of legal or constitutional devices to remove or insulate substantially the new economic institutions from popular scrutiny or democratic accountability"; Stephen Gill, "The Emerging World Order and European Change," in Leo Panitch and Ralph Miliband, *Socialist Register 1992, "New World Order?"* (London:

Merlin Press, 1992), 165.

43. Beckman, Agarwala, Bermeister, and Serageldin (1991).

44. Concerning the revival of the ideas about the white man's burden, see for example, Paul Johnson "Colonialism's Back, and Not a Moment Too Soon" *New York Times Magazine*, (18 April, 1993), 43.

45. Marx is quoted from the Inaugural Address of the IWMA, in *Karl Marx and Fredrich Engles: Collected Works*, (New York: International Publishers) 20, (1975): 12.

46. *Paris-Journal* (30 May, 1871), 1.

47. André Gunder Frank and Marta Fuentes. "Civil Democracy: Social Movements in Recent World History," in Amin, Arrighi, Gunder Frank, and Wallerstein (1990), 139–80.

48. Ralph Miliband and Leo Panitch, "The New World Order and the Socialist Agenda," in Miliband and Panitch (1992), 1–25.

REFERENCES

Amin, Samir, Giovanni Arrighi, Andres Gunder Frank, and Immanuel Wallerstein. 1990. *Transforming the Revolution: Social Movements and the World-System*. New York: Monthly Review Press.

Arrighi, Giovanni. 1990. "Marxist Century, American Century: The Making and Remaking of the World Labor Movement." *New Left Review*, no. 179:29–63.

Arrighi, Giovanni, Terrence K. Hopkins, and Immanuel Wallerstein. 1986. "Dilemmas of Anti-systemic Movements." In *Social Research*, 1, no. 53:185-206.

Bank for International Settlements. Various years. *Annual Report*. Basle: Bank for International Settlements.

Beckman, David, Ramgopal Agarwala, Sven Burmester, and Ismail Serageldin. 1991. *Friday Morning Reflections at the World Bank: Essays on Values and Development*. Washington, DC: Seven Locks Press.

Braudel, Fernand. 1985. Une lecon d'histoire de Fernand Braudel. Paris: Arthaud-Flammarion.

Burke, Edmund, III, ed. 1988. *Global Crises and Social Movements: Artisans, Peasants, Populasts and the World Economy*. Boulder, CO: Westview Press.

Canadian Union of Public Employees (CUPE). 1992. *Union Aid: A Member's Guide to Global Solidarity*. Ottawa: CUPE.

Cameron, Duncan, and François Houle, eds. 1985. *Canada and the New International Division of Labor*. Ottawa: University of Ottawa Press.

Coates, Ken. 1986. *Joint Action for Jobs: A New Internationalism*. London: New Socialist/Spokesman.

Committee for the Study of Economic and Monetary Union. 1989. *Report on Economic and Monetary Union in the European Community* (Delors Report). Luxembourg: Office for Official Publications of the European Communities.

Cox. Robert W. 1981. "Social Forces, States and World Orders: Beyond International Relations Theory." *Millennium: Journal of International Studies* 10, no. 2:126–44. Reprinted, with a postscript, in Robert O. Keohane, ed., *Neorealism and its Critics.* New York: Columbia University Press, 205-254.

———. 1983. "Gramsci, Hegemony and International Relations: An Essay in Method." *Milleniun: Journal of International Studies* 12, no. 2:162–75.

———. 1987. *Production, Power and World Order: Social Forces in the Making of History.* New York: Columbia University Press.

———. 1991. "The Global Political Economy and Social Choice." In Daniel Drache and Meric S. Gertler, eds., *The New Era in Global Competition: State Policy and Market Power.* Montreal: McGill–Queen's University Press, 335–50.

Deutsch, Regine. 1929. *The International Woman Suffrage Alliance: Its History from 1904 to 1929.* London: n.p.

Drainville, André C. 1994. "International Political Economy in the Age of Open Marxism." *Review of International Political Economy* 1, no. 1:105–32.

Eeghen, Louise C. A. van. 1938. *The Spirit and Work of the I.C.W.* Aberdeen, Scotland: International Council of Women.

———. 1993b. *Pour un nouvel ordre économique international.* Brussels, Belgium: Vie et Conscience.

———. 1993. Fédération générale des travailleurs Belges. 1993. *Et si nous changions le cour de l'histoire?* Brussels, Belgium: Vie et Conscience.

Fleming, J. Marcus. 1975. "Floating Exchange Rates, Asymmetrical Intervention, and the Management of International Liquidity." *IMF Staff Papers* 22, no. 2:263–83.

Foreman-Pack, James. 1983. *A History of the World Economy: International Economic Relations since 1850.* Totowa, NJ: Barnes and Noble.

Gorz, André. 1994. *Capitalism, socialism, écology.* Translated by Chris Turner. New York: Verso.

Hajnal, Peter J., ed. 1989. *The Seven Powers Summit: Documents from the Summits of Industrialized Countries, 1975–1989.* New York: Kraus International Publications.

Jay, Martin. 1988. *Fin de Siècle Socialism.* New York: Routledge.

Laclau, Ernesto, and Chantal Mouffe. 1985. *Hegemony and Socialist Strategy: Towards a Radical Democratic Politics.* London: Verso.

Linden, Marcel van der; and Frits van Holthoon. 1988. *Internationalism in the Labor Movement 1830-1940.* 2 vol. Leiden, Holland: E. J. Brill.

Lipietz, Alain. 1985. *Mirages et miracles; Problèmes de l'industrialisation dans le tiers-monde.* Paris: Maspero/La Découverte.

Luijken, Anneke van, and Swasti Mitter. 1987. *Unseen Phenomenon: The Rise of Homeworking.* London: Change.

Mies, Maria. 1986. *Patriarchy and Accumulation of a World Scale: Women in the International Division of Labor.* London: Zed.

Mies, Maria, V. Bennholdt-Thomsen, and Claudia von Werlhof. 1988. *Women, the Last Colony*. London: Zed Books.

Miliband, Ralph, and Leo Panitch eds. 1992. *Socialist Register 1992: New World Order?* London: Merlin Press.

Murphy, Craig N., and Roger Tooze. 1991. *The New International Political Economy*. Vol 6 of *International Political Economy Yearbook*. Boulder, CO: Lynne Rienner Publishers.

Rowbotham, Sheila. 1972. *Women, Resistance and Revolution*. London: Penguin.

Sen, Gita, and Caren Grown. 1987. *Development, Crises and Alternative Visions: Third World Women's Perspectives*. New York: Monthly Review Press.

Ward, Kathryn, ed. 1990. *Women Workers and Global Restructuring*. Ithaca, NY: ILR Press, Cornell University.

Waterman, Peter, ed. 1984. *For a New Labor Internationalism: A Set of Reprints and Working Papers*. Birmingham, UK: Third World Publications, with the International Labor Education, Research and Information Foundation.

Waterman, Peter. 1988. "The New Internationalisms: A More Real Thing than Big, Big Coke?" *Review (Fernand Braudel Center)*11, no. 3:289–28.

———. 1990. "One, Two, Three, Many New Internationalisms! On a New Third World Labor Internationalism and Its Relationship to Those in the West and the East." Working paper no. 76. The Hague, Holland: Institute of Social Studies.

———, ed. 1992. *The Old Internationalism and the New: A Reader on Labor, New Social Movements and Internationalism*. The Hague, Holland: Institute of Social History.

Young, Kate, Carol Wolkowitz, and Roslyn McCullagh, eds. 1981. *Of Marriage and the Market: Women's Subordination in International Perspective*. London: CSE Books.

Index

About the Editors and Contributors

JÓZSEF BÖRÖCZ is Assistant Professor of Sociology at the University of California, Irvine, and Senior Research Associate (on leave) at the Institute for Political Science at the Hungarian Academy of Science. One of the first Hungarians to receive an American Ph.D. in sociology (Johns Hopkins, 1992) since World War II, his scholarly interests lay in comparative economic sociology, the collapse of state "socialism," and the study of tourism as leisure migration.

STEPHEN G. BUNKER is Professor of Sociology at the University of Wisconsin in Madison. Most of his research deals with local, national, and global aspects of the economy.

SING C. CHEW is Professor of Sociology at Humboldt State University. His main research interest focuses on the process of accumulation in world history and its impact on the environment. He is the author of *Logs for Capital: The Timber Industry and Capitalist Enterprise in the 19th Century*.

PAUL S. CICCANTELL is an Assistant Professor in the Department of Sociology, Anthropology and Social Work at Kansas State University. His current research examines Japanese raw-materials access strategies and the role of transport industries and systems in the construction of hegemony in the world-system.

FREDERIC C. DEYO is Professor of Sociology at the State University of New York, Brockport. He currently (1995) chairs the Political Economy of the World-System section of the American Sociological Association. He is also the author of *Beneath the Miracle: Labor Subordination in the New Asian Industrialism* and editor of a forthcoming volume entitled *Social Reconstructions of the World Automobile Industry*.

ANDRÉ C. DRAINVILLE is an Assistant Professor of International Political Economy at Laval University in Québec, Canada. His current research focuses on contemporary resistance movements in the world economy. His latest article was published in the inaugural edition of the *Review of International Political Economy* (Spring 1994) and is entitled, "International Political Economy in the Age of Open Marxism."

KUNIKO FUJITA is a visiting professor of Japanese Studies at the National University of Singapore. Her current research focuses on Japanese multinational corporations and East Asian Development. She recently coedited *Japanese Cities in the World Economy* with Richard Child Hill.

RUCHIRA GANGULY-SCRASE teaches sociology at Deakin University, Australia. Currently on leave from Deakin, she is at present a research fellow at the Asia Centre, University of Tasmania. She has published articles on fieldwork, the ethnographic method, the anthropology of gender in South Asia, and Indian immigrants in Australia.

WALTER L. GOLDFRANK is Professor of Sociology and Provost of College Eight at the University of California, Santa Cruz. He is currently studying the consequences of the boom in Chilean fruit exports.

RICHARD CHILD HILL is a Professor of Sociology at Michigan State University. His current research focuses on Japanese multinational corporations and East Asian Development. He recently coedited *Japanese Cities in the World Economy* with Kuniko Fujita.

STEFAN KIPFER is a graduate student at the Faculty of Environmental Studies, York University, Toronto, Canada. His current research interests are in neo-Gramscian political economy, the political economy of urban space and comparative politics.

PHILIP MCMICHAEL is an Associate Professor in Rural Sociology at Cornell University. He is the author of *Settlers and the Agrarian Question* (1984) and is the editor of *The Global Restructuring of Agro-Food Systems* (1994) and *Food and Agrarian Orders in the World-Economy* (1985). His research focuses on the restructuring of world capitalism, with an area interest in the Pacific Rim.

CYNTHIA SIEMSEN MAKI is a doctoral student in sociology at the University of California, Santa Cruz. Her research interests include the sociology of development, world systems, and women in family law.

DENIS O'HEARN is Lecturer in Sociology at Queen's University of Belfast and Associate Professor of Sociology at the University of Wisconsin–Madison. His recent research focuses on innovation in world-system zones, Irish political economy, and the world aluminum industry. He is editor (with Brad Barham and Stephen Bunker) of *States, Firms, and Raw Material: The World Economy and the Ecology of Aluminum* (1994).

ROBERT J. S. ROSS is Professor and Chair of Sociology at Clark University in Worcester, Massachusetts. With Kent Trachte, he is the author of *Global Capitalism: The New Leviathan* (1990). His most recent work is on the state of Massachusetts through boom and bust.

TIMOTHY J. SCRASE currently lectures in Sociology at the University of Tasmania, Australia. He holds a Ph.D. from LaTrobe University in Melbourne and has taught and done research in the area of globalization and Third World development for more than a decade. He recently published *Image, Ideology and Inequality* (1993) and is currently editing *Social Justice and Third World Education.*

DAVID A. SMITH is an Associate Professor of Sociology and Urban Planning at the University of California, Irvine. His research interests include comparative urbanization, development and underdevelopment in the Third World/periphery, the political economy of the Asian Pacific Rim and global trade and commodity chains. He is currently finishing a book entitled *Third World Urbanization in Global Perspective.*